How to
Teach Balanced
Reading
& Writing

Second Edition

How to
Teach Balanced
Reading
& Writing

Second Edition

Bonnie Burns

CORWIN PRESS
A SAGE Publications Company
Thousand Oaks, California

For information:

Corwin Press, Inc.
A Sage Publications Company
2455 Teller Road
Thousand Oaks, California 91320
www.corwinpress.com

Sage Publications Ltd.
1 Oliver's Yard
55 City Road
London EC1Y 1SP
United Kingdom

Sage Publications India Pvt. Ltd.
B-42, Panchsheel Enclave
Post Box 4109
New Delhi 110 017 India

Printed in the United States of America.

This book is printed on acid-free paper.

Library of Congress Cataloging-in-Publication Data

Burns, Bonnie. How to teach balanced reading and writing / Bonnie Burns. — 2nd ed.
    p. cm.
Includes bibliographical references and index.
ISBN 1-4129-3741-8 (cloth) — ISBN 1-4129-3742-6 (pbk.)
    1. English language—Study and teaching. 2. Language arts. I. Title.
LB1576.B8935 2006
372.6—dc22   2006001770

06 07 08 09 10 10 9 8 7 6 5 4 3 2 1

Acquisitions Editor:	Cathy Hernandez
Editorial Assistant:	Charline Wu
Project Editor:	Kate Peterson
Copy Editor:	Bonnie Freeman
Typesetter:	C&M Digitals (P) Ltd.
Indexer:	Judy Hunt
Cover Designer:	Lisa Miller

Contents

To all those I love who have been so patient, and with special thanks to Pat Braun and Dana LaRocco for research assistance.

—B. B.

Preface

The concept of balanced reading and writing has developed into a more mature philosophy over the past few years. Its roots were in the reading wars, those rancorous debates between whole language advocates and phonics supporters, but teachers have always known that the needs of their diverse learners could not be met with any single end-of-the-spectrum method.

Today, balanced reading is able to skillfully blend skill-based instruction and meaning-based instruction through a whole-part-whole philosophy. Balanced reading also includes integrating the language arts and balancing teacher- and student-centered activities. An expanded definition of balance includes adjusting levels of support and intensity of instruction, which were added in this edition to promote differentiation of instruction to meet the needs of various learners.

The second edition, written for preservice and practicing teachers, includes several new sections as well as updated resources. There is a new chapter on fluency and a new section on language acquisition. Resources for determining readability and locating children's literature, all with easy-to-use Web sites, are other additions. There are new teaching activities in every section, Web sites, and updated tests for phonemic awareness.

Chapters are generally organized in a similar manner. They start by explaining the background and developmental nature of the topics. Activities that teach a skill or strategy follow. Beginning teachers often ask for just the activities but, without knowing why the activities work and when they work, are not able to successfully adapt the procedures for their classes. Teachers need knowledge of both underlying principles and engaging activities to make the right lesson plans for their classes.

The first chapter gives a definition of balanced reading and the role that explicit instruction plays. Chapters 2 through 5 are about primary readers and older students who still need to develop the skills of emergent reading, phonemic awareness, word recognition, and fluency.

The remainder of the book applies to all grades. Guided reading and grouping for reading are addressed in Chapters 6 and 7. They include strategies for teaching the whole class, small groups, and individual students. This section also includes methods for finding the readability of books and locating children's literature.

Comprehension strategies, with ideas for before, during, and after reading, and a vocabulary chapter come next. They are followed by Chapter 10, on spelling, and Chapter 11, which includes strategies to teach both teacher- and student-centered writing. The book concludes with chapters on reading and writing in the content areas and assessment.

Choose the sections that are needed for your classroom, but read Chapter 1 first to understand how theories and activities can be balanced successfully. Learning to read is a long and complicated process, but there are research-based strategies that can make the entire process more coordinated and effective in your classroom.

Publisher's Acknowledgments

Corwin Press gratefully acknowledges the contributions of the following reviewers:

Roxie R. Ahlbrecht, Second Grade Teacher
Robert Frost Elementary School, Sioux Falls, SD

Barbara Smith Chalou, Associate Professor, Teacher Education
University of Maine at Presque Isle, Presque Isle, ME

Betty Ann Collinge, Kindergarten and First Grade Teacher
Green Acres Elementary School, North Haven, CT

Linda L. Eisinger, Third Grade Teacher
West Elementary, Jefferson City, MO

Karen Heath, Literacy Coordinator
Barre Schools, Barre, VT

Sherri Strawser, Associate Professor, Special Education
University of Nevada–Las Vegas, Las Vegas, NV

Jennifer Trujillo, Assistant Professor, Teacher Education
Fort Lewis College, Durango, CO

About the Author

 **Bonnie Burns** is currently Director of the Reading Specialist Program at Dominican University in River Forest, Illinois. She works with both undergraduate and graduate students who are studying to be reading specialists. She has authored or coauthored several books and articles and an online column. Her current interests are establishing school district–university partnerships and reading clinics. She has served for 30 years as an elementary teacher, reading specialist, and principal in Illinois, Florida, and Arizona, working with a wide variety of students. She was a trainer for the Illinois state assessment in writing and the New York State Effective Teaching Program. She has been a presenter of professional development workshops nationally. She received her EdD in Educational Leadership from Loyola University of Chicago.

1

Balanced Reading and Writing

Reading maketh a full man.

—Francis Bacon

Reading is a complex process that takes several years to learn, and the more advanced aspects of reading, such as analysis or synthesis of ideas, take several years more. Readers come from a multiplicity of backgrounds, with divergent levels of knowledge, verbal skills, motivation, and reasoning abilities. How could there be a single method of instruction that would make every child a successful reader?

Nevertheless, new methods in the field of reading continue to be proposed. Some are new and well researched, others are recycled and renamed, and a few are philosophies without much to back them up. Although each method may contain worthwhile elements for certain learners or particular situations, many new ideas tend to be adopted wholesale. The information then filters down to classroom teachers in the form of mandates, one-day workshops, or teaching materials that arrive without explanation or training. Many teachers have had only a single undergraduate course in teaching reading and thus lack the background that might help them interpret new trends. Essential parts of the theory get lost, and some flashy component is all that is left. These flashy leftovers may become popular, but they are usually not rich enough in philosophical content to accomplish the complex task of teaching reading or complete enough to meet the variety of student needs. Teachers are tired of trendy innovations and competing theories and are looking for a balance of methodologies that is rich and flexible enough to meet the needs of all their learners.

■ THE READING WARS

The 1990s, when whole language advocates publicly battled with supporters of phonics, was one of the most contentious eras in education. Whole language was considered a meaning-based philosophy, while phonics advocates supported a skill-based philosophy. Whole language used literature-based basals (the word used to describe graded reading texts for children), children's literature, and shared reading of big books. Due to the literature base, which was not constructed specifically for reading instruction, the first- and second-grade books afforded relatively little control of vocabulary. The basals advocated whole-class, teacher-guided reading, followed with rereading in pairs. Systematic teaching of phonics was deemphasized in favor of a more contextualized approach to help students learn letter-sound relationships (Morris, 2005). Primary teachers especially were uncomfortable with competing theories, particularly when end-of-the-spectrum philosophies did not validate their experiences about how their diverse children actually learned. And they were especially uncomfortable about their slowest learners.

Parts of the whole language philosophy came to an end with the *Report of the National Reading Panel* (National Reading Panel, 2000), which compared years of research through a technique known as meta-analysis, a way to compare studies that use different research methods. Phonics found its rightful place in reading instruction once again.

Reading experts are now recommending a balanced approach. The most important outcome of the reading wars is that reading programs now blend both phonics and literature. That outcome, however, seems like a shallow resolution and fails to provide direction for teachers, either in *how* to combine phonics and literature or in how to teach reading in the intermediate and upper grades. Let's start with some background about combined methods and then move toward a more encompassing definition of balanced reading.

■ COMBINED APPROACHES

Reading instruction that combines elements of reading is not really a new idea. In 1960, Helen Robinson, one of the coauthors of Scott Foresman's Dick and Jane readers, wrote the following, which advocates both skills instruction and reading for meaning:

> Neither is competence in reading acquired in a short time or by learning specific aspects of reading in isolation. Phonics is of little value unless it is a tool used consistently in recognizing words. Word perception is not an isolated skill, but a tool in securing meaning. On the other hand, thoughtful reaction to, and assimilation of, what is read cannot be effective without accurate word perception and acquisition of correct meanings. (p. 239)

In 1998, Timothy Shanahan identified 12 research studies that have influenced reading instruction. Included was the "Cooperative Research Program in

First-Grade Reading Instruction" (Bond & Dykstra, 1967), which compiled data from 27 individual studies of differing approaches to beginning reading, such as phonics, linguistic readers, basals, initial teaching alphabet, individualized reading, language experience approaches, and various grouping schemes. Shanahan reported, "These studies found that none of the instructional methods were superior to the others for students at either high or low levels of readiness." But a big "however" was attached to his conclusion: "[These studies] did find that some combinations of methods (such as including phonics and writing with other approaches) were associated with more learning" (Shanahan, 1998, p. 51).

> Surveys of practicing teachers find the majority using eclectic or balanced approaches.

Surveys of practicing teachers find the majority using eclectic or balanced approaches (Baumann et al., 1998; Worthy & Hoffman, 1997; Pressley, Rankin, & Yokoi, 1996). In a survey conducted by Baumann of more than 1,200 teachers of prekindergarten through fifth grade, 89% said they used a balanced approach, blending phonics and skills instruction with holistic principles and practices. They also allocated classroom time in a balanced way, spending moderate amounts of time on reading strategy instruction and moderate amounts of time in more holistic activities, such as reading aloud to students, independent reading, responding to literature, and writing. Eighty-three percent also balanced instructional materials with a combination of basal reading programs and children's trade books.

It is apparent that combining phonics and literature is a part of balanced reading instruction, but how to combine them is not apparent. One answer for a cohesive approach is the whole-part-whole model of instruction.

WHOLE-PART-WHOLE MODEL OF INSTRUCTION ■

A long-standing concern about reading and writing instruction has been the isolated teaching of skills: phonics, comprehension, or any other type of literacy skill. Although children accumulated the skills, they had little ability to apply them during actual reading or writing. The whole-part-whole model provides a framework for integration and application of skills in context so that they become strategies actually used in literacy. I was first introduced to this idea in 1985 in *Becoming a Nation of Readers* (Anderson, et al.), and Dorothy Strickland, prolific author and professor of education at Rutgers University Graduate School of Education, advocated this framework in 1998.

The whole-part-whole approach replicates the way people learn anything new. To start, students or adults need to see the big picture (the first whole), what "it" is and why it would be useful to learn such a thing. Then learners ask, "So exactly what do you have to do?" and they discover specific parts and skills that make up the whole idea. Finally, they are able to successfully assemble the parts into their entirety (the second whole). When the entire concept is understood, the details make sense and are relevant; they can be applied correctly within the overall concept.

The First Whole in Literacy Instruction

The big picture in reading, or the first "whole," involves the idea that print represents spoken language and is used to communicate meaningful thoughts. Many concepts about literacy are learned by watching adults read and write. Children become aware of print in books, magazines, signs, notes, newspapers, and advertisements and on computer screens. By being read to, they learn the more formal language structures used in books, story structure, and genres of writing. They learn the power of a wonderful story, and they learn that useful information can be conveyed through print. The genres of writing are learned through wide reading and exemplars. Children learn that reading makes sense and serves a useful purpose. Although beginning readers cannot do all these things by themselves, they can see where they are going, what it will look like, and why they might want to learn to do it. When children learn this first meaningful concept of literacy, they learn that completing worksheets is not the primary goal of reading.

The Parts of Literacy Instruction

The parts in whole-part-whole instruction—the specific reading skills and strategies—need to be taught. For most children, these skills do not develop naturally, as speech does, or develop simply through exposure to print. Sometimes kids have unusual misconceptions; for example, most three- and many four-year-olds think the story is told through the pictures rather than the print (Strommen & Mates, 1997). Some do not realize that when the question says, "What do you think . . . ?" the answer is not in the book. Although some children learn naturally through immersion in a literacy-rich environment, most need instruction. Seeing a lot of "it" does not necessarily mean that children are going to "get it" by themselves. This is especially true for children who do not come from a background of literacy or who do not see the purpose of becoming readers.

Many children need **explicit instruction and coaching**. Explicit instruction, also known as direct or systematic instruction, includes letting children know what is being taught, why it is being taught, how they can connect this information to other things they already know, and how the procedure works. Explicit instruction provides enough sustained, focused practice to enable students to learn and use strategies effectively. These ideas from the explicit instruction model fit very well with the first whole.

Although children do learn skills, many do not have the background or maturity that helps them realize that they should transfer those skills to future reading tasks, that is, that they are supposed to actually use what they have learned. Explicit instruction not only includes specific directions and modeling for learning a skill but also shows children how to use the skill in actual reading situations. This idea from the explicit instruction model fits well with the second whole.

In explicit instruction, teachers explain, model, think aloud, demonstrate, and guide students to learn and apply skills. The teacher helps children practice the strategy in actual reading situations. It can be as simple as telling the child that ch sounds /ch/ and *chair* starts with that sound. Later, she might say, "I see you're stuck on that word. It starts with the same sound as *chair* does, just like we practiced this morning." Or the teacher may say, "In order to make an inference, readers must use knowledge they already possess plus information given by the author. In order to figure out what Julie wanted, look at what Julie said and combine it with how she acted. How do you think she is really feeling?" The children's attention is focused on a single reading strategy for enough time for them to learn how it works. This is different from just giving directions to complete a worksheet.

Instruction that is explicit and systematic is essential for some students to succeed (Pressley, 1996). Explicit instruction is especially important for struggling readers. Students with learning disabilities, English language learners, and many students who struggle with reading for a variety of reasons often find it difficult to infer a process or generalize a rule from a simple discussion or one or two examples. They benefit the most from direct instruction. Direct instruction at its best teaches strategies that help "make reading and writing more doable and, hence, less frustrating" (Pressley, p. 282).

Research does not offer guidelines about how much time to spend in explicit instruction versus how much in actual reading. Children's needs determine how direct the instruction should be and how much instruction is needed. However, in a study of an urban school district that was adopting balanced reading, Frey, Lee, Tollefson, Pass, and Massengill (2005) found that although the teachers adopted many aspects of balanced reading, such as independent reading and writing, the amount of time devoted to instruction and modeling effective strategies seemed too limited for students with poorly developed reading and writing skills.

Skill instruction is not just for phonics. Students also need instruction in comprehension skills and how to apply those skills in texts. This is also true for the other components of literacy: listening, speaking, spelling, fluency, writing, and vocabulary. Not surprisingly, extensive research indicates that clearly defined objectives and teacher-directed instruction are characteristics of effective literacy programs. Explicit instruction does not preclude on-the-spot coaching, and it does not encourage mindless, rote learning.

The Final Whole in Literacy Instruction

The isolated teaching of skills has received much well-deserved criticism. Nothing is wrong with selecting a skill and working with it for a while until children learn what it is and how to do it. The problem has been that in some classrooms, the entire process stops right there. I clearly remember teaching a skill from a basal and then searching for an appropriate story in the book where the students could apply and practice the skill they had learned; skills and stories were never very coordinated. In a balanced classroom, skills are not decontextualized (taught or used out of context) for very long. Children need to move from knowing about a generalization to using that knowledge in a purposeful way (Strickland, 1998).

Children need considerable time to practice the skills they have learned. Skills won't "stick" or be used seamlessly unless the children read a lot and have the opportunity to use the skills in real reading. (Of course, some need reminders that the upcoming story will be perfect to use the skills they just learned.) When they can apply a skill in a rewarding way, students will see why they learned the skill and how it is useful in reading.

Children need to read a lot. In reviewing various research studies, Allington (2002b) found that the higher-achieving students read approximately three times as much each week in school as their lower-achieving classmates. The classic study of out-of-school reading by fifth graders was carried out by Anderson, Wilson, and Fielding (1988). Students at the 90th percentile of achievement read, on the average, 2,357,000 words per year while students at the 10th percentile read 51,000 words per year. The more children read, the easier it becomes.

Children need to read a rich variety of interesting texts: challenging books, easy books, magazines, informational books, series books, newspapers, and all the types of materials people find useful in their lives. If children see only practice materials, they may not understand the big picture.

> Children need books at their instructional level and lots of easy books for independent reading that are fun to read and help build fluency.

Children need books at their instructional level and lots of easy books for independent reading that are fun to read and help build fluency. Allington's study of exemplary teachers (2002b, p. 743) found that outstanding teachers taught their students with appropriately leveled texts and made sure that students "received a steady diet of 'easy' texts—texts they could read accurately, fluently, and with good comprehension."

Children need sufficient time and practice to consolidate and unify reading skills if they are to use those skills purposefully and selectively. In real text, readers never use just one skill at a time. When skills are purposely used in reading, they become strategies rather than isolated skills.

Similarly, children need to write whole compositions for real purposes, use precise vocabulary to communicate, and speak and listen in real situations. They need lots of practice in all these skills too.

Teacher coaching seems especially important in transferring the skills to reading. In a study of low-income schools, Taylor, Pearson, Clark, and Walpole (2000) found that teachers in the most effective schools were three times more likely to encourage students to use the strategies they had been taught to figure out unknown words when they encountered them in reading. This finding contrasts with practices in schools of lesser effectiveness, where phonics was explicitly taught but coaching was seldom observed. In a study of outstanding primary teachers (Wharton-McDonald, Pressley, & Hampston, 1998), the best teachers reminded children how the skills could be used in the children's writing and reading. Pressley et al. (2001) found the most effective first-grade teachers frequently reminded students to use previously taught word identification skills during reading activities. Coaching bridges direct instruction and application when students do not make the connection by themselves.

Although not everyone uses the whole-part-whole term, evidence from studies of outstanding teachers (Pressley, Wharton-McDonald, & Hampston, 2002) shows the integration of skills and application.

> Literacy instruction [provided by the most effective teachers] was exceptionally well balanced with respect to the elements of whole language—reading of outstanding literature, writing—and the explicit teaching of skills. Reading, writing, and skills instruction were very well integrated

in these classrooms. Although there were lessons dedicated specifically to certain skills, the skills instruction observed in the three best classrooms in this study was anything but decontextualized. The skills lessons were filled with reminders about how skills related to the children's writing and reading. Moreover, the children had many opportunities to use the skills as they read and wrote. (pp. 193–194)

The whole-part-whole model can be seen easily in the practices of effective teachers. "Moving from whole to part and back to whole again thus provides a framework for planning that addresses skills in a manner that is meaningful, strategic, and more characteristic of the way proficient readers actually use skills when they read and write" (Strickland, 1998, p. 8).

Teaching With a Whole-Part-Whole Approach

Teaching with a whole-part-whole approach requires considerable knowledge of ways to provide effective skills instruction as well as ways to provide holistic reading and writing. Coaching, knowing just when to give that reminder about using a skill, takes intuition or experience—which doesn't come with the teacher's manual. Integrating all these elements into a cohesive classroom takes skill too. Pressley, Roehrig, Bogner, Raphael, and Dolezal (2002) found that the most effective teachers integrated skills instruction and literature, in contrast to less-effective teachers, who had a skills block and a reading block without apparent connection. The more effective teachers also integrated the language arts.

Teaching with literature, rather than with basals, can be even more challenging. Unless a novel is assigned for independent reading, the teacher must determine the skills to be taught. Application is no problem. Most pieces of literature or content texts can be used for a variety of purposes, but some are especially suitable for learning a particular sound-symbol relationship, such as *Sheep in a Jeep* (Shaw, 1986); for learning cause and effect, visualization, or predicting; or especially for inferring and interpreting. Sometimes, teachers choose a particular story just because it requires making inferences, for example, and that is one of the standards that must be met as well as one of the skills readers need.

Since novels do not have a mandated or sequenced set of comprehension skills, as a basal does, teachers can use their professional judgment to match instruction to the needs of the class, which also requires keeping track of what has been learned and what still needs to be taught.

CONTINUING TO DEFINE BALANCED INSTRUCTION ■

Balanced literacy instruction is more than combining skills and literature, although that is a good beginning. To be a rich, cohesive, and flexible philosophy, balanced reading should include integrating the language arts, providing varying levels of support and intensity of teaching, and blending teacher- and student-centered activities. It is not just the presence of a variety of activities that makes a program of reading instruction effective or ineffective. It is the way in which its pieces are fitted together to complement and support one another, always with full consideration of the needs and progress of the young readers with whom it will be used (Adams, cited in Stahl, Osborn, & Lehr, 1990, p. 122).

■ INTEGRATING THE LANGUAGE ARTS

If it makes sense to integrate reading skills and application, then it certainly makes sense to integrate the language arts—listening and speaking, word recognition, spelling, writing, vocabulary, comprehension, and fluency. The components feel less disjointed to both the teacher and the learners, and each skill enhances the others.

When literacy instruction is integrated in a primary classroom, a teacher may read a story aloud as the children listen and make predictions. They then discuss the story together, talking about unfamiliar vocabulary words. An aspect of word recognition based on the words in the story is taught and practiced. The story is reread with partners or in shared reading, with the support of the teacher, for practice and fluency. The teacher may explain the importance of sequence, and the children place sentence strips in order to retell the story. The students write about the story or about personal experiences connected to the topic. As they write, knowledge of decoding affects their spelling, and learning to spell influences their decoding. Children then orally retell the story to ensure they comprehend the meaning.

When literacy instruction is integrated in an intermediate classroom, the teacher may use guided reading for the first section of the story. Children are asked to read for a purpose and discuss both the content and the strategies they used to comprehend the selection. The teacher may model connecting prior knowledge to the selection and then ask students to try the strategy in the next section. Vocabulary words from the selection are discussed, predicted by context, or sorted. Students finish the story independently and return to the group to discuss the content. They respond to the story in writing by retelling from another character's perspective or connecting the theme to personal experiences. The first draft may be examined for logical paragraph structure. Students may use unusual or complex sentence structure from the story as a model to develop original but structurally similar sentences in their compositions. They turn a scene into a Readers' Theatre script (discussed in Chapter 5) and practice for fluency before performing, or they make oral presentations about related topics as their classmates listen and ask questions. Writing in particular is no longer an add-on when the children are writing about what they read. Teachers who have been teaching thematic units have known this for years.

Integrating the language arts places considerable responsibility on the teacher because integrated materials are not always available. Although publishers are moving in this direction, teachers often find themselves with a literature anthology, a spelling book, an English book, a variety of trade books, and perhaps a separate vocabulary or phonics program, each from a different publisher and each bearing no relation to the other. It often takes considerable time to coordinate materials and instruction. Perhaps nowhere is it more challenging to integrate successfully than in first grade, when teachers are often faced with a systematic phonics program and an unsystematic collection of little books and trade books.

Nonfiction is finally working its way into the integrated curriculum. The style of writing used in expository text differs significantly from narrative text in organizational patterns, in concept and vocabulary loads, in the use of visual aids such as charts and graphs, and even in sentence complexity. Developing literacy with expositional text takes considerable teacher support and direct instruction so that students will eventually be able to learn the content independently.

However, the benefits of integrated instruction are numerous. Children see how all the aspects of literacy are coordinated. They discover that what is learned in one area can be used in another. The teacher does not have to start each activity with new background introductions, and interest is already established. It is also more time efficient, and time is always a precious commodity.

LEVELS OF SUPPORT ■
AND INTENSITY OF INSTRUCTION

Balancing reading skills and literature and integrating the language arts make for a more unified and cohesive classroom. However, those aspects alone do not specifically address the diversity of children in every classroom. One of the surprising findings in Pressley, Rankin, and Yokoi's survey (1996) of effective first-grade teachers was that instruction for struggling readers did not differ qualitatively from instruction for other students. The struggling students also had skills instruction and plenty of reading and writing activities. What differed was the extensiveness and intensity of instruction. In a similar study, special education primary teachers

> Teachers meet the needs of diverse learners by adjusting the level of support and the intensity of instruction.

nominated for their effectiveness in teaching literacy were surveyed, and the conclusions were similar. It was not that they used different educational practice but that they taught with greater explicitness and completeness of skills instruction. Teachers meet the needs of diverse learners by adjusting the level of support and the intensity of instruction (Pressley, Roehrig, et al., 2002).

Teachers are always scaffolding (providing support). When students learn a new skill, they require considerable support at first, but the support fades as the learner becomes more competent. It is easy to see the level of support being adjusted in first grade. At the beginning, the teacher assumes all the responsibility when she reads aloud. Soon, students participate in shared reading, in which both the teacher and the students read the text together. This progresses to guided reading, in which the students do all the reading and the teacher provides purpose setting, specific instruction, clues, feedback, and so forth. Students partner read, and finally they are able to read more difficult books independently.

In reality, the process is not quite this linear; support is adjusted daily and in different ways for different children. Children who struggle need continuing levels of high support and the most direct instruction. Those who have stronger backgrounds often learn a new skill easily, so they do not usually require continued high levels of support.

Another way of adjusting support and differentiating instruction is establishing leveled guided reading groups, in which small groups of children who use similar reading processes and are able to read similar levels of text with support meet together with the teacher for instruction and reading (Fountas & Pinnell, 1996). Children learn best when the text is only a little challenging. Students who struggle with books that are too hard to understand have little chance to use comprehension or word attack strategies. It is senseless to think about balancing skills and literature if both are just too hard to understand. Continuing assessment ensures that students are matched to books they can read.

Intensity has two meanings. The first definition is the intensity of meaningful classroom instruction and activity. Students are constantly engaged in productive literacy tasks. Pressley, Wharton-McDonald, and Hampston (2002) describe it as high-density instruction and very little downtime due to transitions or classroom management issues. "The best teachers [in an effective teacher study] were masterful classroom managers. They were so good, in fact, that classroom management was hardly noticeable" (p. 192). Pressley et al. (2002) describe high-density instruction as the 90/90 rule, meaning that 90% of the children are on task 90% of the time. Allington (2001) recommends, as Pressley does, that lessons be paced to take advantage of every minute of time available.

Allington (2002a) provides the second meaning of intensity, viewing it in terms of teacher-pupil ratio—the smaller the better for students who are struggling. This means that the readers who struggle are in the smallest reading group, and students who receive special services should be in very small groups. These groups need to meet daily. He also suggests that specialists might consider longer blocks of time for fewer weeks per year to achieve the necessary intensity of instruction.

Maybe level of support and intensity of instruction are a little hard to fit into a definition of balanced reading, but if teachers don't take these components into consideration, there is not much hope for meeting the needs of all learners.

■ BALANCING STUDENT- AND TEACHER-CENTERED INSTRUCTION

Successful balanced literacy programs combine teacher-directed instruction and student-centered activities (Frey et al., 2005). This last component fits quite easily into the definition of balanced instruction, and choice and autonomy are important in balancing the classroom climate.

In traditional classrooms, the teacher is the focus of instruction, and the content and sequence are determined by the teacher and state standards. This is not entirely bad. Adults have a broader perspective than eight-year-olds do for making informed decisions about the reading process, and adults understand the scope of abilities that a mature reader is going to need. But the teacher does not have to decide everything.

Student choice is also important. Interest, choice, and a degree of autonomy about daily activities are powerful factors in motivation, which affects the classroom climate. Students can choose books for literature circles or independent reading. Writers' workshop topics are chosen by the children. Many teachers provide choice about how students can respond to text. Even given the choice about doing the odds or the evens in an assignment is a big deal! Students can self-determine who will take the roles in Readers' Theatre or which spelling words they will add to their lists for all the ones that were correct on the pretest. Classrooms that allow for choice have a positive climate.

In a balanced program, many teachers choose a blend of activities and materials for direct instruction, and other materials and activities are chosen by the students. The ratio of teacher-directed to student-choice activities can be adjusted depending on the needs and independence of the class.

Balanced reading and writing solves the skills-based versus meaning-based dilemma by using a whole-part-whole approach, integrates the language arts, provides varying levels of support and intensity, and blends teacher- and student-centered instruction. It requires skillful and knowledgeable teaching and a great degree of creativity and ingenuity, especially when the materials that are available were not designed specifically to meet the purposes of balanced reading and writing. The rewards are substantial, however, when children understand the relevancy of reading and writing and explicitly understand how the processes work. They are able to see relationships among the components—reading, writing, listening, and speaking—because each is used to complement and reinforce the others. When children have some degree of choice and control, the classroom climate is balanced, too. Balanced reading and writing is a very strong model for instruction in literacy.

2
Getting Ready to Read

Dear little child, this little book
Is less a primer than a key
To sunder gates where wonder waits
Your "Open Sesame!"

—Rupert Hughes

Learning how to read seems to happen in a moment of magic. One day a student does not know how to read, and the next day that student does. Although it may seem that way, the experiences that lead to reading occur over an extended period. The ease with which a child learns is dependent on several factors. The crucial factors include attaining the concept of reading, as well as language acquisition and sociocultural factors.

■ CONCEPT OF READING

Linda Teran Strommen and Barbara Fowles Mates (1997) conducted a three-year longitudinal study to explore young children's ideas about reading. Although the children reached the various stages at different ages, the progression of increased understanding of reading concepts was similar in all children.

The first idea developed by some of the readers was that reading was one aspect of a social routine rather than a distinct activity. "We take a bath in the shower, and then we go to bed. We read the story, then when my light is off, I call Daddy," noted one three-year-old in the study (Strommen & Mates, 1997, p. 100).

Students next perceived that reading was an interaction between a person and a book. For example, when asked to "read," children turned the pages and looked at the pictures. Sometimes they did this silently; sometimes they commented on the pictures. Children subsequently noticed that reading involved telling an event in sequence, but they thought that the story was created by the reader through the pictures. As they picture read, children often used the type of language and sentence patterns found in children's books. Sometimes their stories were close to the author's and sometimes not. The children who had reached this stage could identify words and letters as "something you can read," but they did not yet connect that knowledge to reading a story. Despite having little knowledge of text, children were willing to "read" because they were confident of their abilities to invent an organized account through the illustrations.

Children begin to develop an **awareness of print** while being read to at home or, for some children, while the teacher reads big books and points to the words. Children learn that print is read left to right and top to bottom. A print-rich environment of words can be developed by labeling classroom objects and developing class charts with names, jobs, birthdays, daily activities, and classroom news.

When children start learning the letters of the alphabet, they do not necessarily connect the letters with words that carry meaning. One child in the study talked about reading a story and then "doing" letters, which to him were two completely unrelated activities.

In Strommen and Mates's next stage, children discovered that a book had a particular story. To many children, this meant that, although the meaning must remain the same, the words could change with each retelling. At this stage, children could often "read" a favorite story from memory, matching the sequence to the pictures. They could even "read" their favorite books with their eyes closed.

Children eventually realized that it is the print that tells the exact wording in a story. "When children achieved this insight they were generally able to read and write their own names, family names, and a few sight words. . . . Most could "sound out" some simple unfamiliar words. However, these skills did not constitute reading in the minds of these young children" (Strommen & Mates, 1997, p. 103). They often had the idea that print was just an aid for memorizing the story. At this stage, decoding skills were so incomplete and laborious that some children abandoned their efforts because it hindered the process of revealing the story. They believed that reading from a text was an ability acquired when you "got big," a mysterious process acquired all at once that was not a matter of decoding.

Children finally reached the stage of using multiple strategies, including pictures, letter-sound relationships, sight words, sentence patterns, and story meaning. One student who had finally gained the concept of reading told the researchers, "[To read] you sound out the letters, or you just know it."

Children may not truly grasp the "whole" (as in the whole-part-whole model of reading instruction) until they have a variety of experiences with language, print awareness, story structure, and at least a partial awareness of the alphabetic principle, that is, that sounds and letters have a dependable correspondence. Strommen and Mates's intriguing study is also a reminder to teachers that young children's concepts of reading may need to be expanded. It is hard to motivate children to learn beginning sounds when they think they should be working on memorizing the story.

■ LANGUAGE ACQUISITION

Spoken language comes naturally; the brain seems "prewired" for language acquisition. Early knowledge of how the brain processes language came from studying patients with brain injuries, but recently, various brain scan technologies have given us much more information. Broca's area, in the left frontal lobe, is believed to be responsible for processing vocabulary, making sense of word order, and applying the rules of grammar. Wernicke's area has to do with processing the meaning of spoken language. Both are located in the left hemisphere, which is responsible for most language processing; however, the emotional content of language is processed in the right hemisphere. Female brains process language in both hemispheres and have a larger and thicker corpus callosum, the bundle of neurons that connects the hemispheres, allowing for easier access between the hemispheres. These two differences may explain why young girls generally acquire spoken language easier and more quickly than young boys do (Sousa, 2005).

Infants can recognize phonemes (basic speech sounds) at six months, when they begin babbling and are able to produce all phonemes available to human speech, but by about one year of age, the phonemes are pruned down to the ones they hear in their environments (Beatty, 2001). Children attach meaning to words by 12 months and express whole thoughts through a single word, such as *cookie*. They begin acquiring seven to ten words a day as Wernicke's area becomes fully functional. Toddlers put together two-word sentences and can recognize noun and verb differences at 18 months. They

Figure 2.1 The language system in the left hemisphere is comprised mainly of Broca's area and Wernicke's area. The four lobes of the brain are also identified.

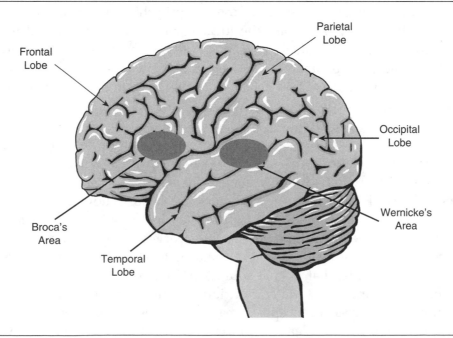

Source: Sousa, David A., *How the Brain Learns to Read.* Thousand Oaks, CA: Corwin Press, 2005.

generate original sentences by generalizing rules rather than through direct imitation of adult speech. For example, few adults would say *Allgone cookie.* By 24 months, children begin to learn other grammatical functions, such as simple subject-verb-object sentences like *Me want cookie.* When parents expand the child's utterances, such as by saying "Would you like a chocolate chip cookie?" language structures increase in complexity. Children learn intonation and are able to differentiate between statements and questions by the rise or fall of the tone at the end of the sentence. They note the regularity of language structures and generalize to irregular words, such as saying *catched* for *caught,* but learn the correct forms through repetition and modeling by adults. By the time a child reaches the age of three, most language activity moves to the left hemisphere of the brain. Between the ages of three and four, children come to understand such numerical concepts as few and many and first and second and may develop a speaking vocabulary of up to 1,500 words (Reutzel & Cooter, 2003).

In addition to vocabulary and syntax, children learn conversational skills, such as how to open a conversation (*You know what?*), and they learn how to take turns; interruptions are rare in a conversation between two children (Richgels, 2004). Young children easily understand subject-verb-object sentences, but they have more difficulty with sentences that include clauses, such as "The boy pushed the girl who took the toy." They may not be sure whether the boy pushed the girl *and* took the toy. Passive structure, "The girl was pushed by the boy," and negative structure, "The toy was taken by the girl, not the boy," are both harder to process (Sousa, 2005). Simple sentence structure is used in beginning texts for these reasons. Through conversational activities with children and adults, young children's language comes closer and closer to approximating the speech patterns of the adults surrounding them.

Recent research indicates that spoken language production is very complex, using multiple areas of the brain. The brain seems to generally process language from the bottom up, distinguishing sounds, the meaning parts of words, and the syntax rules for forming sentences and then making sense of it all. Image-loaded words are processed in the front area while abstract words are processed in the top central and rear areas. Words that are closely related in meaning appear to be grouped and stored in adjacent neurons so that words that connect to one another can be rapidly accessed. A recent discovery is that the neurons in Wernicke's area are spaced about 20% farther apart and cabled together with longer interconnection axons than are neurons in the corresponding area in the right hemisphere. "The implication is that the practice of language during early human development results in longer and more intricately connected neurons in the Wernicke region, allowing for greater sensitivity to meaning" (Sousa, 2005, p. 27).

Vocabulary Growth

Language development flourishes in environments that are rich in vocabulary and language interactions. Hart and Risley (1995) followed the vocabulary growth of 42 children from the age of one year to the age of three. The children came from professional, middle- to lower-class, and welfare families. The children from professional families heard more words, heard more different words, and had larger vocabularies than the other groups; the middle group heard more and acquired more words than the welfare family group. The researchers projected that these differing trajectories of vocabulary growth would continue, with a larger gap developing every year. In addition to the amount of vocabulary, children in professional families heard about six times as many affirmations (encouraging words) and half as many prohibitions as children in welfare families did. See Figure 2.2. When these children were retested six years later, the quantity of vocabulary learned at age three correlated with language, vocabulary, and reading tests at ages nine to ten. The effects of language development are cumulative and long term.

> Language development flourishes in environments that are rich in vocabulary and language interactions.

Figure 2.2   Comparative language acquisition

	Professional families		Middle-class families		Welfare families	
	Parent	*Child*	*Parent*	*Child*	*Parent*	*Child*
Recorded cumulative vocabulary	2176	1116 at 36 months	1498	749 at 36 months	974	525 at 36 months
Average words/hour	487	310	301	223	176	168
Different words/hour	382	297	251	216	167	149

Source: Hart, B. & Risley, T., "The Early Catastrophe," *American Educator*, Spring 2003. From *Meaningful Differences in the Everyday Experiences of Young American Children*, 1995. Copyright © Paul H. Brookes. Reprinted with permission from the Spring 2003 issue of the *American Educator*, the quarterly journal of the American Federation of Teachers, AFL-CIO.

English Language Learners

In 2005, there were at least 5.1 million English language learners in public K–12 schools. Although the size of the general school population remains fairly stable, the number of English language learners continues to increase. Currently 14% of the U.S. population is Latino, and the projection is that it will be 25% by 2050 (Goldenberg, 2005). There is considerable unresolved debate over whether children should receive instruction in their first language before moving to instruction in English. English language learners face a variety of challenges in addition to vocabulary as they learn to read. Some must learn a new alphabet, Chinese students must learn an alphabetic language system, and learners who share mostly the same alphabet must learn different sounds for some letters. Sentence structure may have a different order. Connotations and idioms are just a bear! It is difficult to generalize or prescribe for the many different situations, but teachers must provide extra support to these learners.

Language acquisition is critical at all stages of reading. When decoding skills are just partially learned, readers can often get the word right because they can come close enough to recognize it as a word known in their mental lexicon (speaking and understanding vocabulary). If the word is unknown, close pronunciation won't do much good. Comprehension depends heavily on vocabulary knowledge.

Activities for Language Development

Language development is especially important for children who are English language learners and for children who have little experience with stories or with the type of language used in school. The variety of language experiences traditionally used by early childhood and primary teachers helps develop language structures and vocabulary and helps children begin to detect sound units within words. These activities include telling stories, doing finger plays, reciting poems and chants, and reading stories aloud. Now, these activities are specifically targeted to develop language skills.

Word study includes exploring word meanings and talking about how words are used. Phonological tasks such as rhyming, counting syllables, and adding and deleting syllables and phonemic tasks such as matching beginning consonants in words, substituting sounds, and identifying that a sound exists in a word are a part of sound study. Specific phonemic activities are discussed in Chapter 3; also check out Webbing Into Literacy at http://curry.edschool.virginia.edu/go/wil/home.html for 30 weeks of full-page nursery rhymes with pictures, illustrated rime cards (cards with hill, ill, Jill, spill), riddles, and daily lesson plans. A sample is "One, two, three, four,/ Mary's at the cottage door./ Five, six, seven, eight,/ Eating cherries off a plate." The rhymes are based on Wylie and Durrell's basic 37 rimes (1970), such as -ill and -ate. (The full chart appears in Chapter 4.) Children who have an abundance of opportunities to expand their language and linguistic repertoires are more likely to decode new words and make sense of what they read (Strickland, 2002).

Reading aloud to the class from a variety of books should be a basic staple of the curriculum (Morris, 2005). Read-alouds provide a model of expert reading and fluency, immerse children in the more formal language of literature, and help them develop a sense of story structure. This is especially important for children who have not had this experience in their homes. Talking about books engages children in many of the comprehension challenges they will meet later: more complex vocabulary than commonly used in conversation and conventions used in written but not spoken language (Snow, 2005).

Many primary teachers read aloud to their classes several times a day, focusing on phonological concepts, vocabulary building, or deriving meaning from text. Kindergarten teachers can immediately tell which children have been previously read to because they are better able to focus on a story, ask questions, and listen with sustained attention. Listening comprehension is a moderately good predictor of reading comprehension.

Read-alouds need to be interactive. Before reading, the teacher should ask for predictions to generate interest and to provide focus. Both during and after reading, students need an opportunity to discuss the characters and sequence of the story and to ask questions. This provides occasions for thoughtful use of language and language acquisition and teaches students how to talk with one another about texts. A rather unexpected side effect is that repeated reading of favorite books may help to confirm in the minds of very young children that reading is memorizing. By reading from a variety of texts or covering the pictures and still reading, the teacher may contribute to a shift in thinking. Children who from an early age learn to love a good story have a head start on becoming avid readers.

■ SOCIOCULTURAL AND OTHER FACTORS THAT AFFECT READING

Children may be at risk of failing to learn to read for a number of reasons. Poverty, health issues, nutrition, homelessness, frequent moves, emotional trauma, and neglect all take their toll. As with vocabulary acquisition, some children have much more opportunity to observe reading and writing than other children do. Some have more stability in their lives, which makes them more likely to enjoy early literacy experiences. The quantity of books in the home and the frequency with which parents take children to libraries and book-stores are strong correlates of early reading achievement (Tracey & Morrow, 2002). Other risk factors are hearing and visual problems, which commonly go unnoticed and untreated. Children who have had tubes put in their ears for drainage have often spent a significant amount of time unable to hear clearly, which has an effect on speech and language development.

These are all challenging issues, and most are beyond the scope of this book. Issues that can be dealt with are developing good instructional practices for the diverse children in our classrooms and knowing how to choose appropriate materials. Highly effective literacy teachers have a deeper knowledge base and are more reflective and conscious of the decisions they make than are less effective literacy educators (Pressley et al., 2001).

■ EMERGENT LITERACY

Children need instruction in reading because learning how to read is not as natural as learning to speak. The brain is not prewired for reading. Phonemic awareness, word recognition, fluency, and comprehension are all discussed in separate chapters in this book (Chapters 3, 4, 5, 6, and 8), so the remainder of this chapter will focus on issues and techniques that seem best suited to kindergarten and early first grade. A child's first reading experiences may be with patterned books, echo reading, or language experience activities. These are typical of the holistic activities used as an introduction to literacy.

Patterned Books

Children are able to "read" predictable books with the teacher from the very first day of school. The stories are simple and use a repeated pattern. Some patterned books rhyme, but others do not. A well-known example is *Brown Bear, Brown Bear, What Do You See?* (Martin, 1967). The pattern is repeated more than a dozen times.

> Brown bear, brown bear, what do you see?
> I see a red bird looking at me.
> Red bird, red bird, what do you see?
> I see a yellow duck looking at me.

Although first books are "read" from memory of the patterns, from known nursery rhymes, and from picture cues, children are able to sound like real readers, starting reading with a feeling of accomplishment and confidence. Children develop word and print awareness, gain a sense of sentence and story structure, increase their vocabularies, learn a few sight words, and develop their first ideas about fluency.

Echo Reading

With echo reading, the teacher first reads and discusses a story with the class. Then she rereads a sentence or two, and the students repeat it using the same intonations. A big book or multiple copies of a storybook can be used. Children have the opportunity to hear the text read correctly before they read it themselves, which aids early word recognition. Pointing to the words as they are read helps the children focus on the print instead of simply relying on auditory memory. This technique helps very young readers establish the concept of what a word is and allows them to "read" an entire text. It also builds confidence and models fluency. Children who are a little more mature than most will incorporate some words into their sight vocabularies. Less experienced readers can echo read with more experienced partners, especially following a group session. As children become more familiar with letters, sounds, and words, they can share the task of reading with the teacher as they work out words and discuss the meaning.

Language Experience Activities

Many children first encounter print by having their words written down during a language experience activity. Language experience stories are stories or texts "written" by the students themselves. After a book has been read or an activity completed, the entire class or a small group discusses it and decides what to write. In kindergarten and early first grade, the teacher usually does most of the writing on chart paper as students dictate the sentences. While writing, the teacher thinks aloud about starting on the left side, beginning with a capital, determining beginning sounds, leaving spaces between words, and including punctuation.

After the text is completed, the teacher points to each word and reads the sentence out loud. The children echo read their story, which is relatively easy to do because they composed it. Individual children can be called on to read single words or sentences.

Language experience stories are powerful tools for beginners because reading, writing, listening, and speaking are all integrated. Students see how their own ideas can be communicated and transformed into print. They learn concepts about words and sentences, see how print is arranged, and review letters. As children become more proficient, language experience stories serve as models for choosing topics, thinking of details, and coordinating letters and sounds.

Choral Reading

As students learn to read but still need considerable support, they can choral read, that is, read in unison. The pronunciation of a tough word is immediately available because others in the group are reading with them. If the students are reading from a big book, the teacher should sweep the index finger across the line to discourage stilted, word-by-word reading.

Effective teachers use balanced instruction incorporating a whole-part-whole model. Read-alouds, patterned books, echo reading, language experience stories, and choral reading are all components of the first "whole" in whole-part-whole instruction. They help children develop a working concept of what literacy is. Emergent readers need this foundation before they start working on the parts (specific skills), or they will not understand why the parts should be studied or how they fit together.

■ LETTER AND WORD RECOGNITION

Because word recognition is so important, the focus of first grade may seem a bit lopsided at times. Although comprehension is always a consideration, much time is spent on learning to recognize words. Beginning readers go through developmental stages, starting with the recognition of words holistically through idiosyncratic features. Then they learn the alphabet and gain partial knowledge of sounds and letters, so they often confuse words starting with the same letter or with similar appearances. As they gain a more complete knowledge of sounds and letters, they come to recognize many words instantly as sight words. Children continue to learn frequent and variant spelling patterns and irregularities, and the process culminates in the ability to recognize most words instantaneously and to pronounce any unfamiliar word. This step happens only when students use their word knowledge during extensive reading of text, the last whole in the whole-part-whole model.

Alphabet Knowledge

Children should be able to recognize both uppercase and lowercase letters in a variety of print fonts and manuscript writing. The names of many letters are also closely related to their sounds, which is helpful in decoding and in developmental spelling. Speed in letter recognition is important because it indicates that the letters are thoroughly learned and can be discriminated at a glance.

Alphabet war is similar to the card game war. It is played in pairs with an alphabet strip on the desk. Each child has a pile of letter cards. They each take a card from the pile, and whoever has the card closer to A wins both cards. The winner must say "___ is closer to A than ___, so I win."

In **alphabet chant**, the teacher says the alphabet with a repeating pattern of voice tone while pointing to an alphabet strip.

AB (loud) CD (soft) EF (loud) GH (soft) IJ (loud) KL (soft) . . . A (low) BC (high) D (low) EF (high) G (low) HI (high) J (low) KL (high) . . .

Alphabet books help students see the letters and hear the sounds that start the selected words. Reading alphabet books to preschoolers also helps to develop phonemic awareness. Look at *Alphabeasts* (Edwards, 2002) or *G Is for Goat* (Polacco, 2003) for inspiration and fabulous illustrations. Go to Webbing Into Literacy at http://curry.edschool.virginia.edu/go/wil/home.html for seasonal alphabet books with full-page illustrations.

> Effective kindergarten and first-grade teachers create rich literacy environments.

Word Recognition

Effective kindergarten and first-grade teachers create rich literacy environments with **environmental print** by labeling everything in the classroom. Labeled objects can always be used as examples. When working with *m,* the markers and the milk crate become perfect examples. The classrooms of effective teachers are also overflowing with a diverse collection of children's books (Pressley et al., 2001).

In first grade, **word walls** are usually composed of high-frequency words or key words for word families. The posted words serve as a reference for beginning sounds, as key words for word recognition, or as a reference for spelling. Word walls can be used effectively for emergent readers, too. Janiel Wagstaff (1997) started a word wall with her emergent readers by using nursery rhymes. After reading, reciting, and dramatizing "Jack and Jill," the class chose three key words, *Jack, water,* and *pail.* The teacher emphasized the initial sounds, and the children made the sounds and practiced writing the first letter. They searched for other words that began with those letters and reread the rhyme. The teacher posted the words below the alphabet with illustrations as cues and displayed "Jack and Jill" for rereading. Each week about three new words were added.

Author and teacher Francine Johnston (1998) used a **word bank** activity in conjunction with little books, the 12- to 16-page trade books for early readers. Students reread a little book every day for a week, but they were also given a text-only copy of the story. The students then underlined words they thought they knew. The teacher held up an index card with one of the selected words printed on it. If the child could name the word, it went into that child's word bank. On the third day, children reread the words, used the book to identify others, and added more words to their banks. On the fourth day, the students read their words again and participated in a word study game. The teacher said, for example, "If you have a word that begins with f, hold it up." Or "Hold up a word that rhymes with *not.*" Students who participated in the word bank study learned more words than those who used sentence strips or repeated reading. Johnston recommends discontinuing word banks when a child has 150 to 250 words because by then children will have developed their own system of internally storing and retrieving words.

Originally suggested by Sylvia Ashton-Warner (cited in May, 1998), **key words** are personal words that children want to know either because they have a need for them or because they find them interesting. The teacher asks each child for a word and writes it down on an index card. Children can keep their card collections in word banks, in word boxes, or on large snap-open key chains (which solves the spillage problem). The key words may be added to sight words or kept separately. The children work with the key words by reviewing their collections, reading words with a partner, or making sentences with the word cards.

Great **word cards** can be made on the computer in a 72-point font. Five words will fit on a piece of paper. The words will look more like the text in a book than handwritten print will. Producing word cards on a computer is especially useful when word cards are made for the whole class or a small group of students. The drawback to this technique is that not all printers take heavy, durable paper. If the teacher has access to a duplicator that takes heavy paper, the computer-printed cards will serve as master copies. To make life easier logistically, glue a library pocket or staple a zip-lock bag into the back of the books to hold all the word cards for that story. Experienced teachers know to write the name of the book on the back of each card so that the leftovers lying on the floor can find their proper places.

Writing and spelling are important paths to word analysis skills. As spellers determine sound-letter relationships, they identify how words look in print. Chapter 10 offers several ideas for working with children who are learning how to spell.

Words With Text Support

Words are easier to identify when used in context. Context is an insufficient and unreliable cueing system for word identification, but it does help limit choices of words to those that are contextually and syntactically appropriate, that is, fit the meaning and the sentence structure.

Use **word cards with text support**. When students are studying words that have been taken from a story, allow the students to keep their books open. Those students with only partial knowledge can use the book for additional clues to identify the words.

A short story or a poem can be rewritten on **sentence strips.** These are presented without the support of the pictures. The strips can be shuffled, and the students must reassemble the story in correct sequence. Large strips written on tagboard can be used in pocket charts, and small sentence strips can be duplicated on paper for individual students. If the teacher makes a line down the edge of each child's paper with a different color of marker before cutting the paper into strips, children can easily identify which strips are theirs when working with a partner or when the strips get spilled on the floor. Even beginning readers can use this technique with a memorized poem. Since students already know what the lines say, partial clues can be used to make the match and to put lines in order.

Individual sentence strips can be cut into **word strips**. The words can be reassembled into the original sentence with the help of the book or rearranged into variations. With large cut-up sentence strips, the words can be given to different children, who need to assemble themselves in a sentence sequence. The period can also be included on a separate card. After the children are in order, other students in the class read the sentence.

Connected flash cards are individual flash cards that make up a sentence when put together. It is easier to recognize the words with some context help, and they can be used to communicate messages:

| *Line* | *up* | *for* | *music.* |

COMPREHENSION AND BEGINNING READERS ■

Because word identification is so important in first grade, it is difficult for both students and teachers to remain focused on comprehension. Nevertheless, it is essential to do so because the roots of reading comprehension are formed during this period (Tracey & Morrow, 2002). Students who have strong language skills and vocabulary have an advantage because they can recognize the meanings of words and the more formal structure of sentences in books. It is especially important to discuss the meaning of new words prior to reading so students with limited vocabularies and students who are English language learners will comprehend. Background experiences also affect comprehension. Read-alouds and shared and guided reading often start with making links between known concepts and the story. These connections need to be made explicit for many primary students who are not used to the idea of searching their own backgrounds for familiar ideas that will help them interpret new ones. Many primary teachers do this with a picture walk, looking at all the pictures and discussing the events and vocabulary before reading.

Readers with good word attack strategies have a better chance at comprehension because working memory is not overloaded by decoding tasks. Working memory is now defined as temporary memory, 5–10 minutes for preadolescents. It lasts longer than immediate memory (reading a phone number from the telephone book, dialing, and forgetting) but shorter than long-term permanent memory. Retaining verbal information depends on one's age, experience, and language proficiency (Sousa, 2005). If too much working memory is taken up by decoding, little is left for comprehension.

Comprehension Development

Primary comprehension skills are learned and practiced during read-alouds, shared reading, and guided reading through teacher modeling, explanation, and guided practice. During shared reading, the teacher and students read together, often from a big book. Children chime in when they can. Repeated reading of a favorite book allows for greater student participation.

Primary skills include monitoring for comprehension, predicting, connecting to prior knowledge, comparing and contrasting, and using fix-up strategies when the text does not make sense. They can be learned best in the context of connected reading. Children learn to read increasingly difficult material because the teacher is there, supporting the process. Readers demonstrate their comprehension through retelling, making reasonable predictions, summarizing, and participating in discussions. Although oral reading is extremely valuable for diagnosis, everyone practices when students read silently or whisper read during guided reading, not just the student whose turn it is.

> Children learn to read increasingly difficult material because the teacher is there, supporting the process.

Monitoring Comprehension

Monitoring relies on three **cueing systems**: graphophonics, semantics, and syntax. Most young readers need cueing to learn the cues. If all the systems are not taught and used, the reader will come to rely on one more than the others and not be successful. Struggling readers tend to rely solely on graphophonics.

Graphophonemic cues are the sound-letter correspondences and spelling patterns used to identify unknown words. If it sounds like a known word, the reader can identify it. Chapter 4 explains developmental stages and provides strategies for teaching word recognition.

Successful readers use **semantic cues** to see if the text makes sense. Semantic cues are meaning cues found in the text and in the pictures. The word must make sense in the context of the rest of the story. All readers must use previous experiences and their meaning vocabulary to make these judgments. Fortunately, most primary stories are straightforward and apparent. The cueing question when a student says the wrong word is "Does that make sense?"

Syntactic cues are given by sentence patterns and grammatical structures. English sentence patterns, especially in primary text, tend to be very predictable. Syntactic cues cannot be used to identify just any real word; the word has to fit a slot in the sentence. Try answering the questions about the following sentence. *The squitly tourmarands vashornly blained the cloughts in the wroked knanflede.*

What did the tourmarands do?
They blained the cloughts.

Where did they do it?
In the wroked knanflede.

What kinds of tourmarands were they?
Squitly tourmarands.

How did the tourmarands blain the cloughts?
They did it vashornly.

Syntactical clues do not provide much help in precise word identification, but they do help in limiting the possibilities. The cueing question when a student says the wrong word is, "Does that sound right?"

Teachers worry about interrupting meaning when they provide corrective feedback of miscued words, but providing **corrective feedback** leads to significantly improved word recognition (Perkins, cited in McCormick & Becker, 1996). In other studies that compared feedback with feedback combined with practice, the combined approach was found to promote better retention. When a student missed a word while reading a story, the teacher wrote it on a card. The cards were practiced until the passage could be read correctly (McCormick & Becker).

Miscues

All the cueing systems need to be used to monitor reading. If the phrase looks like *little red boot*, but the story is about sailing a toy on a pond, the reader needs to notice the conflict between the cueing systems and take a second look. Teachers can judge which systems students are using by their miscues, that is, the occasions when a child's response does not match the text. The following samples and related explanations point out miscues and the reasons behind them.

Original text: James put the little red boat in the water.

Irene: The boy is sailing the boat in the pool in the park.

Mike: Jack puts the pretty little sailboat in the pond.

Julie: James put the late red boot in the water.

Maya: Jamie putt the little ready beat in the wait.

Albert: James put the little red boat in the water.

Based on the responses, we can determine which cueing systems each child is using. Irene is picture reading. She uses appropriate sentence patterns and makes sense, but she is not using any print cues, not even the number of words in the sentence. Mike is matching the number of words, using the picture and partial cues as the *J* in James. He probably knows *the* and *in* by sight and is monitoring for syntactic and semantic cues. Julie knows the words, but she is not monitoring for sense or using prior knowledge. Maya is relying solely on graphophonemic cues. She knows something about initial, medial, and final consonants, but she is not paying attention to sentence patterns or meaning. Albert reproduced the text exactly, but the teacher cannot tell which cueing systems he used.

Practice, Practice, Practice

Students strengthen word recognition and comprehension through extensive independent reading. Children who read extensively (which almost always means willingly) develop larger vocabularies, learn more concepts, and have greater opportunity to practice comprehension strategies than those who do not.

Children can read in pairs or independently with books that the class has studied or books of their own choice. Choice in independent reading gives some control to students and strengthens their motivation. The National Academy of Sciences' report on preventing reading difficulties, published by the National Research Council (Snow, Burns, & Griffin, 1998), recommends daily independent reading. Richard Allington (2001, p. 44) reminds us, "The evidence available has convinced me that lots of easy reading is absolutely critical to reading development and to the development of positive stances toward reading."

Even beginning readers can make good use of independent reading time when they are taught how to select books and how to pretend read or picture read. Children can pretend read by telling a story from a familiar story book, picture read by looking at a book with lots of pictures and talking about all that they see, or actually read by reading the words (Cunningham, Hall, & Defee, 1998).

Children love to share what they have read, and opportunities for children to tell or write about their books should be provided. In addition to giving the reader a chance to report, these opportunities let other children learn about books they might like to read.

■ CHOOSING TEXTS FOR BEGINNING READERS

Reading texts are not created equally. Beginners' texts are based on the author's or publisher's philosophy of what would make it easy for children to learn to read. Some children's books are not written with instruction in mind at all. It is a balancing act to write books for beginning readers that are enjoyable, create enthusiasm, and use natural language yet provide practice in letter-sound relationships that have been taught. These multiple requirements have made beginning reading quite controversial. Most teachers choose a variety of texts so that their students have opportunities to use all their word recognition strategies.

Predictable Text

Beginning readers who start with predictable text do experience early success in "reading," but they often do not pay much attention to the print, which does not optimize word learning. Word learning is assumed to happen as children read and reread the text, but evidence for this assumption is limited (Johnston, 1998). Where context is strong enough to allow quick and confident identification of the unfamiliar word, there is little incentive to pore over letter-sound relationships.

Johnston also found insufficient repetition of words. Although this seems contradictory on the surface, the set of words used in one patterned book may be completely different from the set used in another. Also, the key word, the one that is different within the pattern, may appear only once; for example, "I saw a robin, I saw a cat, I saw a lion." Certain words, such as *possum,* may be used to make a story charming or creative, but they may not occur in text again for quite some time. More than half (52%) of the words in the predictable books used by Johnston occurred only once. Johnston concluded that beginners are more likely to learn words that are repeated and are easily decodable, and those words were not the most common words in the predictable books used in her study.

Decodable Text

Decodable words follow regular patterns of letter-sound relationships. They are words such as *can*, *then*, or *make*. Decodable text includes a high percentage of words that follow the regular patterns and a few sight words so that children can practice decoding or word attack patterns that they have been taught. Even with just short vowels and a few sight words, the following story can be read.

Josh has a cat, Sam. Josh and Sam go to shop on a ship. Josh had cash to shop. The big ship sells the best fish. On the ship, a big fish is in a pan. The cat did a mad dash. Sam bit the fish! The man is mad. "That cat is bad!" Josh did not shop.

The following mid-first-grade text has 18 different words, of which 16 could be decoded entirely on the basis of sound relationships (Anderson, Hiebert, Scott, & Wilkinson, 1985).

Ray loads the boat. He says, "I'll row."

Neal says, "We'll both row." They leave, and Eve rides home alone.

Today's texts are an improvement over a 1970s version that read, "Dan can fan the man. Can Dan fan Nat?" Exceptionally attractive and meaningful decodable texts come from the Books to Remember series by Flyleaf Publishers; visit www.flyleafpublishing.com.

Texts With High-Frequency Words

High-frequency words occur the most often. Unfortunately, many of them are irregular, such as *said* or *come*, and do not follow predictable spelling-pronunciation rules. There are several very similar lists of high-frequency words, or "instant words." See Figure 10.3 in Chapter 10. Anderson, Hiebert, Scott, and Wilkinson (1985) cite an example of a high-frequency text that could be read in approximately November of first grade.

"We have come, Grandma," said Ana. "We have come to work with you."

"Come in," Grandma said. "Look in the book," said Grandma. "Mix this and this."

This text uses 17 words, of which only three to eight could be decoded entirely on the basis of letter-sound relationships, depending on how far a first grader has progressed in phonics. None of the stories is very memorable, but they are readable. It is hard to write terrific stories with a limited vocabulary, whether that vocabulary is limited by high-frequency words or by reliable phonetic relationships. This is why teachers use good literature for read-alouds and for instruction when the children are ready.

Aesthetically Constructed Text

Literature-based stories can be described as using aesthetically constructed text (Cole, 1998) to be read for enjoyment and appreciation. Many basals and primary anthologies have switched to these stories, to the delight of countless children. In these books, the language is rich and varied and has structural complexity that can be appreciated by children who have the experience to understand it. Aesthetic and beginner texts differ noticeably in vocabulary. While aesthetically constructed texts use vivid verbs such as *demanded*, *tucked*, *wailed*, *observed*, and *capture*, the beginner-oriented texts settle for *said*, *put*, *saw*, *went*, *came*, and *hop*, all higher frequency and easier to decode. Although *Where the Wild Things Are* (Sendak, 1964) is loved by thousands of children, it has 67 words within one sentence strung across four pages (Cole), which can be daunting for some children. It does make a great read-aloud, however.

Vocabulary Control, Repetition, and Sentence Structure

Vocabulary control and repetition affect comprehension. In basals published prior to 1990, initial vocabulary was repeated and gradually expanded through the second grade. Basals published during the whole language era used more natural language but less vocabulary control and repetition. Darrell Morris (2005) wonders about the effect on low readers when first-grade basals increase the number of words while decreasing the repetition of these words within and across stories. Many first-grade teachers are concerned too. While word control may no longer be needed by mid- or late second grade, it is of special concern for struggling first-grade readers. Teachers of early readers supplement basal instruction with texts that offer various kinds of support for their students.

Teachers supplement with **little books** of 12 to 16 pages for beginning readers. The stories are simple, and the pictures help to carry the story line. They provide either high-frequency text or decodable text, often featuring a key letter-sound correspondence. Oxford, Wright, Rigby, Sundance, Modern Curriculum Press, and Scholastic are some publishers of little books. The vocabulary from book to book in the series is not especially repetitive, but children do get additional practice reading beyond the basal.

Books such as the "I-Can-Read" series can be thought of as **beginner-oriented text** (Cole, 1998). They may not have thrilling stories, style, or beautiful language, but they offer certain advantages, especially for struggling readers. Cole found they offer repetition, simple language, simple sentence structure with fewer words per sentence, fewer words on a page, and larger print. Furthermore, new sentences begin on a new line, which is very helpful to some readers. The simplicity and controlled vocabulary of these books can provide success for young readers who are overwhelmed by too many unfamiliar words and what must seem to them a tangled web of long and complicated sentences. Cole argues that the kind of language structure offered in beginner-oriented texts may segue into fluency for struggling readers.

No matter the type of text, a key element of success is controlled difficulty. Morris (2005) compares two successful models for reading intervention, Reading Recovery, a one-on-one tutorial program, and Success for All, a school-wide intervention program. While they differ in philosophy, materials, and teacher training, they both include a large set of carefully graded reading material (15 or more readers for first grade). With 10 or more Reading Recovery books at each level, there is ample practice of high-frequency vocabulary. In Success for All, phonetically regular words are gradually introduced and systematically repeated at each level. Morris concludes, "Effective classroom instruction for low readers is impossible without a set of carefully graded reading materials geared to the children's interests and needs" (p. 191). Both Reading Recovery and Success for All also provide ongoing help in mastering the letter-sound relationships. These two elements, controlled vocabulary and ample practice, are essential for supporting struggling readers and may prevent reading difficulties for many more.

EMERGENT WRITING ■

Writing is almost inseparable from early reading, and effective teachers integrate their language arts literacy program (Tracey & Morrow, 2002). Children write about what they are reading and thus extend their comprehension.

> Writing is almost inseparable from early reading, and effective teachers integrate their language arts literacy program.

Modeled Writing

Learning about writing often starts by watching the teacher model the process as she verbalizes her thoughts about content, spelling, and mechanics. Primary teachers start the day with a "morning message," in which the day's schedule, a list of special events, or a personal anecdote is communicated to the students by the teacher in a written format. Modeling writing about everyday occurrences lets children know that their daily happenings are suitable topics for writing. Children see how writers think and what the product looks like even if they cannot do it themselves yet.

Shared Writing

Shared writing is among the very first writing experiences in which children participate. It is very similar to a language experience story except, as students begin to learn more about sound-symbol relationships and sight words, they are the writers. After the topic is chosen, a sentence is developed. Children are called on to write the beginning letter, a blend, a vowel sound, the ending sound, or the rime part of a word-family word as the teacher guides the children in letter formation and matching letters to sounds. More difficult vowel sounds, /ou/, /ow/, /oo/, and /igh/, are often written by the teacher.

It is a good idea to place white tape over any misprinting or misspelling. The child gets a second chance to write the letter, and the finished story is quite legible. In contemporary educational jargon, the tape is placed over a "preconventional attempt." Letter formation needs to be taught. Children who use unusual directionality patterns will be handicapped when trying to learn cursive writing, which requires movement from left to right only.

Words are counted, spacing discussed, and capitals and punctuation put into place. Sometimes the entire text is only a single sentence long because constructing it takes considerable time. "The power of the lesson lies not in the length of the text constructed but in the quality of the interaction" (Button, Johnson, & Furgerson, 1996, p. 449). The teacher can provide instruction at the exact point it is needed. Stories are posted in the room for rereading or can be duplicated for at-home reading practice. Topics suitable for shared writing include transcribed nursery rhymes and poems, class observations of pets or plants, class rules, and stories modeled after patterned text.

After the shared writing is completed, the class reads the text in echo, choral, or real reading, depending on the maturity of the students. Many teachers also have students write their own copies of the day's text on white boards with markers or on primary paper on clipboards.

All students, regardless of their abilities, can participate in shared writing. When the teacher works through the process rather than just taking dictation, close examination of print concepts and word analysis is encouraged. Children also learn about the process of composing and see themselves as successful writers. Ideas for older writers may be found in Chapter 11.

Genres and Purposes in Primary Writing

Primary writers need to write for a variety of purposes. A list of ideas is presented by Duke and Stewart (1997) (see Figure 2.3).

Figure 2.3   Purposes of writing

Writing for Obtaining and Communicating Information

morning message	lunch counts	lunch choices
cards	notes	weekend news
surveys	labeling	journals

Writing for Literary Response and Expression

retelling stories	story recommendations
favorite scenes	story extensions based on theme or topic
poems	expression of personal events
story maps	writing original stories

dialogue journals, in which the student and teacher respond back and forth

Writing for Learning and Reflection

exit slips or quick writes about what was learned in a content lesson
reflecting about classroom conflicts
listing or grouping content area facts

Writing for Problem Solving and Application

letters requesting a solution to a dilemma
researching a problem and writing the solution
brainstorming topics and writing the list
brainstorming what is known about a topic or problem and writing the list

---

Source: Adapted from Duke, N., and Stewart, B., "Standards in Action in a First-Grade Classroom," *The Reading Teacher* 51(3), 1997.

SUCCESS IN FIRST GRADE IS CRITICAL ■

First-grade success in reading is critical. Despite teachers' unfailing optimism that a poor student will catch up, this is generally the exception, not the rule. When learning to read becomes frustrating, children avoid the task and limit their opportunities to improve.

Research suggests that students who are having the hardest time benefit the most from focused, intensive, organized instruction. Those kids who are at risk and those who always seem a little vague about the entire process do better with a straightforward approach. In a report from the National Academy of Sciences commissioned by the U.S. Department of Education and the U.S. Department of Health and Human Services (Snow, Burns, & Griffin, 1998), the blue ribbon panel advised, "There is little evidence that children experiencing difficulties learning to read, even those with identifiable learning disabilities, need radically different sorts of supports than children at low risk, although they may need much more intensive support. Excellent instruction is the best intervention for children who demonstrate problems in learning to read" (p. 3).

Excellent instruction is the best intervention for all children who are learning how to read.

3

Developing Phonemic Awareness

What greater or better gift can we offer the republic than to teach and instruct our youth?

—Cicero

"Learning to read is much easier when children have acquired three prerequisite understandings about print: print carries messages, printed words are composed of letters, and letters correspond to the sounds in spoken words" (Lapp & Flood, 1997, p. 698). However, kindergarten and first-grade children who lack the language competency known as phonemic awareness may not be ready to profit from instruction in those early literacy understandings. Intensive research, much of it in the 1990s, has demonstrated that children who lack phonemic awareness often experience subsequent difficulties learning to read. Fortunately, phonemic awareness skills can be learned through instruction, with clear benefits for subsequent acquisition of decoding, spelling, and reading skills (National Reading Panel, 2000; Pressley, 2002).

Phonemic awareness is the ability to notice, think about, and manipulate the individual sounds in words (Torgesen, 1998). English consists of 41–44 phonemes, which are the smallest units of *spoken* language. Children need to understand that spoken words can be divided into individual sounds (phonemes), and phonemes can be blended together to form words.

Phonemes represent sounds whereas graphemes are written letters. Usually graphemes represent one sound with one letter: M is /m/. (Slashes are used to indicate a sound rather than a letter name.) Multiple-letter graphemes, such as PH, can also represent one phoneme, /f/, as in *phone*. Matching graphemes (letters) to sounds is called phonics. Phonics requires written letters or words.

Phonemic awareness is manipulating sounds orally. As some children say about phonemic awareness, "You can do it with your eyes closed!"

It is difficult for many young children to think of words as being composed of sounds because they have previously considered words only as whole, meaning-carrying units. Dog is the furry creature that licks your face, not a composite of the sounds /d/, /o/, and /g/. Most preschoolers do not acquire phonemic awareness naturally. They have had no need to notice and ponder individual sounds; they have been concentrating on the meaning of the whole word in spoken language. When asked the beginning sound of *pizza*, preschoolers may answer *hot* or *mmm* (Moats, 2005).

Children who lack phonemic awareness are able to hear the phonemes, but they are not yet aware of the concept that words are composed of smaller units, which are the individual sounds. When children can repeat a word with all the sounds intact, they have auditory acuity and discrimination, but being able to separate and combine sounds consciously is a different skill from auditory discrimination. Steven A. Stahl (1992) relates a story about a young child who was asked to say *coat* but without the /c/. She answered, "jacket." Since she had not yet learned that words could be thought of as a composite of individual sounds, something less than a coat must be a jacket.

For an emergent reader, hearing the individual sounds is not easy. When a word is analyzed by means of a spectrograph that displays sound waves visually, the sounds blend into one another and are not identifiable in isolation without distortion. Several sounds—/b/, /p/, /d/, /k/, and /t/—are difficult to produce without adding a vowel sound. Thus identifying sounds in isolation is an abstraction, something that does not happen in actuality in the way we conceptualize it in print.

DEVELOPING PHONEMIC AWARENESS ■

Although some children acquire phonemic awareness without direct instruction, many do not. Children who are exposed to a great deal of language and have large vocabularies have had many opportunities to play with language and discriminate sounds (Goswami, 2001). Because of their extensive contact with print and initial word play, often through exposure to rhyming words in nursery rhymes and patterned rhyming books, they begin to think about the sounds of words—their similarities, their differences, and their combinations.

Black and Hispanic children of low socioeconomic status are more likely than Anglo children of low socioeconomic status to have poor phonemic awareness of school English. This may be attributed to greater differences between home and school language as well as to cultural differences involving the time spent with word play and exposure to print (Juel, 1988).

The most advanced levels of phonemic awareness develop in conjunction with and reciprocally with formal reading instruction. However, "phonemic awareness seems to contribute more to learning to read than learning to read contributes to phonemic awareness" (Pressley, 2002, p. 114).

■ THE ALPHABETIC PRINCIPLE

The idea that written spellings systematically represent spoken words is called the alphabetic principle. Purely alphabetic languages have one symbol for each phoneme, and learning to read an alphabetic system requires the ability to analyze words into phonemes. Chinese is a language that is not alphabetic and instead requires memorization of symbols. It is fairly easy to see why children have difficulty with phonics if they do not understand the concept of separating out the phonemes within a word. "In order to apply the alphabet principle to 'sounding out' words, children first have to realize that words can be 'sounded'" (Busink cited in Smith, 2003). The alphabetic principle includes these components:

1. Words are made up of individual sounds.

2. Words are made up of individual letters.

3. Letters can be reliably matched to sounds that can be blended together to identify words for reading.

4. Word sounds can be separated and reliably matched to letters for spelling.

5. The sequence of the letters represents the sound sequence.

6. Changing the letter changes the sound and makes a new word.

7. Changing the sound changes the letter and makes a new word.

Although English is an alphabetic language, it is not a language of exact one-to-one correspondences. English includes multiple variations of sound-letter correspondences, which makes both reading and spelling more challenging. Because English sounds do not match spelling precisely, phonemic awareness training has a greater impact on English-speaking students than on students of languages that have a closer match and a system that is easier for a new reader to decode (National Reading Panel, 2000).

Visual memory of words is not as important in learning words as once thought unless the reader does not understand the alphabetic principle. Then reading becomes a memory-intensive act, with each word being memorized by its visual characteristics. This method is sufficient for learning perhaps 50 or so words, and it was once the basis of the look-say method. However, it is not sufficient for learning to read the 6,000 words that most first graders have in their speaking vocabulary.

Phonemic awareness is the best overall predictor of first-grade reading success. If children do not develop phonemic awareness, they will have a very difficult time understanding the concept of phonics and are likely to have difficulty learning to spell. Without rapid, automatic word recognition, fluency and comprehension will be affected. Study after study has demonstrated that children with phonemic awareness make better progress in learning to read.

PHONOLOGICAL AWARENESS ■
AND ALPHABET KNOWLEDGE

Phonological awareness has several components, which develop hierarchically. Phonological awareness includes rhyming and the ability to separate syllables, whereas phonemic awareness is limited to consciously manipulating individual sounds.

Alphabet Knowledge

> Knowledge of letter names and phonemic awareness are the two best predictors of reading success in first and second grade.

Knowledge of letter names and phonemic awareness are the two best predictors of reading success in first and second grade (National Reading Panel, 2000). Knowing both is better than knowing one or the other. Many phonemic awareness programs also teach the alphabet.

Rhyming

Rhyming belongs under the classification of phonological awareness rather than phonemic awareness because a larger unit of sound is processed rather than a single phoneme. Many sound awareness activities start with rhyming because the ending part of the word—the rime—is a more psychologically cohesive unit, more similar to a syllable than a phoneme.

Separating the **onset and rime,** or partial segmentation, is often the first word analysis skill that young children can execute, and it can be accomplished by many preschoolers. In *wink,* /w/ is the onset and /ink/ is the rime. Separating onset and rime is more complex than syllabic awareness, but only slightly. Children who are unable to rhyme may be lacking the skill of separating the onset from the rime.

Rhyming becomes important in learning to read. Children who cannot rhyme will not be able to understand the relationships among words in word families. They will have a hard time learning new words by analogy to a known word in the family. An example of making an analogy is, "If this is *time,* then that is *dime."*

Learning to isolate the initial sound is the phonemic skill most related to beginning reading because the initial consonant is the first clue used to identify unknown words. Partial segmentation corresponds to the initial stages of learning sound-letter relationships whereas accuracy in word identification requires full segmentation abilities. Unless a child has a basic awareness that the sounds in words can be segmented, he will not be able to understand a question as simple as "What is the first sound in *ball*?"

PHONEMIC AWARENESS SKILLS ■

These skills tend to develop hierarchically in the following order: phoneme identity, detecting the odd word in a set of words, blending phonemes together, segmenting a word into its component sounds, deleting individual sounds from an intact word, and substituting or inserting sounds.

Phoneme Identity and Phoneme Isolation

Phoneme identity requires recognizing the common sound in different words; for example, a teacher may ask, "Tell me the sound that is the same in *bell*, *bite*, and *button*." Phoneme identity is needed for matching phonemes to letters in reading and spelling. Phoneme isolation requires recognizing individual sounds in words; for example, the teacher may say, "Tell me the first sound in *mask*." Children can isolate the first sound long before they can isolate (segment) all the sounds in a word.

Differentiating, or Odd One Out

In odd-one-out tasks, children are orally given two or three words that have the same beginning sound and one that has a different beginning sound. For example, "Which word doesn't start the same: *man, moon, saw, mom*?" This task is easier than many of the other phonemic skills because it requires only comparison and contrast; therefore it is a suitable task for prereaders.

Many of the differentiating activities are based on Bradley and Peter's seminal study (cited in Pressley, 2002), in which five- and six-year-olds who lacked phonemic awareness were taught to categorize different sets of words by initial, ending, and middle sounds. An important principle was that words could be categorized in different ways: *hen* could belong with *hat* and *hill*, or with *men* and *sun*, or with *bed* and *leg*. With pictures in the first 20 ten-minute sessions and aural words in the next 20 sessions over two years, these children outperformed the children in the control group, who grouped words by meaning categories, by about a year. In a five-year follow-up, children trained in sound categorization still demonstrated striking advantages.

Blending

When children are presented with separate sounds, such as /f/ /a/ /n/, they blend, or combine, the sounds into a word. Blending is easier than separating a word into sounds (see next section), and blending phonemes into nonsense words is harder than blending into real words. In clinic, I have found some children very frustrated and confused by nonsense words. Blending is one of the most important skills as children learn to decode unfamiliar words.

Full Segmentation

Segmentation is the opposite of blending; when children are presented with a word, they must separate it into its sounds. Full segmentation is the ability to break apart an entire word into its constituent sounds. For example, the word *sat* is composed of /s//a//t/. *Game* is /g//ā//m/. *Sight* is /s//ī//t/. In English, there are often more letters than sounds in words. The ability to fully segment words is more predictive of reading ability than are the more simple forms of phonemic awareness (Nation & Hulme, 1997). Sound segmentation is the skill that will later be needed for spelling.

Linnea Ehri and Simone Nunes (2002) reported on several studies that taught just blending, just segmenting, or both blending and segmenting. Results showed that groups learned the skill(s) they were taught but performed poorly on the untaught skill; in other words, teaching one skill will not automatically enhance the other. The segmenting and combination groups performed similarly on measures of reading and spelling and outperformed the blending-only group and the control group (which had no phonemic awareness training). Segmenting and blending really are different skills, and segmenting may be the more powerful.

In a study by Liberman (cited in Adams, 1991), none of the four-year-old participants and only 17% of the five-year-old participants were successful at full segmentation. However, the task was completed successfully by 70% of six-year-old participants. Full segmentation apparently develops as a result of learning to read as children begin to decode. Thus more complex phonemic awareness tasks may not be suitable for kindergarten children or for those who have not yet begun to read.

Sound Deletion

Sound deletion involves removing a sound from a word and then pronouncing the remaining sounds. When children are asked to delete sounds, they are usually asked to remove the first or last sound from a word. Say *hill.* Say *hill* without the /h/. Say *pink* without the /k/. Some sound deletions are harder than others. It is especially difficult to delete one sound from a consonant blend such as /bl/. Deleting just one sound of an ending cluster such as *-nt* or *-mp* is also very difficult.

Sound deletion is a strong predictor of reading achievement but has been found to be beyond the ability of children before the end of first grade (Adams, cited in Stahl, Osborn, & Lehr, 1990). Deletion does develop into an important skill, and Byrne and Fielding-Barnsley (1993) found a relationship between success at sound deletion and success at spelling in first grade. Deletion may be another result of learning to read rather than a prerequisite.

Sound Substitution

Sound substitution requires both segmenting and blending. An example of a sound substitution task is to ask the student to say *side.* Take off the /s/. Add /r/. What word is it? The ability to delete, transpose, or add phonemes to a syllable continues to develop at least through high school (Adams, 1991).

WHEN SHOULD PHONEMIC ■ AWARENESS BE TAUGHT?

Phonemic awareness instruction seems most beneficial between the ages of four and six, but should it be taught prior to formal reading instruction or simultaneously with reading instruction? The answer is both. Phonemic awareness instruction is usually started with kindergartners and can be taught with success simultaneously with the alphabet and letter sounds. Letter manipulation helps children acquire phonemic awareness (National Reading Panel, 2000), perhaps because it adds a visual component. (Have you ever tried to learn a foreign language without seeing it written down?) Phonemic awareness activities are so intensely auditory that almost any kind of visual or tactile manipulative helps.

Phonemic awareness continues to be taught in first grade as students start formal reading instruction; however, nonreaders will require more explicit phonemic awareness instruction and support than those who are reading successfully. In first grade, the combination of phonemic awareness and beginning phonics has produced consistently positive effects. Schneider, Roth, and Ennemoser (2000) taught German students who were at risk because of low phonemic awareness abilities. One group received instruction in phonemic awareness combined with sound-letter correspondence, one in phonemic awareness only, and one in sound-letter correspondence only. The "combined" group had a small but consistent advantage. It is not until students have a sound grasp of letter-sound relationships that they are able to perform all the phonemic tasks, especially segmentation, deletion, and substitution. This makes sense, as a true grasp of the alphabetic principle requires both awareness of phonemes and association with the letters that represent the sounds.

Teaching techniques that have been most successful are those that aim to teach only one or two phonemic tasks at a time. More may be too confusing, or the added tasks may be above the level of the child. Small-group work was more effective than individual or whole-class work, and the optimum length of training was 10–18 hours (National Reading Panel, 2000), which is surprisingly short.

■ BALANCING PHONEMIC AWARENESS

Without doubt, phonemic awareness helps the beginning reader, but remember Keith Stanovich's reminder (1986). Phonological awareness may be a necessary but not a sufficient condition for the acquisition of reading. Learning phonemic concepts does not alleviate the need for multiple exposures to and practice with sound-letter correspondences and word identification strategies as well as extensive experiences with print in reading and writing. Barbara Foorman and colleagues (1998) found that at-risk emergent readers benefited from phonemic awareness training combined with direct instruction in the alphabetic principle and literature activities. Without these other aspects of emergent literacy, it is not likely that phonemic awareness training and sound-symbol relationships will generalize to actual reading and spelling skills.

In order for phonemic awareness skills to generalize to reading, children may have to be made metacognitively aware of how matching, blending, and segmenting apply to reading and spelling. Cunningham (1990) included explicit instruction for transfer and achieved large gains in phonemic awareness and significant transfer to reading.

This brings us back to the whole-part-whole principle of balanced reading. Children need to understand the broader concept of reading (the whole) so that they know why they are learning discrete skills (the parts). They also need the

> Teaching phonological and phonemic awareness can be fun for both children and teachers.

opportunity to apply what they have learned (the whole). Readers are successful when the teacher integrates the instruction and coaches for transfer.

INITIAL ACTIVITIES FOR LEARNING ■ PHONOLOGICAL AWARENESS

The activities in this section deal mostly with phonological awareness, working with units of sound larger than the individual phoneme. Teaching phonological and phonemic awareness can be fun for both children and teachers. The usual recommendation is that it be taught for 10–20 minutes daily. The intense auditory nature and the attention span of primary students make this just about the right amount of time.

Environmental Sounds, Whole Words, and Syllables

To begin teaching phonemic awareness, Marilyn Adams, Barbara Foorman, Ingvar Lundberg, and Terri Beeler (1998) suggest starting with environmental sounds, then moving on to word and sentence awareness, rhyming, segmenting syllables, and breaking onsets from rimes. They suggest working with all these activities before even starting with phonemes.

Environmental sounds are those sounds from common, everyday activities that can be found in a young reader's surroundings. Have children listen to a familiar sound with their eyes closed or their back to the teacher. Sounds could include cutting paper with scissors, turning on a computer, sharpening a pencil, writing on the board, pouring water from a glass, crumpling paper, or snapping fingers. Next, the teacher asks the children to identify two sounds in sequence. A classic book to accompany these early activities is *The Listening Walk* (Showers, 1961).

Because **whole words** are easier to identify than phonemes, it is best to begin listening activities at the whole-word level. The teacher can read familiar nursery rhymes that are mixed up. As children hear the error, they raise their hands and explain what is wrong (Adams et al., 1998).

Song a sing of sixpence	reversed words
Baa baa purple sheep	substituted word
Humpty Dumpty wall on a sat	switched word order, ungrammatical
Jack fell down and crown his broke	switched word order, ungrammatical
One, two, shuckle my boo	switched initial consonants
Five, six, pick up sticks One, two, buckle my shoe	switched order of events

In **compound word deletion**, the teacher says a compound word, for example, *sailboat*. Students repeat the word. The teacher says, "Without *boat*, what is left?

Tapping out **syllables** is a way to teach simple segmentation. Two cubes can be placed on a table. As the teacher says a two-syllable word, she taps the two cubes and asks the student to repeat the word and say the first or last syllable. Three-syllable words can be done next by adding a third cube and the word *middle* to the instructions, that is, ask the student to say the first, middle, or last syllable. (If the teacher sits facing the student, the cubes must be arranged from the student's left to right.)

In **syllable segmenting**, children clap the syllables in their own names and in the names of items in the room. A game using this idea is called "King's/Queen's Successor." The children circle the teacher, who is wearing a crown, and she issues an order, which is an action. She repeats the word rhythmically, accentuating the syllables: march ing, march ing, march ing. The children perform the action in rhythm. Then a child is chosen as the royal successor and gives the next order (Lundberg, Frost, & Petersen, 1988).

Rhyming

Nursery rhymes and **rhyming books** provide students with a vehicle for learning about rhyming. Children these days seem less familiar with the classic English nursery rhymes than prior generations were, but they will be just as delighted by them as children have been in the past. Contemporary rhyming books such as *If I Were a Lion* (Weeks, 2004) and *The Little School Bus* (Roth, 2002) are also filled with delightful rhymes. After reading a couplet, the teacher can stop to ask the children which words rhymed. Or, just before the second rhyme in a couplet, the teacher can ask the students what the rhyming word will be.

The following provides an example of a **rhyming poem**:

> Two little feet go tap, tap, tap.
> Two little hands go clap, clap, clap.
> A quiet little leap up from my chair,
> Two little arms reach up in the air.
> Two little feet go jump, jump, jump.
> Two little fists go thump, thump, thump.
> One little body goes round, round, round,
> And one little child sits quietly down.
>
> —Adams et al., 1998

First, the teacher reads the poem for the children, emphasizing the rhythm and rhyme. Then the teacher rereads the poem, and the students repeat each line in unison. Many repetitions are necessary. Variations on this exercise include reciting the poem in whispers but saying the rhyming words in a loud voice, reciting the poem in a loud tone but whispering the rhyming words, asking different groups of children to say different lines, having each child in a circle recite one line each, and having each child in a circle recite one word each.

In **nonsense rhymes**, the teacher says a rhyming nonsense word for objects in the room, such as "I see a *jable*," and the students respond, "Oh, you must mean a *table*." Students practice rhyming and initial sound substitution.

In the rhyming game called **Did You Ever See?** the teacher thinks of a rhyming question, and the students fill in the last word.

Did you ever see a boy play with a ___? (toy)

Did you ever see a mouse that lived in a ___? (house)

Did you ever see a fish that was lying on a ___? (dish)

Did you ever see a bear with long brown ___? (hair)

Did you ever see a pig wearing a ___? (wig)

Thumbs up is a simple way to monitor rhyming responses from the whole class. Thumbs are up if the words rhyme and down if they do not. The teacher says the pairs *run-fun* or *rip-bag* and asks for a thumbs-up or thumbs-down response from everyone (Heggerty, 2004).

PHONEMIC AWARENESS ACTIVITIES ■

These activities generally progress from the easier to the more difficult tasks.

Phoneme Isolation

Stahl (1997) recommends that teachers start with a small set of sounds, possibly teaching them one at a time. The consonant sounds that are continuant, or can be stretched, such as /m, s, n, f, z, v, th, sh, l, r/, can be worked with more easily than stop-consonant sounds, /t, d, b, k, p, g, ch, j/, which are harder to manipulate.

At the most basic level, ask "Is there /w/ in *watch?*" "Is there /s/ in *tooth?*" For children who are just learning to identify sounds, it may be less confusing if the teacher asks, "Is there /w/ in *watch?*" rather than "Is there a /w/ in *watch?*" Beginners sometimes think the word *a* is part of the sound.

Differentiating, or Odd One Out

To teach the concept of identifying a word that is different from other words in a series, the teacher may start with words that rhyme (except for one): *rake*, *make*, *pen*, and *take*. Many children already know this activity from a *Sesame Street* game called "One of these isn't like the other ones."

Move on to initial sounds and play odd one out, asking students which word begins with a different sound: *turtle, nut, toaster, tent.* This activity can be done with a set of four pictures, which very closely resembles the *Sesame Street* segment. Oddity tasks are easier than segmentation or blending because they require only comparison and contrast, so they are excellent initial activities for the study of sounds.

Phoneme Identity and Partial Segmentation

Phoneme identity tasks teach children to identify and match sounds. For example, the /s/ heard at the beginning of *sand* and *sister* is the same sound. It is also the same as the /s/ at the end of *miss*. Children can match initial sounds to pictures. Starting with a picture of the key word, ask, "Which of the pictured objects, *shoe, lock, heart*, starts the same as *lamp*?" Both beginning and ending sounds can be matched to the key word, and initial practice items are often compound words such as *football* and *footprint* to ensure that children understand the phrase "starts the same as."

Slightly more advanced questions require **matching**. The teacher can ask children if the beginning sound of a word is the same as or different from the beginning sound of another word or words. "Does *ring* begin the same as *river* and *race*? Does *pen* begin the same as *cup* and *can*?" Identifying location in a word is still more complex. Does *lamp* have /l/ at the beginning or the end? Does *fall* have /l/ at the beginning or the end? A slightly more complex exercise is to say two words: *nap, dip.* The students must then say /p/, which is the ending sound the words have in common.

In **concentration**, children lay out five pairs of picture cards face down. Each pair has matching initial sounds. A student turns over two at a time. If they match in initial sound, and the child can say "These are *sun* and *sock*. They both start with /s/," the child keeps the cards. If they do not match, they are turned face down again. More advanced students can play concentration with final sounds.

Alliterative phrases and tongue twisters draw children's attention to matching initial letters, as in *Silly Sally snores*. Hallie Kay Yopp (1995a) has identified a long list of read-aloud books that are excellent for developing phonological awareness.

The class can play **I Spy**. The teacher says, "I spy something in the classroom that starts the same as *door*." All matching answers may be accepted.

In **What Was on the Tray?** several objects that start with the same sound are placed on a tray. Ask children to remember them and remove the tray from sight. The students can draw and name the items. Having students use a patterned sentence response such as "This is a *key*, and it starts with /k/," helps them to make an explicit connection. Paying close attention to items on a tray or letters in a word is a skill worth encouraging.

To teach students how to **compare and contrast** the sounds, start with two different sets of picture cards. Each set should start with the same single consonant: *nail, nut, nest, net, nurse.* Have a child pick a card and draw out the initial sound, /nnnnest/. Have the children repeat and notice how their tongues and lips are placed. Ending sounds can also be separated. After both sets of cards are completed, they can be mixed up and sorted by initial sound.

Troll at the Bridge is a charming game for teaching partial segmentation. A troll puppet says, "Only children whose names start with /d/ may cross the bridge." Of course, the troll eventually says all the beginning sounds of the names of the children in the class. More advanced students can play the game with ending or middle sounds (Stahl, 1997). For a variation, ask students to line up for recess by saying the initial sounds of their first names.

To make an **alphabet book,** write one letter on a large sheet of drawing paper. Children draw pictures or cut out magazine pictures of objects starting with that sound. This is tricky with c, g, and the vowels. Later, pictures can be labeled—if anyone can still figure out what the drawing represented. Selected pages can be assembled into a class alphabet book.

To **match sounds and separate initial phonemes,** try this song. The words are sung to the tune of "Jimmy Cracked Corn and I Don't Care."

Who has a /d/ word to share with us?   *Dog* is a word that starts with /d/.

Who has a /d/ word to share with us?   *Dog* is a word that starts with /d/.

Who has a /d/ word to share with us?   *Dog* is a word that starts with /d/.

It must start with the /d/ sound.   *Dog* starts with the /d/ sound.

—Yopp, 1992, pp. 699–700

Riddles can be used to teach partial segmentation. The teacher asks riddles (questions) in which all the answers must start with a certain sound: On what do you put a stamp? *Mail.* What does a boy grow up to be? *Man.* With what do you light a fire? *Match.* What do you take when you're sick? *Medicine.* What animal is chased by a cat? *Mouse.* What is between the beginning and the end? *Middle.*

In an activity known as **Every Student Response**, students are given identical sets of four to six picture cards, each with a different beginning and ending sound, which are placed face up on their desks. The teacher asks, "What begins the same as tiger?" Each child must hold up the appropriate picture. For one more round, the teacher can ask the class, "Which one begins with /t/?" With more advanced students, ask for the ending sounds. As children learn sound-symbol relationships, the teacher can ask, "Which one begins with t?" The children all hold up their cards, and one can be called on to respond, "*Turtle* begins with t. It sounds /t/." If all the *turtle* pictures are colored green and all the *bear* pictures are brown and so on, the teacher can check everyone's response by the color when it is hard to see the pictures of students sitting in the back of the room.

Teachers who have no qualms about singing before the class can try **singing the beginning sounds** for a set of words. For example, to the tune of "Old MacDonald Had a Farm," sing the following verse. (This exercise can be adapted to final sounds also.)

What's the sound that starts these words

Turtle, time, and teeth? [Wait for a response.]

/t/ is the sound that starts these words:

Turtle, time, and teeth.

With a /t/,/t/ here and a /t/,/t/ there,

Here a /t/, there a /t/, everywhere a /t/,/t/.

/t/ is the sound that starts these words:

Turtle, time, and teeth.

—Yopp, 1992, p. 700

In **partial segmentation bingo**, students have 9-square or 16-square bingo cards with pictures of objects beginning with different sounds. The teacher says a sound, such as /r/, and if the students have a picture beginning with that sound, they use a marker to cover it. Sometimes old phonics books can be cut and pasted together to make bingo cards. Since each card must be different, it is a daunting task to assemble the cards. However, once made and laminated, they can be used over and over for various tasks. Another idea is to have several sets of loose identical pictures that the children can place in blank divided squares, but with loose pictures and loose markers, the whole thing gets a little wiggly. Once the children learn sound-letter relationships, they can write their own letters on a bingo card, and the teacher can call words that start with the sounds of the letters.

Blending

Because it is very hard to avoid adding vowel sounds to certain consonants when we try to say the consonants in isolation, the most difficult part about teaching the blending of individual phonemes is saying them in segmented form. Remember it is /t/, not /ta/, and /r/, not /er/. It is no wonder children have trouble figuring out the word when *bed* comes out ba-eh-ed. Teachers often start with blending together compound words, then syllables, and next onsets and rimes. What word is /g/ /ate/? /t/ /ub/? /b/ /est/? The rimes are stronger psychologically, and the idea of blending can still be accessed.

Some sounds are easier to extend than others when blending; for example, *van* is easy to stretch out (/vvv/ /aaa/ /nnn/). For those short stop sounds, /t, d, b, k, p, g/, it is easier to repeat the sound multiple times (/t-t-t/ /iii/ /nnn/). While words to be blended can be said at first with silence between the phonemes, the secret of blending is not to let go of one sound before adding the next.

Begin with a simple blending exercise known as **echo and blend**. The teacher says a sequence of sounds, such as /l/ /e/ /g/, and the students echo the sequence, blend the sounds, and then say the whole word.

In **Troll Talk** the teacher tells the students a story about a troll who likes to give presents, but the child must first guess what the present is. When the teacher (as the troll) segments the name of the presents, such as /d/ /o/ /l/ or /tr/ /u/ /k/, the student must blend the sounds together. For beginners, the consonant blends, such as /tr/, can be preblended, but for more experienced students, segment the consonant blends (Adams et al., 1998).

I like the phrasing of the teacher query that Heggerty (2004) uses for group unison responses because it makes it easy for the children to know when to give their response. To blend onsets and rimes, the teacher says a rime, such as *reeze*. The students repeat. The teacher says, "Add /f/ at the beginning and the word is . . ."

Teachers can also teach **blending using words in context**. Read a sentence from a book that is being read in class. Omit a word, segment it, and ask the children to blend it back together. The words should not be ones that could be guessed from context.

Full Segmentation

Initial consonants are easiest to segment, then final consonants, and finally medial sounds. Vowels are the hardest to hear, and young children are resistant to the idea that blends such as /pl/ are two sounds. A simple activity to teach full segmentation involves **stretching words**. The teacher simply asks the child, "Say *sun* so that I can hear all the sounds." /Sssuuunnn/. Using a big rubber band as a prop can help.

For some children, sound segmentation is easier if they notice the position of their tongues and lips. Mirrors can help the children see the changes in the shape of their mouths and thus the change in sounds. LiPS, the Lindamood Phonemic Sequencing Program (Lindamood-Bell, 2005), and speech pathologists have been doing this for years.

In **say it and move it,** children identify individual phonemes by moving blank markers. Provide the students with sheets of paper with sets of empty squares, one square for one-phoneme words, two squares for two-phoneme words, and three squares for three-phoneme words. A picture card is placed above the squares, and the teacher says the word. The children repeat the word, and as they repeat it a second time, they each move markers one at a time from the bottom of the paper into the empty squares. Make sure there is a long distance between the markers and the boxes so the sounds can be really stretched out as the marker is moved. The children repeat the word again. Plastic letters or letter cards replace the markers in later stages.

An interesting intermediate technique was developed by Eileen Ball and Benita Blachman (1991). They suggested that as children learn their first sound-letter correspondences, they should use one letter tile and allow the other markers to remain blank. Begin with no more than two tiles with letters in a lesson. Heavy-duty laminated cardboard survives all this sliding and moving better than ordinary paper. After any of the above activities, children can be asked to count the sounds or tap out the number of sounds.

Body movement can help with segmentation. The children can open the fingers on their hand, one-two-three, as they segment sounds. Saying the segmented sounds as the children touch their shoulder, elbow, and wrist works the same way. After segmenting, the children should repeat the whole word with a final movement of a closed fist or a clap.

As children learn sound-letter correspondence, **invented spelling** is a natural follow-up to stretching words since one must stretch out the sounds in a word in order to spell it. Invented spelling allows children to spell words as best they can, according to the sounds they hear, even though the spelling may not be standard. Invented spelling also improves segmentation skills.

Sound Deletion and Sound Substitution

Simple sound deletion works as follows: "Say *moon*. Now say it without the /m/. Say *coat*. Now say it without the /t/."

A very basic substitution activity is to change the words in the chorus of familiar songs. "Fe-Fi-Fiddly-i-o" in "Someone's in the Kitchen with Dinah" can become "Ze-Zi-Ziddly-i-o"; "Ee-igh, ee-igh, oh!" in "Old MacDonald" can become "See-sigh, see-sigh, soh"; and "Happy Birthday" can become "Bappy Birthday bo bou" (Yopp, 1992, p. 701).

Pig Latin is another deletion task. It is of course more complicated because the deleted sound must be added to the end of the word. It is such fun that most children will work to learn the system. Trying to decode someone else's word in pig Latin is a great sound manipulation task also. An interesting note to pig Latin is that both consonant digraphs, such as /ch/, and consonant blends, such as /pl/, stick together, as in *ickenchay* and *ateplay*. It is never *latepay*. Their psychological cohesiveness as units explains why it is difficult for children to split blends apart. This exercise may be beyond the abilities of many primary children.

Sound substitution is complicated because it requires both deletion and blending. The directions are "Say *boat*. Take off the /b/. Add /c/. What is the new word?" Once students get the idea, the directions can be shortened to "Say *fat*. Change the /f/ to /b/." It seems much easier to do this with written words than to do it orally. Since deletion and substitution are two of the most difficult phonemic skills, it may be best to try this task after students have a grounding in sound-letter relationships.

In written form, it is called **making words.** Give children a limited number of letter cards or tiles. Every child should have the same letters. Start by saying a three-letter word such as *sit*. The children move the appropriate letters into a working space on their desks. The teacher should write the word on the board so children can check if they are right. Then remove the /s/ and replace it with /b/. Have the children say the word *bit*. Other words can be formed by changing the beginning or ending letter. The really advanced students can change the vowels.

■ AT-RISK READERS

Phonemic awareness is important for all readers and especially for at-risk readers. One study more than any other focused attention on the role of phonemic awareness. Connie Juel (1988), in a four-year study of 54 children, found an 88% probability that children who were poor readers at the end of first grade would remain poor readers by the end of fourth grade. The probability that an average reader in first grade would become a poor reader in fourth grade was 12%. The children who entered first grade with little phonemic awareness and became poor readers did not reach the ceiling of the phonemic awareness test until the end of third grade, whereas the good readers had nearly reached that ceiling by the end of first grade. Nine of the poor readers, who had little or no phonemic awareness on entering school, could read no pseudowords at the end of first grade despite a year of phonics instruction.

By the end of fourth grade, the poor readers had not reached the level of decoding achieved by the good readers at the beginning of second grade, which prevented the poor readers from reading as much text as the good readers, both in school and out of school. Juel estimates that by the end of fourth grade, good readers had read 178,000 words of running text in their basals, but poor readers had read only 80,000, and the gap in out-of-school reading widened each year.

On attitude questionnaires, 40% of the poor readers said they would rather clean their rooms than read, and one stated, "I'd rather clean the mold around the bathtub than read." Interestingly, 70% of both groups said they would rather watch television or play with their friends than read. Do not underestimate the competition!

English language learners who are beginning readers also benefit from phonemic awareness, but the teacher has to be sensitive to their first-language sounds. For example, Spanish speakers may fail to distinguish /ch/ from /sh/, and Chinese speakers may not discriminate between /r/ and /l/ as these differences do not occur in their native languages.

> Failure in beginning reading has a snowball effect.

The Matthew Effect

Failure in beginning reading has a snowball effect. Keith Stanovich (1986) coined the much-used term *the Matthew effect*, which is a variation on the old maxim that the rich get richer, and the poor get poorer. Readers who experience early success read more, so they become even more successful. Children who have had difficulties in learning to read tend to be exposed to less text.

Due to their slower start, struggling readers get less practice with reading. They are often asked to read materials that are too difficult, they have difficulty with decoding, and they are less motivated to read than their more successful peers are. Lack of exposure and practice delays the development of automaticity and speed at the word-recognition level. Readers who must spend their time decoding have less cognitive energy for comprehension. "Thus, reading for meaning is hindered, unrewarding reading experiences multiply, and practice is avoided or merely tolerated without real cognitive involvement" (Stanovich, 1986, p. 364). Because uninvolved readers read less, they miss out on vocabulary, language development, and content knowledge. These readers do not catch up.

Early Intervention

Many schools are screening their kindergarten and first-grade students for phonemic awareness. The extra help that can given to these students in the primary grades often means the difference between a successful primary student and one who faces frustration with learning to read, write, and spell.

Intensive support of primary children may prevent reading difficulties. Vellutino et al. (1996) tutored first-grade poor readers in letter identification, phoneme awareness, word reading skills, and practice in connected text. The majority of these students became average readers. A balanced approach of phonemic awareness, direct instruction in sound-symbol relationships, and reading in connected text seems to hold particular promise for at-risk readers as well as average readers.

However, for the very most at-risk students, the Committee on the Prevention of Reading Difficulties in Young Children recommended that phonemic awareness training and other emergent literacy skills may have to be supplemented with language training, additions to background knowledge, memory skills, and vocabulary in order for intervention to make a difference in reading (Snow, Burns, & Griffin, 1998).

■ RESOURCES FOR PHONEMIC AWARENESS

Two excellent books that provide a year's curriculum in phonemic awareness are *Phonemic Awareness in Young Children: A Classroom Curriculum* (1998), by Adams, Foorman, Lundberg, and Beeler (http://www.brookespublishing .com), and *Phonemic Awareness: The Skills That They Need to Help Them Succeed!* (2004) by Heggerty. There is a kindergarten version and a Grade 1–2 version at http://www.literacyresourcesinc.com.

If children have begun developing sound-symbol relationships, invented spelling can be used as an informal assessment of phonemic awareness. As young children improve in their ability to segment and identify sounds within a word, they spell more accurately. For example, S, SP, SAP, and STAP for *stamp* all represent increasingly more complex levels of spelling and thus higher levels of phonemic awareness.

A number of formal assessment tools are available to test phonemic and phonological awareness.

1. Assessment Test, included with *Phonemic Awareness in Young Children*, listed above. This screening test can be given to groups of six kindergarten children or up to 15 first graders. It includes rhyming, counting syllables, matching initial sounds, counting phonemes, comparing word lengths, and representing phonemes with letters.

2. The Phonological Awareness Test, developed in 1997 by LinguiSystems, http://www.linguisystems.com. It contains subsections on rhyming, segmentation, isolation, deletions, substitution, blending, graphemes, and decoding. It is administered individually.

3. Test of Phonological Awareness, TOPA-2+, developed by PRO-ED (www .proedinc.com) has updated 2002 and 2003 norms. It can be administered individually or to a group and is suitable for children 5–8 years of age. There are kindergarten and early elementary versions.

4. Test of Phonological Awareness in Spanish, developed by American Guidance Service, http://www.agsnet.com. This test consists of initial sounds, final sounds, rhyming, and deletions. It is individually administered and suitable for ages 4-0 to 10-11.

5. Comprehensive Test of Phonological Processing, also developed by American Guidance Service, http://www.agsnet.com. There is a version for ages 5 and 6 and one for ages 7 through 24, and each is administered

individually. There are 13 subtests that assess phonological awareness, phonological memory, and rapid naming.

6. Yopp-Singer Test of Phoneme Segmentation (Yopp, 1995b), printed in its entirety in the September 1995 issue of *The Reading Teacher*. The test is administered individually and requires about five to ten minutes per child.

As teachers become aware of phonemic awareness and provide appropriate instruction and activities, primary students will learn the skills that underlie beginning reading. There is a high probability that with these skills, more children will be successful readers throughout all the grades.

4

Teaching Word Recognition

Good readers decode rapidly and automatically.

—Marilyn Adams

Accomplished readers identify words through a combination of strategies, switching from one to another as the need arises. Beginners blend individual letter-sound correspondences: /j/ /e/ /t/ is *jet*. They then use larger units as they become more familiar with word structure: /sh/ /eep/. Many words are read by pattern and analogy—if this is *dime*, then that is *time*—and they use their knowledge of roots and affixes. Readers also confirm words by using the context: Ed petted the big black ____. Finally, words are instantly recognized as sight words.

■ THE DEBATE ABOUT PHONICS

Instruction in phonics has been emphasized more in some eras than in others. It is now recognized as an essential component of beginning reading. In Colonial times, beginning readers started with the alphabet, often in combination with key words and phrases, such as, "A, In Adam's fall, we sinned all." Children learned the letters, then some syllables, and then learned to read text from memorized passages from the Bible and patriotic essays.

In 1836 the first McGuffey Readers were introduced. They were a series of five books of graduated difficulty. It was the first time vocabulary was controlled. Word families, such as *play*, *pray*, *bray*, and *gray*, were taught. Articulation and correct pronunciation were stressed. Over a period of 50 years, 122 million McGuffey Readers were published (Kismaric & Heiferman, 1996). By the middle of the 1800s, Horace Mann was pleading for children to be taught whole, meaningful words first and for teachers to stop the drill of isolated letter-sound correspondence.

Dick and Jane first appeared in the 1930 Elson Basic Reader preprimer. These readers used sight words first, which were to be learned as entire words, and they featured stories with a simplistic, highly controlled vocabulary. Dick, Jane, Sally, Spot, and Puff became part of Scott Foresman's New Basic Reading

Program. By the 1950s, 80% of the first graders in the United States were learning to read with Dick and Jane (Kismaric & Heiferman, 1996).

During the 1950s, prompted by Rudolph Flesch's book, *Why Johnny Can't Read*, which strongly advocated a phonics approach, educators began to reexamine what advantages phonics might offer. Flesch provided the motivation. "There is a connection between phonics and democracy—a fundamental connection. Equal opportunity for all is one of the inalienable rights, and the word method [sight words] interferes with that right" (Flesch, cited in Adams, 1991, p. 24).

It was time for a serious look into beginning reading methods and strategies. The U.S. Office of Education Cooperative Research Program in First Grade Reading Instruction was a compilation of 29 individual studies of various approaches to beginning reading reported by Bond and Dykstra in 1967. The studies were coordinated with common research questions, pretests, and outcome assessments.

> According to Bond and Dykstra's analyses, the approaches that, one way or another, included systematic phonic instruction consistently exceeded the straight basal programs in word recognition achievement scores. The approaches that included both systematic phonics and considerable emphasis on connected reading and meaning surpassed the basal alone approaches on virtually all outcome measures. (The exceptions were in the speed and accuracy of oral reading for which there were no significant differences between approaches.) In addition, the data indicated that exercise in writing was a positive component of beginning reading instruction. (Adams, 1991, p. 42)

No approach proved to be superior for students with higher or lower degrees of reading readiness. School, community, and teacher characteristics did not predict success, but certain student characteristics were strong predictors of end-of-the-year achievement. The best predictor was the student's ability to recognize and name uppercase and lowercase letters. This ability accounted for 25–36% of the variation despite the instructional approach. The next best predictors were the students' scores on an auditory phoneme discrimination task and a general intelligence test. Another important finding was that some pupils learned to read with thorough success and others experienced difficulty with every instructional method studied.

Jeanne Chall confirmed the findings of the First Grade Instruction studies in *Learning to Read: The Great Debate* (1967). Although the students taught by the look-say (sight word) method had an early advantage in rate and comprehension, students who were taught phonics caught up and surpassed the sight word group in comprehension, rate, and vocabulary by the end of second grade. In addition, Chall found that systematic instruction in phonics, compared with teaching letter-sound correspondence as the need arose, resulted in significantly better word recognition, better spelling, better vocabulary, and better reading comprehension at least through the third grade (Adams, 1991).

Despite the thoroughness of these studies from the 1960s, dissatisfaction about isolated drill and the simplicity and meagerness of early stories led in the 1980s and early 1990s to the whole language movement, in which phonics was taught within the context of literature only as teachers decided it was needed.

Whole language programs emphasized meaning-based reading and writing activities (National Reading Panel, 2000). Margaret Moustafa (1998) believed that words that arise from meaningful contexts are more memorable than words that don't. However, the idea of incidental phonics felt a little wiggly and haphazard to many classroom teachers, especially beginning teachers. They were unsure of exactly what to do and how often to stop to analyze a word. While discovery learning is a highly effective way to learn, students may not make all the discoveries that they need to make about phonics (Gunning, 2005).

Marilyn Jager Adams's work in 1990, supported by the U.S. Department of Education Cooperative Agreement with the Reading Research and Education Center at the University of Illinois, was a major turning point for research-based instruction.

> Deep and thorough knowledge of letters, spelling patterns, and words, and of the phonological translations of all three, are of inescapable importance to both skillful reading and its acquisition. By extension, instruction designed to develop children's sensitivity to spellings and their relations to pronunciations should be of paramount importance in the development of reading skills. This is, of course, precisely the goal of good phonics instruction. (Adams, 1991, p. 416)

The National Reading Panel report (2000) compared 38 studies over the preceding 30 years. One conclusion was that several types of systematic phonics programs are about equally effective, and all contribute more to students' growth in reading than do incidental phonics programs. Whole-class, small-group, and tutoring situations are all effective, but the smaller the group, the larger the effect. Early phonics instruction in kindergarten and first grade was more effective than phonics introduced after first grade. Instruction to prevent reading difficulties had significant effects for at-risk kindergartners and first graders but no significant impact for low-achieving readers in Grades 2–6. Children from lower socio-economic groups made greater gains than did middle-class students.

■ HOW DOES WORD RECOGNITION DEVELOP?

Students progress through distinct stages of word recognition, which are very similar to the stages of spelling. They move from global to analytic processing, from approximate to specific linking of sound and letter, and from context-driven to print-driven reading (Moats, 2005), or in other words, from hazy to precise. Teachers who are aware of the stages and are good diagnosticians can teach children word-identification strategies that are appropriate to their developmental needs.

> Studies of readers as they proceed through the phases of word learning suggest that the more functional knowledge students have about the alphabetic system and how words are structured systematically to represent speech, the more fluent and automatic they become as readers. Research indicates that students having difficulty learning to read are the ones who understand the least about the alphabetic system. (Gaskins, Ehri, Cress, O'Hara, & Donnelly, 1997a, pp. 172–173)

Through learning visual features, context, letter-sound correspondences, common spelling patterns, roots and affixes, and sight words, children can achieve automatic and efficient word recognition. Students need to become fluent with these strategies to be able to concentrate on meaning, an ability which is never automatic and never without active attention and thought.

Visual Features

Children first learn some words by visual features, such as the McDonalds' logo. However, when *McDonalds* is written in regular type, children at this stage are unable to recognize the word. Because there is no systematic link of spelling to pronunciation, this form of "reading" is memory intensive. These visual cues usually precede phonetic cues.

Using the Context for Word Recognition

When analyzing the mistakes of beginning and struggling readers, researchers have found that many of the errors make sense in the context. These readers rely heavily on context because their decoding skills are not sufficiently developed to provide enough phonetic clues. Context is never sufficient as a sole strategy to reliably identify unknown words but works best as a tool to monitor word recognition. It is not a substitute for information provided by the letters in a word (Snow, Burns, & Griffin, 1998). Good readers also use context to decide on the meaning of a word with multiple definitions (e.g., *The princess went to the ball* versus *Harry hit the ball*).

Sight Words

The term *sight words* has two related but different meanings. Throughout the sequence of word recognition instruction, some words just have to be learned by sight or by visual memory. These are usually words such as *want*, *come*, or *they* that do not sound out according to the rules. Although these words are irregular, phonics instruction is still helpful because the consonants maintain their sounds (National Reading Panel, 2000). Other sight words are unusual words needed for a story, such as *hippopotamus*, or word patterns that will be studied later but are needed now, such as *boy*. The other meaning of *sight words* is words that have been studied and read so many times that they are recognized instantaneously. A minority of reading-disabled students who are unable to learn phonics can learn to read with sight words.

Letter-Sound Correspondence, or Phonics

Phonics is the principal way readers identify unknown words. While phonics is the most common name for this word recognition strategy, it is also referred to as sound-symbol relationship, word attack, the graphophonemic cueing system, letter-sound correspondence, decoding, and the orthographic processing system (although this term has more to do with spelling patterns). Some terms are a bit broader than others, but they all have to do with the system of how letters and spelling patterns represent speech sounds.

The squitly tourmarands vashornly blained the cloughts in the wroked knanflede. You probably did not have much trouble "reading" the previous sentence. It is fairly straightforward to anyone who has broken the code. *Cloughts* may be /clowts/ or /clawts/. *Wroked* may be /rok-ed/, /rokd/ or /rokt/, but the other words are simple to pronounce once the system is known. Phonics allows readers to pronounce words that they have never seen before. Of course, pronouncing does not mean knowing the meaning or being able to comprehend the message, but comprehension will certainly be hindered if the words cannot be identified.

Phonics includes the consistent letter-sound matches (*n* is always /n/) and the patterns of multiple sounds for certain letters, such as *c* in *caught* or *city* or *ou* in *doubt* or *cough*. It also includes learning multiple spelling patterns for the same sound, such as long *e* in *meat, mete,* or *meet,* or that /r/ can be represented by *r* or *wr*.

Systematic phonics aids the comprehension of young readers and reading-disabled students the most (National Reading Panel, 2000). "The ability to sound out new words accounts for about 80% of the variance in first-grade reading comprehension, and continues to be a major factor in text comprehension as students progress through the grades" (Foorman et al., cited in Moats, 2005, p. 81).

> Systematic phonics aids the comprehension of young readers and reading-disabled students the most.

Mature readers process every single letter of the text (Pressley, 2002). Their eyes leap from word to word, taking in about three letters to the left of center and six to the right. Good readers also habitually translate spellings to sounds as they read. This is very useful for those words that are less frequently seen and end up being processed auditorily, and even expert readers resort to subvocalization with very difficult texts. If it sounds familiar, the meaning is accessed, and the word is known.

General Progression in Learning Phonics

Phonics instruction starts with **distinguishing between letter names and sounds**. Common reading and spelling errors are made when these are confused. The letter *y* sounds like /wī/, *u* sounds like /yū/, so *your* is spelled *ur*. *W* is often spelled and read as *u*, and *x* sounds like /eks/.

Beginning reading starts with **a few consonants and one or two vowels** so that children can start learning the letter-sound correspondence and blend them together into simple words. Instruction usually begins with the consonants that are continuous or can be stretched, such as *m, s, n, f, z, v, l,* and *r*. The stop-consonant sounds, *b, d, k, t, p,* and *g,* are harder to work with without adding vowels sounds. The letters *c* and *g* usually are studied much later because their sounds depend on adjacent letters. The idea is to establish the alphabetic principle, which is that when certain letters are seen, they can be expected to consistently produce a specific sound. Initial consonants are easiest to hear, then final, and then consonants in medial (middle) positions. Beginning instruction minimizes *c, q,* and *x* as redundant letters. The letter *c* sounds /k/ or /s/. The letter *q* is redundant for /k/, and *x* sounds /ks/ or /z/. In good phonics instruction, decoded words are immediately used in sentences for meaningful practice, and children read real text in which they can apply their newfound knowledge.

Beginning readers tend to select one or two salient letter-sound cues to identify a word. However, too many words are too similar, such as *were*, *wear*, *we're*, and *where*, for this strategy to be effective for very long. Students who notice only a few letters, who are unable to blend the sounds together to form recognizable words, or who guess from the context will not have a reliable or efficient enough system for rapid decoding (Gaskins et al., 1997a).

After children learn most consonants and vowels, other elements are added. The sequence of introduction varies with different programs but includes the following:

Short vowels: Short vowels are more consistent but harder to hear and learn than long vowels are. Instruction in the short vowels *a*, *e*, and *i* usually precedes instruction in *o* and *u*.

Consonant clusters and blends: *bl, cl, fl, gl, pl, sl, br, cr, dr, fr, gr, pr, tr, sc, sk, sm, sn, sp, squ, st, sw, tw, scr, spl, spr, str, thr, -ct, -ld, -lf, -lk, -lm, -lp, -lt, -lve, -mp, -nce, -nch, -nd, -nt, -rd, -sp, -st* (not necessarily in this order). Letter combinations that blend their sounds are learned after cvc (consonant-vowel-consonant) words. Spanish has *l*-blends (*blusa*), but because it has no *s*-blends, Spanish-speaking children learning English tend to add an *e* before the *s* (*espot* for *spot*) to make them sound more natural.

Long vowels with silent *e*: Both Spanish- and Chinese-speaking students will have difficulty with long *e*. Start them with long *o*. Some teachers now call the silent *e* "bossy *e*" because it tells the vowel what to do.

Inflectional endings: *-ed, -ing, -s*

Consonant digraphs: These are pairs of letters that make a new sound rather than blending their sounds: *ch, sh, th, wh, ph, gh, -ng, -nk.* These are harder to learn than blends.

Two letter–one sound pairs: *-ck, kn, qu, ph, wr*

As children add more letter-sound associations, they can decode simple words and predictable syllables. With practice, they begin to process larger chunks, such as *-and, -ame, -ine, -ing,* and *-ed.* In the complete alphabetic stage, readers analyze all the letters in a word.

More advanced phonics includes learning the lower-frequency vowel combinations and spelling variations that can be used to represent sounds. Figure 10.2 in Chapter 10 lists the alternate spellings of the vowel and consonant sounds. It is an important chart of all the patterns of phonics.

R-controlled vowels: *ar, er, ir, or, ur.* The *r* changes the vowel sound so that it is neither long nor short.

Vowel diphthongs: *aw, ew, ow, ou, oo, oi, oy*

Vowel teams: *ai, ea, oa, ee, eigh, ay, ey, igh,* and the infamous *ough* as in *bough, though, through, rough,* and *cough.* These usually represent short or long vowel sounds but are not always consistent in sound.

Vowel patterns: The vowel patterns are useful for both single and multi-syllable words. Vowels generally follow these patterns:

1. cvc, ccvc, cvcc, or ccvcc. The vowel is usually short (*top, thin, sink, think*).
2. cvce. The vowel is usually long (*face*).
3. cvvc. The first vowel usually "does the talking" or is long (*mail*). There are several vowel teams for which this is not true.
4. cv. The vowel sound is usually long (*he, no*).
5. Sometimes *y* and *w* act as vowels. The key word for *y* is *crybaby,* which uses both sounds of *y* as a vowel. The letter *w* is used in vowel digraphs *aw, ew,* and *ow.*
6. The sound of the vowel can be controlled by *r, l,* and *w* (*are, call, few*).

English has so many spelling-phonics patterns because it has 40-some phonemes and only 26 letters to represent those sounds. In addition, English words were derived from many different languages, and the letter-sound rules in one violated the letter-sound rules in another. For example, *ch* is used to spell /ch/ in Anglo-Saxon words such as *chair;* it is used to spell /k/ in Greek-derived words such as *chorus;* and it sounds /sh/ in French-derived words such as *charade* (Moats, 2005).

Word Families, Pattern, and Analogy

As readers progress, words are more often identified by pattern and analogy. Successful decoding is not really done letter by letter or by memorizing rules but by patterns of letters that represent units of sound. At this stage, word families are learned—the rhyming words that share a common rime. In the "squitly tourmarands" sentence, you probably said *blained* to rhyme with *rained.* The last syllable in *tourmarands* rhymed with *bands* or *sands.* Later on, students can make generalizations about internal parts of the word. You probably pronounced the *ough* in *cloughts* to rhyme with the *ough* in *bought* or *bough.* When the reading process is repeated on a daily basis with a variety of texts, children begin to form generalizations about written language and internalize the rules.

The research on phonics reports that the rules apply between 40% and 85% of the time, and even those rules that are useful are not memorized but generalized. Rosso and Emans (cited in May, 1998) gave students a list of 14 words, each exemplifying a different phonetic rule. The children could identify an average of 75% of the words but could explain the rule only 15% of the time. It is only through extensive reading that the rules turn into generalizations.

Sight Words: The Stage of Automatic Decoding

Sight word reading is the principal way that familiar words are read (Gaskins, Ehri, Cress, O'Hara, & Donnelly, 1997b), but this is not the same as learning words by their shape or even as a whole, as with a Chinese logograph.

The word is learned first through analysis of the sounds and then by multiple encounters until the word becomes so well known that it seems to be processed as a whole—as a sight word. The pronunciation, spelling, and meaning are accessed at a glance. Students need substantial practice with words to store them in memory and be able to retrieve them with ease. As children read more and more text, even the less frequently encountered words become sight words. Thus the word recognition sequence is visual, phonetic, and then visual again.

What is a familiar sequence of word recognition to primary teachers is now being explained through brain scans. Novices process words differently than skilled readers do because novices need to analyze each new word. The visual cortex images the word *pig*, for example, and sends the information to the parietotemporal area, located slightly behind the left ear. In that area, spoken language sounds and letters are matched. The parietotemporal area and Broca's area work together (see Figure 2.1 in Chapter 2) to segment the sounds /p/ /i/ /g/ and encode the sequence to its visual word form, *pig*. Meaning is accessed from another part of the brain, and the word is recognized. Because all these steps— sound-symbol match, pronunciation, and meaning—are processed separately, the process is slow.

Skilled readers store learned and processed words in a different part of the brain, the occipitotemporal area. Visual information is sent directly to that area, where all the relevant linguistic information is stored, and the word is retrieved in less than 150 thousandths of a second as a sight word. (My many thanks to David Sousa's book *How the Brain Learns to Read* (2005) for helping me begin to understand this field.)

Syllabication and Morphology

Advanced study of word recognition includes studying syllabication; roots and affixes that affect meaning, such as *-tion* and *-ly* or *pre-*; morphology (meaning-carrying word parts); and foreign-derived roots. Learning common letter patterns helps readers syllabicate. For example, the letters *dn* are not a common sequence, so good readers know those letters will define a syllable boundary, as in *midnight*. About 60% of words in running English text are derived from Greek or Latin (Henry, 1997).

> Extensive reading is the necessary balance to instruction in word recognition.

WORD RECOGNITION IN A ■
BALANCED READING PROGRAM

No matter which word recognition stage students are in, they need extensive practice with whole text. Extensive reading is the necessary balance to instruction in word recognition. Teaching isolated phonics first is like teaching batting to a child who has never seen a baseball game. The child can learn to do it but can't figure out what it's good for (Stahl, 1992). Children first need to understand the "whole" concept of reading. Learning that reading is meaningful can be accomplished through read-alouds and other early literacy experiences.

Figure 4.1   These diagrams show the brain systems used for reading. The novice reader uses the parieto-temporal area to slowly analyze new words with considerable help from Broca's area. However, the skilled reader uses the occipito-temporal area to quickly identify previously learned word forms, with just a little help from Broca's area, as indicated by the dotted arrow. Both types of readers activate the frontal lobe to generate meaning.

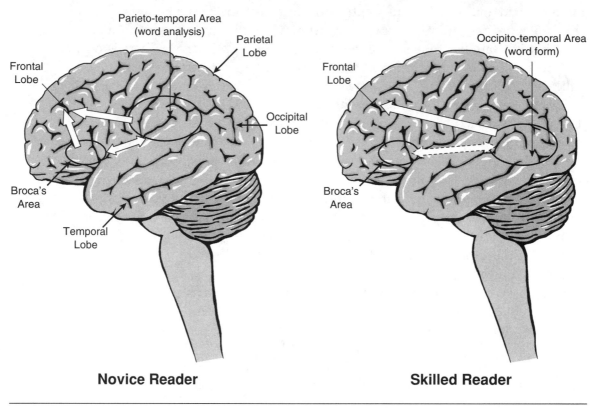

Novice Reader   **Skilled Reader**

Source: Sousa, David A., *How the Brain Learns to Read.* Thousand Oaks, CA: Corwin Press, 2005.

The "parts" in whole-part-whole instruction are the skills and strategies of reading, and students require explicit instruction in them to learn them thoroughly. Phonics is no exception. Nothing is intrinsic in the symbol *h* that gives it an /h/ sound. In Spanish, *h* is silent, and /h/ is represented by the letter *j*. These agreed-on conventions in a language need to be taught. Explicit instruction means not only clear instruction; it also means explaining to children why anyone would want to use a particular strategy and how it can be of use. This is especially helpful for children who come from environments in which reading is not a priority.

Coaching during application may be especially important for struggling readers who do not automatically transfer skills. In a study of low-income schools, Barbara Taylor and colleagues (2000) found teachers in the most effective schools were three times more likely than teachers in the less effective schools to encourage students to use a range of strategies to figure out unknown words when reading. The opposite was observed in schools of lesser effectiveness: Phonics was explicitly taught, but coaching was seldom observed. Coaching for application is important for all students. Robert Gaskins and colleagues (1995) found significant relationships between success on decoding tests and the amount of time outside of word identification lessons that teachers spent encouraging use of decoding strategies. Michael Pressley and colleagues (2001) found the most effective first-grade teachers frequently reminded students to use previously taught word identification skills during reading activities. Coaching bridges the gap between instruction and application when students do not make the connection by themselves.

The last "whole" in whole-part-whole instruction is extensive reading and application of skills in text. Practice does make perfect or at least better. Newly decoded words need to be practiced in sentences, in writing, and through repeated opportunities to read. While the position statement from the International Reading Association recognizes that phonics is an essential part of beginning reading instruction, it also says, "However, effective phonics instruction is embedded in the context of a complete reading and language arts program" (International Reading Association, 1997).

What proportion of a balanced program should be devoted to word recognition? Of course more time is devoted in the earlier grades, when children are learning to break the code, but experts recommend about 25%. Cunningham and Cunningham (2002) recommend the four block approach—guided reading, self-selected reading, writing, and working with words—with each receiving about one fourth of the time allotted for reading class.

A balanced reading program includes reading to children from quality literature, building background and language skills, discussing and responding, writing, independent and guided reading, and of course word study.

APPROACHES TO TEACHING PHONICS ■

There are several approaches to teaching phonics. The **synthetic method** starts with isolated letters and sounds, which are blended into words. This is the method used in current basals. Louisa Moats (2005) suggests **sound to spelling**. In this method, instead of the alphabet, sounds are listed on the word wall. Thus under /s/, *see*, *fuss*, *city*, and *science* would all be listed. See a list organized this way in Chapter 10, Figure 10.2. This approach helps children see the variations with greater dependability in the sound-letter relationships. In the **analytic method**, children analyze letter-sound relationships once a word is identified. Some approaches use the words in context from the beginning, and some do not. **Analogy phonics** programs teach children to use parts of words they already know to identify new words. These are all **systematic, explicit methods** that teach the sounds through a planned, explicitly taught approach that progresses from easier to more difficult. **Embedded** or **indirect teaching** of phonics occurs during shared or guided reading or during writing experiences as the need occurs.

> An experienced phonics teacher sequences instruction so that easy and dependable letter-sound correspondences are learned first, and children come to understand there is a correspondence between letters and sounds.

In a survey of 1,207 teachers of kindergarten through fifth grade, James Baumann and colleagues (1998, p. 641) found, "66% of the kindergarten through second-grade teachers used systematic instruction in synthetic phonics, 40% used analytic phonics, and 19% taught phonics on an as-needed basis." Leslie Mandel Morrow and Diane Tracey (1997) studied 76 preschool, kindergarten, first-grade, and second-grade classrooms and found that indirect methods were used most often in preschool classrooms. As children progressed through the grades, the instruction in phonics became more explicit.

■ ACTIVITIES TO TEACH WORD RECOGNITION

I met a very young primary teacher and asked her how she taught phonics. She said it was too difficult to keep track of the odd order in which the sounds were presented in the phonics program, so she just started in alphabetical order, *a, b, c, d, e,* and so on. She did not realize that she was starting instruction with mostly inconsistent letter-sound relationships that make it difficult for children to form generalizations. The vowels *a* and *e* have short and long sounds. The letter *c* represents the /k/ or /s/ sound, and *b* and *d* look just alike to young readers. An experienced phonics teacher sequences instruction so that easy and dependable letter-sound correspondences are learned first, and children come to understand there is a correspondence between letters and sounds.

Using Context

Context can help limit the choices for word identification. To teach this, the teacher writes several sentences on the board and covers one word in each sentence with sticky notes. Children read the sentence and guess several words that would make sense in context. The guesses are written on the board, and then the first letter of the mystery word is uncovered. Guesses that did not start with that letter are erased. The remainder of the word is uncovered, and the word is confirmed (Cunningham, Hall, & Defee, 1998).

Sounds to Words

In synthetic phonics, the teacher might say, "This is the letter *m.* It sounds /mmm/." The children write the letter and make the sound. A key word such as *mop* is shown, and the teacher sounds it out, pointing out that the first sound in *mop* is /m/, which is written *m*. The teacher might ask the children to think of other words beginning with /m/, which are written on the board. The common spelling pattern is noted. Several simple words, *mat, mob, map, man, mad, met, men,* and *mom,* are listed by the teacher, and the class sounds them out, blends the sounds, and says the words. The students might write the words, use them in sentences, and if the children are advanced enough, read whole sentences containing the words. The synthetic method is explicit because the children are told the letter-sound correspondence and do not have to discover it by themselves.

To **blend sounds,** students can use alphabet tiles or letter cards placed a few inches apart from each other. To teach *met,* the letters *m e t* are separated and then pushed together as the students say /mmm/ /eee/ /ttt/. The process is repeated several times, each time a little faster, until the word is pronounced normally.

To play **I Spy,** say "I spy with my little eye something beginning with *d.*" Children must then guess what object in the room has been spotted that begins with the letter *d*. Writing a list of *d* words on the board helps children notice the letter-sound match, and the list can be read again. **Tongue twisters** also emphasize initial sounds: Little Lucy likes licking lollipops. **Jump rope rhymes** offer many possibilities, as in M, My name is Molly. My brother's name is Mike. We eat mustard, and we live in Moscow. The geography part is a lesson in itself.

Words to Sounds

Can Kate <u>please</u> come out to <u>play</u>?
The <u>plastic</u> <u>plane</u> was red.
The <u>plump</u> dog <u>plopped</u> down on his bed.
The teacher reads the sentences aloud and has the students echo read them. Next she reads the underlined words and has the children repeat them. She asks which sounds are the same in the words and which letters are the same so as to establish the letter-sound correspondence. The teacher can ask the students to produce the sound that *pl* makes and think of other words that begin with /pl/. The children return to the sentences and read them chorally and then individually. The students then do a word search, looking through books to find and write other examples of *pl* words. This sample lesson is adapted from Frank May (1998).

In **stretching sounds**, teachers start with words with one-to-one correspondence, such as *man*, /mmm/ /aaa/ /nnn/, and move to words that have multiple letters for single sounds: *will* /w/ /i/ /l/, *snail* /s/ /n/ /ā/ /l/, *phone* /f/ /ō/ /n/. Rubber bands or hand motions accompany the stretching. This technique helps children segment and identify all the sounds.

Another analytic technique is **fully analyzing words**. It includes "stretching out the pronunciations of words to analyze the constituent sounds in the words, analyzing the visual forms of words, talking about matches between sounds and letters (and grouping letters into chunks where necessary), noting similarities to sounds and letters in other words already learned, and remembering how to spell the words" (Gaskins et al., 1997b, p. 319).

The teaching of fully analyzed words can be done by modeling the process in a **Talk-to-Yourself Chart** (Gaskins et al., 1997b). When students are guided through the following process with teacher modeling and support, they soon learn to replicate the process by themselves.

1. The word is _____.

2. Stretch the word.   I hear _____ sounds.

3. I see ___ letters because _____.

4. The spelling pattern is _____.

5. This is what I know about the vowel. _____

6. Another word on the word wall like _____ is _____.

7. They are alike because _____.

The full process sounds like this: The word is red, /rrr/, /eee/, /ddd/. I hear three sounds. I see three letters because every letter has a sound. The spelling pattern is cvc. The vowel will sound /ĕ/ because it's a single vowel between consonants. Another word like *red* is *let*. They are alike because both have two consonants with a vowel in the middle, so they both sound /ĕ/.

As children learn to fully analyze a word, relating all the sounds to the letters, they begin to see the one-to-one correspondences and to see which sounds require two letters. *Back* has three sounds but four letters. They notice the consistencies as they compare words and also notice which words are irregular and how they are different from expected patterns.

Gaskins believes that it is only when words are fully analyzed phonetically that they will become true sight words. Without thorough analysis of all the letters in the word, children do not seem to recognize similar patterns and are unable to take advantage of word families. Partners can use the talk-to-yourself chart to work on new words. Comparing old and new words to words on the word wall (see below) reinforces the patterns.

The spelling part of fully analyzed words is done through **Elkonin boxes**, as in Figure 4.2. Students have worksheets that contain groups of boxes, each containing the same number of empty boxes as there are sounds. For *chick*, there would be three boxes, for *ch*, *i*, and *ck*. As the teacher stretches the sounds in the

Figure 4.2 Elkonin boxes

ELKONIN BOXES

1	r	e	d				
2	d	i	me				
3	ch	e	s	t			
4	s	l	igh	t			
5	sh	ou	t	e	d		
6							
7							

target word, the students write the letters. Clues are given about how many letters it takes to make a particular sound. For example, to make /k/ at the end of a word, two letters are needed. Spelling in first grade is most impacted by phonics instruction (National Reading Panel, 2000).

For **Secret Word**, select a word from a pattern and give five clues. Students number their papers and write a guess after each clue. For example, "The secret word is in the -*at* family. It has three letters. It is an animal. It can fly. Into the cave flew the ____" (Cunningham & Allington, 1999).

In **Ready-Set-Show** (Gaskins et al., 1997a), students prepare four key-word cards that are copied from the board. These words are analyzed and placed face up on each student's desk. The teacher pronounces a new word, and the students stretch the sounds and analyze what they hear. They then compare what they heard with their key words. When the teacher says, "Ready, set, show," each student holds up the card that contains the word with the same sound(s), which can be beginning or ending sounds, vowel matches, or pattern matches, depending on the maturity of the students. The steps are repeated for approximately 12 words, providing students with practice in phonemic segmentation and sound-letter matching. An advantage to this technique is that every student is involved with each match.

Word walls are a display of words listed above or below an alphabet chart. These words are thoroughly learned and can be used as key words for word families, or they may be words that do not follow regular patterns, such as *have*. Usually no more than five words are added each week. Word walls may be color coded so that there is a different-colored background for each vowel letter and for irregular words. For example, if students wanted to find a word to decode *dent*, they could limit the search to just the "blue" words, with the letter *e*, instead of searching the entire wall (White, 2005). Students need to be coached to use the word wall for comparison to new words for both reading and writing.

Manipulating Words

After children have learned a body of words, teachers use a combination of analytic and synthetic phonics and work both from word to letter and from letter to word. Several activities actively involve children in manipulating words so that they begin to notice that small changes make big differences.

When **Making Words**, children are given a set of six to eight letters that will eventually be combined into a secret word. The students make words with magnetic letters or tiles as directed by their teacher. The vowels are a different color from the consonants so that children learn that they must include a vowel in every word. The teacher prepares all the words on word cards for later use. For the letters *a, i, m, n, r,* and *t,* the directions might start like this: "Take two letters and make *am. I am your teacher.* Change one letter and spell *at. We are at school.*" The changes continue so that the children make *rat, mat, man, tan, ran, ram, rim, trim,* and *tram.* Then the teacher starts again with *main, rain, train.* Children see if they can find the secret word, *Martin,* which was chosen for a unit on African American heritage.

Next the students sort the word cards. Word cards can be sorted by beginning sounds, paying special attention to the *tr* blends, and by rhyming words. New words that follow the given pattern can be added, such as *swim* and *Spain*. Children "learn to pay attention to all the letters because changing just one letter results in a new word. They also learn that it matters where you put the letters" (Cunningham & Cunningham, 2002, p. 100).

Word Sorts help children pay attention to patterns and variations. Sorting activities are determined by the students' stage in word recognition. Beginners sort pictures and initial sounds, ending sounds, blends and digraphs, and then vowel patterns. Second- or third-grade students who are confused about the various sounds and spelling patterns of *o*, for example, might sort *shout, brown, old, cone, boat, fold, roast, spout, rope, cow, pound, road, hole, now,* and *couch*. The teacher provides the two main categories: long o and /ow/. The students will find the *ou* and *ow* spelling patterns under /ow/ and the *-old,* o-silent-*e,* and *oa* spelling patterns under long *o.* To avoid just sorting by spelling, students must say the word and explain the pattern: "This is *couch*. It has the /ow/ sound because it's spelled with *ou*." For words they can't figure out, the direction is reversed: "This word has *ou* like *sound*, so it must have the /ow/ sound and be *couch*."

Manipulatives

Teachers can give children a variety of helpful hands-on ways to learn word recognition. Children can write words on the board as the words are analyzed; the children can write on individual white boards or chalk slates; and they can use letter tile cards or plastic letters, pocket charts, or hand gestures for blending. Post (2003) recommends using lowercase letters, which are easier to combine visually into a unit. Those with serifs, the fine strokes attached at the ends, lead the eye in a left-to-right direction.

The teacher can turn **word games** into board games by using the insides of file folders as the boards. A series of squares drawn on the makeshift board act as the spaces that the children advance through as they play the game. Each square has a word written in it. Add a spinner and a set of tokens to move as game pieces. Students move the markers around the board as they correctly pronounce the words written in the spaces.

Technology

There are several low-tech and high-tech tools for phonics practice, such as *Write: OutLoud,* a talking word processor (Don Johnston, Inc.), and *Dr. Peet's TalkWriter* (Interest-Driven Learning, Inc.), which will say words that have been typed in. *Kidspiration* (Inspiration Software Inc.) has a speech component, and LeapPad books (Leap Frog Enterprises) use an electronic device that speaks individual sounds or words when a special pen is passed over them. Sunburst has CD-ROM software such as *Max's Attic* to help build students' vowel recognition skills. Starfall, http://www.starfall.com, features activities and stories to introduce single-syllable patterns and also has a speech component.

Word Families, Phonograms, and Analogies

Learning the sounds of common spelling patterns (*-ime, -ate, -ish*), alternate spellings for the same sounds (*-eat, -eet*), and alternate sounds for the same letter combinations (*fought, though*) is the second stage in phonics instruction. These patterns should be taught after students already possess the skills of rhyming, onset-rime awareness, initial phoneme identity, and letter-sound knowledge (White, 2005).

Word families are also called phonograms or onsets and rimes. In the word *bank*, *b* is the onset and *-ank* is the rime. *Bank* is part of the word family *tank, sank, drank, thank,* and so on. Onset and rime division develops early, and this approach may be easier for some children than full-segmentation phonics. The strategy of identifying new words by comparison to a known word in the family is called word recognition by **analogy**. Even beginning readers are able to make analogies (White, 2005). Betty Levy and Linda Lysynchuk (1997) found rime-based and phoneme-based training equally effective in both short- and long-term retention and generalization.

Letter-sound correspondences in word families are more dependable than sounding out words letter-by-letter, especially vowel sounds. The combination *ea* has multiple sounds but is regular in all rimes except *-ead, -eaf, and -ear.* "Of the 286 phonograms that appear in primary grade texts, 95% of them were pronounced the same in every word in which they appeared" (Stahl, 1992, p. 623).

Figure 4.3   Wylie and Durrell's phonograms to generate 500 words

ack	ail	ain	ake	ale	ame	an	ank	ap	ash	at	ate
aw	ay	eat	ell	est	ice	ick	ide	ight	ill	in	ine
ing	ink	ip	it	ock	oke	op	ore	ot	uck	up	ump
unk											

Less-Common Phonograms and Useful Endings

ace	ad	ade	age	ail	ait	al	all	am	and	ance
are	art	as	ask	aw	azy	eak	eam	ean	ear	eck
ed	een	eep	eet	em	en	end	er	et	ew	ib
ice	id	igh	ile	im	ime	imp	is	ish	ive	old
og	on	one	ong	ony	ood	ook	ool	orn	ose	ough
ould	ound	own	ub	ue	un	up	ut			
ed	ing	ie	ly	tion	y					

Source: R. E. Wylie and D. D. Durrell, "Teaching Vowels Through Phonograms," *Elementary English*, 47, 787–791. Copyright (c) 1970 by the National Council of Teachers of English. Reprinted with permission.

Richard Wylie and Donald Durrell (1970) found that only 37 rimes were necessary to generate 500 words frequently used by children and that it was easier for children to identify rimes or word families than to learn individual vowel sounds. See Figure 4.3.

Wylie and Durrell (1970) found other interesting characteristics about learning word families.

1. All types of long vowel families (*-ail*, *-eed*, *-oke*) are equally easy to learn and are as easy to learn as the short vowel families (*-ap*, *-og*, *-et*).

2. The odd vowel combinations (*ou*, *ar*, *all*, *aw*) are a little harder to learn than regular long and short vowel families but not so much harder that they should be postponed.

3. Those word families that end with a single consonant (*-ap*, *-it*) are easier to learn than the word families that end with consonant blends (*-ump*, *-ank*).

Of course, many of the most common words do not follow the word family patterns: *gave*, *save*, and *have*; and *maid*, *paid*, and *said*. Those words need to be taught as sight words or as infrequent patterns. Still, the patterns are common enough that children benefit from learning word families when decoding both single-syllable and multiple-syllable words.

In **rhyming word sorts**, several words from three or four word families are listed in random order on the top of a worksheet or pocket chart. Key words are already in place at the tops of columns, and children must sort the words according to their spelling patterns. The words are pronounced by the analogy strategy: "When I come to a word I don't know, I think of a word I do know. If this is *sight*, then that is *fight*." It seems critical that the key words are well learned or overlearned, and placing them as key words in a word wall will be helpful (White, 2005).

Practice word families with **sliding sleeves**. A sleeve can be made from a manila folder that is open at both the top and bottom. The word family rime (*-ink*, for example) is written on the outside to the right of a hole that has been cut in the sleeve and which will reveal the different onsets. A sliding piece of paper can be fit inside the sleeve with the onsets *p*, *m*, *dr*, *l*, *r*, *st*, *s*, *th*, and *w* written in a column. The resulting words can be pronounced, written, spelled, and used in context. Multiple examples help children attend to all the letters in a word.

Reading/writing rhymes is done with a chart that has the same rime written eight times. A pack of onsets is distributed to the children; it includes all the single consonants, blends, digraphs, and other combinations of two letters that produce one sound, such as *ph*, *wr*, *kn*, *and qu*. Children are asked to come up and place their onset next to the rime if they think it will make a word. If the word is real, the word is used in a sentence and written on the chart. The reason rhyming words that are not real words or that use a different spelling pattern are not put on the chart is given. The teacher can add two-syllable words that follow the same pattern. When the chart is completed, the class writes sentences with lots of rhyming words, and the children can write sentences of their own. The chart can be kept for future practice (Cunningham & Cunningham, 2002).

Secret Messages are substitution exercises that focus on onset and rime. Once these messages have been modeled, students can create their own (QuanSing, cited in Gunning, 2005).

Take *H* from *He* and put in *W*.	We
Take *l* from *lot* and put in *g*.	got
Take *p* from *pen* and put in *t*.	ten
Take *st* from *stew* and put in *n*.	new
Take *l* from *looks* and put in *b*.	books

Children love **word games with rhymes**. Find a copy of the 1960s song "The Name Game" or use hink pinks, riddles with rhyming answers. An example of a hink pink is, What do you call Hawaiian punch? A pink drink.

Books with rhymes provide vivid oral language and enjoyable stories. Dr. Seuss books are a natural source for decoding new words in families. Read the story and discuss the meaning first. Word study follows when the story is reread. The rhyming words are listed on cards and placed in a pocket chart, and spelling and sounds are compared. Care needs to be taken to use words that match in spelling and sound, such as *say*, *today*, and *away*, especially when children are first learning the pattern. *Sheets* and *seats* can also be noted, but one card can be dramatically torn and discarded because it does not match the spelling pattern of the day. Patricia Cunningham, Dorothy Hall, and Margaret Defee (1998) recommend that children brainstorm other words that have the same pattern (*play*, *lay*), so that generalization and transfer of the pattern occur.

Kids can write variations of book patterns such as Brown's *Good Night Moon* (1947). The story tells of several characters saying good night in a rhyming pattern. The following is an excerpt from a classroom adaptation (Morrow & Tracey, 1997).

There were three big crickets, sitting on tickets

And two big frogs, sitting on logs.

There were three gold fish, swimming in a dish

And a bowl full of jello, and a bird that said "hello" . . .

Good night crickets, good night tickets;

Good night frogs, sitting on logs.

Phonics instruction that includes whole text is not only more interesting but also improves children's identification of words. This is because whole text makes available additional cueing systems, both syntactic and semantic, which help children confirm words.

Go to the Web site Webbing Into Literacy: A Headstart Program, http:// curry.edschool.virginia.edu/go/wil/home.html, for a fabulous array of rhyming words with full-size illustrations, riddle cards for rhymes, and several month-by-month activities.

Vowels

Vowels are always a problem. They are harder to discriminate and remember than consonants. Key words and phonograms seem to be easier to remember than the vowel rules, which work only fairly well. Many one- and two- syllable words follow the basic patterns: cvc for short vowels and cv, cvvc, and cvce for long vowels. Children who have had experience with phonograms are much more likely to be able to generalize and apply the vowel rules.

Cheryl Harding (1998), a speech and language pathologist, advises that teachers should not fear working with vowels in isolation, especially with children who are having a difficult time discriminating the sounds. Key words work well, and she uses *Ed* for short *e* because the usual *elephant* and *egg* cause problems; the *l* makes it difficult to isolate the sound of *e*, and some children say *egg* with a long *a* sound. The diphthongs and vowel teams are best taught after other generalizations are established and are easiest to teach as phonograms.

More advanced primary students can do **vowel sorts**. Fifteen to 20 words encountered in reading and that contain the same vowel letter can be gathered and sorted by vowel sound. It usually turns out there are only two or three categories and an exception or two. This activity can be done with cards and a pocket chart or with pencil and paper. The good thing about sorting with sturdy cards is that the words can be resorted by parts of speech (a simplified version), syllables, or other word patterns for extra practice.

Frank May (1998) recommends matching patterns across vowels so that *face*, *nice*, and *bone* are grouped together. (Words with *e* or *u* are uncommon in a silent *e* pattern.) Irene Gaskins and colleagues (1997a) recommend word play in which the vowel is changed but the other letters must remain the same, such as *treat* to *trout*.

Syllables

Syllable boundaries (where syllables are divided) cause more problems than the number of syllables in a word, so start teaching syllables with easy affixes, such as *-ing* and *-ful*, and then compound words. Continue with closed and open syllable patterns: A closed syllable, cvc, ccvc, cvcc, or ccvcc, makes the vowel short (*top*, *thin*, *sink*, *think*). An open syllable has a vowel at the end of the syllable, cv, which makes the vowel long (*he*, *no*). With two-syllable words with two consonants in the middle, divide the vowels, one to each side, as in *cu-rr-ent* and *whi-mp-er*, and split the two middle consonants, one to each syllable: *cur-rent*, *whim-per*. Blends and digraphs stay together: *vi-brate*, *hun-dred*.

When there is only one consonant, syllable boundaries get a little trickier. Again, divide the vowels, for instance *mo-m-ent* or *ro-b-in*, and try the middle consonant with the second syllable, which is the more common placement. It works for *mo-ment* (one open and one closed syllable) but not for *robin*. Since *ro-bin* is not a recognizable word, try attaching the middle consonant to the first syllable *rob-in*. The accent will be on the first syllable in a two-syllable word 83% of the time (Rastle & Coltheart, 2000). Add the other syllable types: the silent *e* syllable, the *r*-controlled syllable, the consonant-*le* syllable, and the diphthong or double vowel syllable. Because there are many exceptions, readers have to check to see whether their word sounds like a real word and makes sense in context.

The time-honored advice of looking for the small words within the big word works reasonably well but not as well as looking for phonograms, which hold together better as units. Finding the little words often leaves leftover letters and does not make use of common rimes.

Writing and Invented Spelling

Writing and invented, or developmental, spelling focus students' attention on sound-letter relationships. The beneficial relationship between reading and writing has been understood for a long time. The comparative first-grade studies of the 1960s found that when writing was included as a component of beginning reading programs, the program had a high degree of success. Cunningham's four block strategy includes writing as one-fourth of the total beginning reading program. "Writing is a principal vehicle for developing word analysis skills" (Adams, 1991, p. 420). As students work to determine the written representation of a word, they are compelled to actively look for sound-letter correspondences.

Both writing words with standard spelling and writing with invented spelling as a part of informal practice help children become more aware of sound-letter correspondences and patterns. As teachers give feedback to developing writers, the students approximate the standard spelling to a greater degree and solidify sound-symbol relationships.

PHONICS AND OLDER STUDENTS ■ WHO STRUGGLE WITH READING

The National Reading Panel defined struggling in three ways: at-risk students who are K–1 students who can achieve with early remediation, disabled readers who achieve in other areas but have difficulty with reading, and low achievers in Grades 2–6 with reading difficulties and possibly other cognitive difficulties that explain their low achievement.

When the National Reading Panel analyzed the effects of phonics instruction on disabled readers in Grades 2–6, they found gains similar to other groups' gains in word recognition, which indicates phonics also benefits disabled readers. Effects on spelling and comprehension were limited, as would be expected with more complex materials beyond first grade. Disabled students with severe difficulties in word recognition often have underlying language deficits. Highly explicit and sequenced instruction such as the Orton-Gillingham method is often used with these students. Analogy instruction has also been found effective, and analogy following decoding or decoding following analogy was better than either separately (Lovett et al., 2000). Low achievers in Grades 2–6 did not benefit very much from phonics instruction (National Reading Panel, 2000).

■ ASSESSING SOUND-SYMBOL RELATIONSHIPS

Figure 13.1 in Chapter 13 shows the BAF test, which uses a series of nonwords to diagnose or assess knowledge of letter-sound relationships. It is set up in the categories of consonant letters, consonant digraphs, consonant clusters, and vowels. Although it is administered individually, a knowledgeable first or second grader can complete the test in about three minutes. Because the "words" in the text have no context and none is a sight word, the teacher knows that only letter-sound correspondences are being tested.

For a more informal assessment that uses context, try *Good Zap, Little Grog* (Wilson, 1995). Young readers who understand phonics love the book, but those who know only sight words or are unsure of the letter-sound relationships stumble through the text. The book is a good diagnostic tool that is fun for children to read, as the following excerpt shows.

Zoodle oop, little Grog,   In the dusk of the garden

give a hug; stretch and yawn   a wild fribbet humms,

The night moons are fading.   and all the blue zamblots

There's shine on the lawn.   are covered in flumms.

The objective of word recognition instruction is to help children recognize words quickly and automatically so their cognitive energy can be spent on comprehension. The idea of merely sounding out words letter by letter is only a partial view of the role of phonics. Children also need to learn to recognize the larger patterns that are useful for both spelling and reading. A balanced approach combines the following elements: immersing children in rich language by reading aloud to them, writing, spelling, providing them with a variety of texts for extensive reading, and explicitly and systematically teaching them letter-sound correspondences. No wonder teaching the primary grades is such a challenging job!

5

Fluency

If time is precious, no book that will not improve by repeated readings deserves to be read at all.

—Thomas Carlyle

Fluent, expressive oral reading is a joy to hear. Disfluent, halting, word-by-word reading is torture for all concerned. However, fluency is much more important than merely sounding natural when reading aloud. In the past, teachers assumed that when children integrated sound-symbol relationships, sight words, and knowledge of language, fluency and comprehension would follow. This is often but not always true. Little attention or instructional time was devoted to teaching fluency until 2000, when the *Report of the National Reading Panel* was published. Fluency became a hot topic. The report defines fluent readers as those who "can read text with speed, accuracy, and proper expression" (National Reading Panel, 2000, p. 3-1). An additional element of fluency is the ability to group words into meaningful units using appropriate pitch, stress, and phrasing, called prosodic reading. In silent reading, fluency becomes reading rate.

FLUENCY IS LINKED TO COMPREHENSION ■

Lack of fluency and a slow rate are obstacles to comprehension. Very slow readers simply forget the gist of the sentence or the meaning of the paragraph by the time they get to the end. Their choppy, plodding reading sounds as if they were reading a list rather than connected text, so the brain, which is designed to pick out patterns and to group ideas, is not able to consolidate everything into working memory and comprehend (Sousa, 2005).

> Although which is the cause and which is the effect is not yet understood, a strong correlation exists between fluency and comprehension.

Table 5.1   Oral Reading Fluency Scale

Level 4	Reads primarily in larger, meaningful phrase groups. Although some regressions, repetitions, and deviations from text may be present, these do not appear to detract from the overall structure of the story. Preservation of the author's syntax is consistent. Some or most of the story is read with expressive interpretation.
Level 3	Reads primarily in three- or four-word phrase groups. Some smaller groupings may be present. However, the majority of phrasing seems appropriate and preserves the syntax of the author. Little or no expressive interpretation is present.
Level 2	Reads primarily in two-word phrases with some three- or four-word groupings. Some word-by-word reading may be present. Word groupings may seem awkward and unrelated to larger context of sentence or passage.
Level 1	Reads primarily word-by-word. Occasional two-word or three-word phrases may occur—but these are infrequent and/or they do not preserve meaningful syntax.

Source: From NAEP Facts, 1995, pp. 3–4.

Fast readers tend to have good comprehension and to be proficient (Rasinski, 2000). The National Assessment of Educational Progress's first large-scale attempt to measure oral reading in 1992 found only 55% of a representative sample of the nation's fourth graders to be fluent. These were the readers who scored at level three or four on the Oral Reading Fluency Scale, shown in Table 5.1. Students who read at level four scored an average of 249 points on a 500-point reading proficiency scale and read an average of 162 words per minute (wpm) whereas students who read at level one scored 179 and read 65 wpm (NAEP Facts, 1995). Although which is the cause and which is the effect is not yet understood, a strong correlation exists between fluency and comprehension.

■ ASSESSING FLUENCY

Fluency can be assessed in wpm or words correct per minute, and the material being read should be at instructional level. The easiest way is to time a child for one minute and count the words. To determine fluency in a longer passage, for example 242 words read in 3 minutes and 14 seconds, change the minutes into seconds and cross multiply: $242/194 = \times/60$, $194\times = 14{,}520$, and $\times = 74.8$ wpm. A more complex measure such as the Oral Reading Fluency Scale, used in the National Assessment of Educational Progress (see Table 5.1), takes phrasing, expression, and fluidity into account.

■ FACTORS AFFECTING FLUENCY

Automatic word recognition is a necessary but insufficient condition for fluency (National Reading Panel, 2000). When readers spend time working out a word, reading rate is reduced, and working memory that could have been used for comprehension is reallocated to word recognition. However, in the case of children with reading disabilities, the inability to identify words is the most important factor in accounting for individual differences in fluency (Torgesen, 2004). Teaching children to say isolated words faster may improve their fluency but not their comprehension (Stahl, 2004).

A second factor is the amount of exposure to fluent models of reading. Children may come from homes in which there are few books and little or no reading, or they may have had little classroom instruction or practice in fluent reading.

Extensive exposure to and practice with text is a third factor. Struggling readers in the upper grades may be taught to increase their reading accuracy but may have a very difficult time increasing their fluency. They may lack fluency due to difficulties in word recognition or lack of vocabulary knowledge, but Joseph Torgesen (2004) speculates that the culprit may be the lesser amount of text they have read over the years. S. Jay Samuels (2002) believes that it is only with sufficient exposure to text that readers come to process words as a whole rather than letter by letter or segment by segment. The cumulative amount of text read, rather than the process of teaching phonics or sight words, is more important for developing automatic word recognition and fluency.

Difficulty of material is another factor. Materials that are too difficult or dense with unfamiliar vocabulary or concepts or contain complex sentence patterns can make any reader disfluent. Teachers can nurture fluent reading by providing lots of books that are at the student's independent reading level, that is, that the student can read with 95–100% word accuracy and 90–100% comprehension (Rasinski, 2000). Good readers are exposed to quantities of text at their independent reading levels, whereas poor readers frequently encounter text at their frustration levels.

> Good readers are exposed to quantities of text at their independent reading levels, whereas poor readers frequently encounter text at their frustration levels.

Other readers may lack fluency because they are concentrating solely on correct pronunciation, have become dependent on the teacher's word prompting (Allington, 2001), or were never taught the skills of rapid and prosodic reading.

INDIVIDUAL METHODS FOR IMPROVING FLUENCY ■

One-on-one methods for improving fluency were developed over the past 40 years. Many of these techniques can also be employed as whole-class methods.

Repeated Reading

The classic and most often recommended method for improving fluency is repeated reading. This method involves reading the same text over and over to increase fluency and rate. With an opportunity for the student to perfect performance and with teacher review of the miscues, fluency increases and word recognition errors decrease. To ensure that the reader also attends to comprehension, different questions may be asked after each rereading. A graph can provide a visual record of progress as individual students compete with their own past performance. Moderate positive effects were found in studies of repeated reading with developing readers in Grades 2–4 and with students with various kinds of reading problems through high school (National Reading Panel, 2000). Multiple rehearsals with teacher feedback are especially helpful for English language learners working to perfect pronunciation, comprehension, and fluency.

S. J. Samuels (1997) found that when a reader moves to a new piece, fluency and rate decrease but not to their level on the original passage. Samuels suggests that teachers choose easy, interesting stories and mark off a 250-word section of the story. The student is told to read the passage aloud as smoothly as possible, and the teacher records on a graph the student's speed in wpm and the number of word recognition errors. The student continues to practice the passage alone; a tape recording may be used as support. The student then rereads the same section aloud, and again the teacher records the data. The entire process is repeated until the student meets the criterion of 85 wpm.

Not surprisingly, just listening to a tape does not have the same effect as working with a teacher. Engagement and accountability are usually lower when a student works alone with a tape rather than with a teacher. However, tapes recorded at slower rates may be more effective than commercially recorded books on tape, which are read by professional readers, often at rates too fast for students to follow (Allington, 2001). For fluency instruction and practice, tapes and CDs at multiple reading levels, a phonics series that emphasizes decodable words, and a Spanish version are available from Read Naturally at www.readnaturally.com. They feature selections recorded at various speeds and come with all the necessary support materials.

For small-group settings, use repeated reading with some variations. Children read orally from multiple copies of the same text for three minutes. They mark their stopping point and discuss with the teacher any words that caused difficulty. When they repeat the same passage, they should be able to read farther and with greater accuracy (Stahl, 2003).

Assisted Reading and Other Similar Plans

In clinic or other one-on-one settings, several similar interventions may be used. Using **assisted reading** and the other techniques discussed below, the teacher and student read simultaneously, with the teacher setting the pace and reading just a little louder and faster than the student. Word recognition ceases to be a problem because the student hears unfamiliar words as they are encountered. The student and teacher stop from time to time to discuss the selection so that comprehension stays in the forefront.

In **neurological impress**, the teacher sits slightly behind the student, reads toward the student's dominant ear, and points to the text as they read together. As comfort with the arrangement increases, the student can do the pointing. Sessions should be short, and after independent practice, the same text can be read again the next day. With **Preview, Pause, Prompt, Praise** (Topping & Ehly, 1998), the teacher previews the text, and the student and teacher read simultaneously. Then, when ready, the student taps the table and continues on alone. If the student miscues, the teacher waits for the end of the sentence, to allow for self-correction. If the student self-corrects, the teacher praises the strategy. If the student does not self-correct, the teacher tries a subtle prompt, such as "Let's read this again." Then the teacher praises the student or corrects the error and begins reading with the student once more. Discussion of the text follows.

Paired reading allows students to choose reading materials from a level higher than they would normally be able to read independently. For a total of 15–20 minutes daily, an adult reads the chosen selection to the child. Then the child and adult read the material together several times. Finally, the child is able to read the text to the adult. This is a simple technique to recommend to parents who wish to work with their child at home. Children who engaged in this form of paired reading made major gains in as little as five weeks, compared with children who received clinical tutoring but no parental paired reading support (Rasinski, 1995). Paired reading can also be a helpful classroom technique when a more-able reader pairs with a less-able reader.

WHOLE-CLASS METHODS ■ FOR IMPROVING FLUENCY

Although many techniques for improving fluency were developed for tutorial situations, they have become part of whole-class lessons. The *Report of the National Reading Panel* noted, "Classroom practices that encourage repeated oral reading with feedback and guidance lead to meaningful improvements in reading expertise for students" (National Reading Panel, 2000, p. 3-3). Instruction can begin as soon as a child has some basic reading ability, but other techniques, such as modeling, echo, and choral reading, can start earlier.

Modeling

Since the most fluent reader in the classroom is the teacher, read-alouds are powerful for modeling fluency and prosodic reading. Young readers and older, less fluent readers may not know what fluent reading sounds like. Read-alouds are especially important for English language learners, and the teacher must speak carefully, clearly, and specifically in order to model the language as well as fluency (Prescott-Griffin & Witherell, 2004). The teacher can point out how a character might say dialogue or how reading is sped up when the story becomes more exciting. Teachers may also model fluent reading while students simultaneously read the same passage silently. Clearly, students need frequent opportunities to see and hear fluent reading.

> Students need frequent opportunities to see and hear fluent reading.

Echo and Choral Reading

To provide fluency practice in the classroom, teachers often use echo and choral reading. Echo reading, in which the teacher reads a phrase or sentence and the students echo or repeat it, provides a model for both accuracy and fluency. In choral reading, the students read a passage in unison. Several fluent readers or the teacher can lead the reading to set an appropriate pace and to model phrasing. Older students enjoy choral reading of poetry.

Readers' Theatre

Using Readers' Theatre in the classroom is one of the most enjoyable ways to practice and teach fluency. In Readers' Theatre, students read orally from a prepared script. There are no costumes, props, memorization, or staging, so attention is focused on the text. Rehearsals for the presentation provide readers with a legitimate reason to reread texts and practice fluency, and the prospect of performing before peers provides the incentive. Working in a team with more skilled readers offers struggling readers an opportunity to boost their confidence and provides them with models of good reading (Reutzel & Cooter, 2003). As students bring characters to life, Readers' Theatre also becomes a vehicle for interpreting literature. Furthermore, activities involving drama encourage the reader to make connections between speech and actions, so they are especially good for English language learners (Opitz & Rasinski, 1998).

Some teachers have students read right out of the text, with a narrator reading any part that is not dialogue. Some teachers prepare a script with dialogue adapted or taken directly from a text. Other teachers have older students write their own scripts and use their own language to retell a story. Commercially prepared scripts and free scripts are available online at http://www.aaronshep .com, http://www.readinglady.com, http://www.loiswalker.com, http://www .storycart.com, and http://www.lisablau.com. Some teachers turn Readers' Theatre productions into radio plays, with a sound person who provides the footsteps, doorbells, and other effects. In all Readers' Theatre formats, the teacher provides instruction in fluency, especially in expression and phrasing.

My favorite adaptation comes from Martinez, Roser, and Strecker (1999). The students in a second-grade class were divided into three repertory companies that each practiced together during the week and presented on Friday. Each group used materials at its instructional level. On Mondays, the teacher, modeling fluent reading, read aloud the complete stories in their original version, discussed them, and taught some aspect of fluency. She prepared a script based on each story and made two copies for each student: one for taking home and one for keeping in school. The students read the entire script independently or with a buddy.

On Tuesdays, the students gathered in their groups, and parts were assigned randomly. (Highlighting a single part on each copy of a script is helpful to the reader.) After the first reading, the scripts were passed to the left, and the play was read again. If time allowed, more rotations would occur. On Wednesdays, every child read two, three, or more parts again. In the last five minutes of the period, the students determined who would play which role in the final presentation.

On Thursdays, the students practiced their roles. Fridays were for performing the plays in front of the whole class and invited guests. In this ten-week study, not only did the students become more fluent, but they also outperformed a control group on informal reading inventories, and most students improved their reading rate.

Students in the upper grades also enjoy Readers' Theatre, and poetry is an alternative. The poetry selections are shorter than an upper-grade play, and poetry provides an ideal opportunity for practicing interpretation and expression. Gay Ivey (2002) recommends adapting high-interest texts for older struggling readers or using *Novio Boy: A Play* (Soto, 1997), which comes in script form.

Fluency-Oriented Reading Instruction

Fluency-Oriented Reading Instruction (FORI) was developed by Stahl, Heubach, and Cramond (1997) as a whole-class program. They conducted a two-year study with second graders from diverse backgrounds and used basal readers. The study focused on fluent and automatic word recognition. First, the teacher introduced a story, read it aloud, and discussed it. Vocabulary and other comprehension features were reviewed. On the next two days, the whole group echo read and partner read the story. During the third and fourth day, children did additional vocabulary, decoding, and comprehension work. A fourth rereading was sometimes made into a performance. Students approaching grade level reread the story at home with an adult three times during the week, for a total of at least five rereadings to different audiences. Self-selected reading was included daily. Yearly gains averaged 1.8 grade equivalents, and those entering with scores below grade level made the largest gains. The study is continuing for five years, with one group reading three books during the week instead of repeating the basal story. Students using either the FORI or the multiple book method are outperforming their peers, suggesting that the increased amount of reading and support contribute to success (Stahl, 2004).

In a follow-up, Melanie Kuhn (2004) compared groups of second graders. The repeated-reading group used a FORI-like format that included modeling, choral, partner, and performance reading of the same story over a three-day cycle. A second group, the wide-reading group, also concentrated on fluency and expression but read three times as many different books. A third group listened to the same books as the wide-reading group. A control group received only the normal instructional program. Both the repeated-reading and wide-reading groups increased their word recognition, rate, and fluency, but only the wide-reading group showed improved comprehension. The listening and control groups did not show these gains. Kuhn speculates that the repeated-reading students may have focused on expression and did not automatically shift their attention to comprehension of the text.

Fluency Prompts

Prescott-Griffin and Witherell (2004) offer some useful fluency prompts for everyday reading:

What does your voice do when you see a period?

Take a breath when you see a comma.

Read that part again quickly.

Listen to me read, and then echo the way I did.

Read this part without taking a breath.

Let me hear the character talking.

Is your reading rough or smooth?

Does the way you're reading help tell the story?

These prompts help readers think about fluency and make adjustments.

Repeated Reading in the Content Classroom

Although instructional and independent-level materials are most often recommended for fluency instruction and practice, McCormick and Paratore (1999) developed a technique that uses repeated reading with grade-level content textbooks that may be too difficult for students to understand independently. Usually the teacher selects key portions rather than an entire chapter, introduces vocabulary, and previews the text. Then, using assisted reading, the teacher and the class read a selection aloud together. The children discuss previously posed questions and predictions. Then they reread the selection using partner, echo, or choral reading. Finally the students read to the teacher individually or in pairs.

All the successful methods for improving fluency and reading in general draw on the last three decades of research, including Berliner (1981), for example, who simply said the more time children are actively engaged with appropriately leveled text, the more proficient they become. This increased time may be spent in repeated reading or just more reading. Past research is echoed by Snow, Burns, and Griffin (1998): Adequate progress in learning to read beyond the initial level depends on sufficient practice to achieve fluency with different texts. These consistent findings have generally brought round-robin reading to an overdue demise and guided oral reading to the forefront.

■ READING RATES

How rapidly should students be reading? Table 5.2, from Tindal, Hasbrouck, and Jones's study (2005) of more than 36,000 students, provides fall, winter, and spring rates for students at the 25th, 50th, and 75th percentiles. Silent rates become faster than oral rates as early as second grade (Prescott-Griffin & Witherell, 2004). The most desirable rate is as rapidly as the student can read without losing comprehension.

■ OTHER FLUENCY ISSUES

Some children may read accurately and relatively quickly but have trouble phrasing or dividing the text into meaningful chunks. **Text segmenting** provides visual clues reminding students when to pause. It can be in done several

Table 5.2 Oral Reading Rates by Grade Level in Words Correct per Minute

Grade	Percentile	Fall wcpm	Winter wcpm	Spring wcpm
1	25		12	28
	50		23	53
	75		47	82
2	25	25	42	61
	50	51	72	89
	75	79	100	117
3	25	44	62	78
	50	71	92	107
	75	99	120	137
4	25	68	87	98
	50	94	112	123
	75	119	139	152
5	25	85	99	109
	50	110	127	139
	75	139	156	168
6	25	98	111	122
	50	127	140	150
	75	153	167	177
7	25	102	109	123
	50	128	136	150
	75	156	165	177
8	25	106	115	124
	50	133	146	151
	75	161	173	177

Source: Tindal, G., Hasbrouck, J. E., and Jones, C., *Oral Reading Rates by Grade Level in Words Correct per Minute.* Oral Reading Fluency, 90 Years of Measurement, Technical Report 33, 2005. Reprinted with permission.

Note: wcpm = words correct per minute.

ways. The text can be retyped and indented to make the divisions more clear, or each phrase can be put on a separate line. In an original text, slashes or periods can be added between phrases to let the student know when to pause. In a review of 24 studies of programs to build fluency in elementary students with learning disabilities, Chard, Vaughn, and Tyler (2002) found that the same techniques recommended for all readers—repeated guided reading, modeling, text segmenting, and peer tutoring—led to increased fluency and comprehension in students with learning disabilities.

Some struggling readers have difficulty visually tracking text from line to line, which causes them to lose their place and to lose fluency. The return sweeps, eye movements from the end of one line of text to the beginning of the next, are difficult for these students. Clark (1995) believes that making an accurate return sweep is necessary to maintain fluency and meaning and recommends using a bookmark above the line being read to avoid added interference with the return sweep movement. On the other hand, bookmarks and finger pointing may impede fluency for some students.

■ THINKING ABOUT RATE FOR OLDER STUDENTS

Fluency is usually thought of as an oral skill to be developed with primary students or with struggling readers, but silent reading rate is important for upper-grade students too. Slower, less efficient readers simply read less. It takes them longer, and every classroom teacher has noticed these children observing their classmates who have finished reading and then pretend they have also finished. Thus they have read less, learned less, and picked up fewer vocabulary words and less content. In independent reading outside school, these children also read less than their peers, enjoy it less, and are less likely to become lifelong readers. Keith Stanovich's classic term (1986) for this phenomenon, *the Matthew effect*, was discussed in Chapter 3. Improving the rate of older readers allows them to read more quickly and thus read more material in the same period of time. Fluency instruction need not be limited to the young.

> Teaching readers to be fluent without attending to comprehension is just plain silly.

Repeated reading of the same text, although effective, does not seem to be the necessary element in building fluency. Increasing the amount of reading at appropriate levels, with teacher guidance, does seem essential. And trying to teach readers to be fluent without attending to comprehension is just plain silly. Fluency should be just one part of a balanced approach to teaching literacy.

6

Guided Reading

Instruction enlarges the natural powers of the mind.

—Horace

To understand the power of guided reading, it helps to think about round-robin reading, the way you probably read in elementary school. The teacher had a student read a paragraph aloud and then had the next student read the next paragraph aloud. You probably remember counting how many children would be called on before you and then counting the number of paragraphs. Once you located your paragraph, you practiced it and waited for your turn to come.

The problem with this method was that only some children followed along, much less read the entire text. Most children practiced one paragraph until they could read it fluently because to be judged a good reader, one had to know all the words and read rapidly. No one stopped to ask if anyone understood what was being read until the selection was completed. Then it was difficult for the children to answer questions because they each had read only one paragraph for fluency and perhaps followed along haphazardly by listening or reading.

Kids need to read the whole text, and they need to read a lot! Anderson, Wilson, and Fielding (1988) reported that fifth-grade students scoring at the 10th percentile read 1.6 minutes per day, or 51,000 words per year. Those at the 50th percentile read 12.9 minutes per day, or 601,000 words per year, and those at the 90th percentile read 40.4 minutes per day, or 2,357,000 words per year. The 2004 National Assessment of Educational Progress found that 13-year-olds who read 5 or fewer pages per day, in school and for homework, scored 249; those who read 6–10 pages per day scored 260; those who read 11–20 pages per day scored 262; and those who read 20 or more pages per day scored 263 (National Center for Education Statistics, 2004, p. 52). "There is an extensive amount of correlational data linking amount of reading and reading achievement" (National Reading Panel, 2000, p. 3-10), meaning that the best readers read the most and that poor readers read the least. Because the studies were not experimental, it can't be claimed that reading more causes improved reading, but intuitively we know that practice does make perfect. Round-robin reading did not encourage a lot of eye-to-text time, much less brain-to-text time.

One of the subsequent patterns for reading in school was silent reading. At least everyone was reading the whole text, or supposedly reading. The problem was that questioning often came at the end, when it was too late. Some students understood it all, some got confused in the middle and gave up, and others just pretended to read until they noticed their classmates finishing. Instruction in comprehension, when there was any, was often limited to isolated practice or workbook passages. Comprehension was seldom taught with the text the students were actually reading, and student-to-student discussion time was limited.

■ WHAT IS GUIDED READING?

Guided reading has several variations, but the common factors seem to be that everyone in a small group reads a relatively short passage that offers only a slight challenge. Most words, concepts, and reading skills are known. To promote reading for meaning, the students and teacher discuss what was read and discuss the strategies that were used. Fix-ups are done on the spot, a comprehension strategy is taught just when it needs to be applied, and when the meaning is secure, everyone goes on to the next passage. Most guided reading time is spent actually reading. Guided reading gives children the opportunity to develop as individual readers while participating in a socially supported activity (Fountas & Pinnell, 1996).

Guided reading is the bridge from direct instruction in skills and strategies to independent reading. The teacher and students share the responsibility of constructing meaning with continuous text. Children read silently while the teacher observes. Little ones "whisper read" simultaneously. The teacher provides support and prompting as students try out reading strategies and discuss both the content of the text and the process of comprehending it. Guided reading is just one aspect of a balanced reading program, which also includes reading to children, giving explicit instruction, and having the children read independently. Vocabulary, word recognition, and fluency are all key components, but guided reading is where everything comes together in a supported environment.

> Guided reading is where everything comes together in a supported environment.

Guided Reading Provides Scaffolding

Providing scaffolding means giving support that enables students to accomplish tasks that would otherwise be beyond their efforts. It usually means providing hints and prompts on an as-needed basis. Difficult tasks require more scaffolding or guidance, and less difficult tasks require smaller amounts of guidance. If the task does not require any guidance, it is considered independent reading. Scaffolding is a metaphor: The scaffolding for a building under construction supports it until it can stand on its own. Scaffolding was one characteristic of the most effective first-grade teachers, who provided it in both whole-group and one-on-one instruction (Wharton-McDonald, Pressley, & Hampston, 1998) when children faltered.

Benefits of Guided Reading

Guided reading is extremely helpful to students who have defined reading only as fluent pronunciation—the word callers. It gives them an opportunity to experience what it is like to make reading for meaning their primary focus and to have a teacher guide the process. Guided reading is also beneficial for students who have difficulty focusing independently on printed material for a sustained period of time. They have expert leadership from the teacher as to what they should pay attention to while reading silently, and they have a short, defined amount of time for concentrated reading. As an added benefit, no student "reads" passively for very long before being prompted to recall, think about, or apply what was read. Guided reading encourages the habit of thinking while reading, which some students seem to think are two separate activities!

LEVELED GROUPS ■

Children learn to read best when they know almost all the words and can understand most of the text; therefore guided reading is usually done with leveled groups, that is, small groups of children who use similar reading processes and are able to read similar levels of text with support (Fountas & Pinnell, 1996). The materials, which could be little books, trade books, or basal stories, should be at the children's instructional level.

Although there is some variation, the long-standing guidelines for reading levels say that if a student can recognize at least 96% of the words in a particular text and read with 90–100% comprehension, the material is at the student's independent level. If the student recognizes 90–95% of the words and can read with 70–89% comprehension, the material is at the student's instructional level. If the student recognizes 89% or fewer of the words and comprehends less than 70% of the text, it is at the student's frustration level (McCormick, 1999).

Although whole-class instruction is usually easier for teachers to manage than guided reading is, the lowest readers encounter so many obstacles in the text that they become frustrated and give up. The chance that they will catch up by reading text that is too hard is negligible at best. On the other hand, the best readers have no opportunity to problem solve if they read text that is at the level of the majority in the class. While the practice is good, they have little opportunity to advance.

To place students in reading groups, teachers take running records or use an informal reading inventory to accurately assess reading level. Teachers with a great deal of experience can rely on informal observation of a student's miscues or errors and comprehension responses to gauge when a child is struggling too much. If students are assessed frequently, it is easy to tell when to move a child to a different group.

Working in small groups provides interaction among students, and they can often clarify meaning for each other better than the teacher can. In small groups, students are more likely both to understand the text and to learn what it means to engage in a discussion (Gambrell & Almasi, 1996).

For second language learners, this social interaction is especially advantageous. Hispanic school-age enrollment jumped from 9.9% in 1986 to 16.3% in 2001 (National Center for Education Statistics, 2001), and many teachers now find the range of reading levels in their classes is widening.

Groups do not always have to be formed by level. For variety (and a chance for children to change their views about reading self-efficacy (their personal view of their proficiency), try interest groups, author study groups, or flexible groups to study or review a particular strategy. Although some experts define guided reading only in terms of small groups, the process may be modified for whole-class instruction, with scaffolding, when the achievement range is small or in the upper grades, where grouping is seldom used (but ought to be).

■ PLANNING AND LOGISTICAL MANAGEMENT

In the primary grades, at least 90–120 minutes daily should be devoted to reading. Intermediate grades should read at least 90 minutes daily, and the more the better. A mixture of small-group and whole-group work may be included in the reading block. Usually there are three groups, but there may be four, depending on how long the children can work independently and how wide the range of reading ability is. Especially in four-group plans, the teacher works with the lowest group daily but may not always work with all the other groups.

Figure 6.1   Possible daily second-grade plan

Time	Teacher group	What the others are doing	
20 min.	Whole class: directions, morning message		
25	Group A: Guided reading	B: Independent reading	C: Word work
5	Change groups, answer questions, get everyone started		
25	Group B: Guided reading	A: Word work	C: Independent reading
15	Phonemic awareness, active activity Change groups, answer questions, get everyone started		
25	Group C: Guided reading	A: Independent reading	B: Word work
5	Closure		

Guided reading takes considerable planning. Figures 6.1–6.4 show what the logistics might look like. They are just samples to show a variety of choices, but they try to use as much time as possible to make comprehension the focus of instruction during group time. Certainly the teacher takes diagnostic notes every day, not just on Friday, but a chart can hold only so much. The key to smooth functioning is to teach students how to do the independent activities independently, which ensures minimal interruptions and profitable use of time.

Figure 6.2   Sample weekly primary plan

Day	One guided reading group	What the others are doing
M	Picture walk Read story aloud Shared reading: big book Discuss meaning and connections	Early in year: alphabet work Later in year: independent book basket reading Practice with sight words
T	Echo read Choral read Phonics lesson Making words	Early in year: picture-sound sorts Later in year: reread a big book Partner read Phonics word sort
W	Picture walk for retelling Partner read Print conventions	Early in year: alphabet work Later in year: independent choice reading Listening center Making words with magnetic letters
Th	Everyone reads for fluency Written response	Early in year: picture-letter sorts Later in year: independent book basket reading Working with cut-apart sentence strips
F	Everyone reads and teacher makes diagnostic notes, or everyone starts a new story	Early in year: read an ABC book Later in year: independent reading of class-published books Story illustration and caption

Figure 6.3   Sample weekly intermediate plan

Day	One guided reading group	What the others are doing
M	Vocabulary, activate prior knowledge and teach new concepts Start text	Independent reading Partner reading
T	Guided reading Teacher modeling of target strategy	Independent reading Vocabulary practice
W	Guided reading Student think-aloud	Independent reading Story map or text structure graphic organizer
Th	Skills practice with text, vocabulary practice, advanced phonics or morphology study, fluency	Independent reading Summarizing or retelling
F	Guided reading, closing critical discussion Teacher makes diagnostic notes	Independent reading Writing in response to reading

PROCEDURES ■

The teacher first introduces the text. In primary grades, this is done by means of a picture walk, which means going through the entire story just looking at the pictures. The students get the gist of the story, discuss key vocabulary or

Figure 6.4   Sample weekly upper-grade plan

Day	One guided reading group	What the others are doing
M	Vocabulary, activate prior knowledge and teach new concepts Explain strategy needed	Choice of independent reading Review skill practice
T	Guided reading DRTA Teacher modeling and think-aloud	Choice of independent reading Continued silent reading
W	Guided reading Student think-aloud	Choice of independent reading Written response to reading
Th	Guided reading Strategy applied in text Literary elements	Choice of independent timed reading Vocabulary practice
F	Guided reading, higher order questioning, Socratic discussion	Choice of independent reading Summarizing

concepts, and are then ready to concentrate on the text, as they already know the story. Intermediate and upper-grade teachers often activate the students' prior knowledge or pose a thought question as an introduction.

After the introduction, in the primary grades, each child reads the whole text "silently," or whisper reads. The teacher can listen to individual children as they progress through a page. Word recognition errors can be corrected on the spot with, "Does that make sense? Does that sound right? Let's read that again" or "Ch makes the /ch/ sound." When everyone finishes, the story can be discussed, and the children can think about the content and the process.

In the intermediate and upper grades, whose texts are much longer, and with some primary readers, the teacher sets a purpose for reading a small passage. How short "a small passage" is depends on the grade level. It could range from a single sentence to several pages. The students read the passage silently, and then the class discusses content and the strategies they used. The teacher may ask a student to prove an answer by finding the relevant passage in the text or may ask how a certain conclusion was reached. Perhaps a prediction is made or the text summarized as students discuss how they decided what was important. A new purpose is set, there is more silent reading, new questions are asked, and additional content and strategies are discussed. Michael Opitz and Michael Ford (2001, p. 3) discuss the importance of conscious strategy use. "Children need to become aware of how reading works, and they need to be able to use this knowledge to make the reading process work for them. This is called metacognition." The class proceeds in this manner until the entire section is read. Teachers observe the children, and listen to their answers and explanations, and take notes to use in planning future lessons.

The best readers tend to dislike guided reading because they "get it" without too much guidance and just want to read; the struggling readers love it because finally they are successful and know what to look for as they read. Once kids have a solid start, it may not be necessary to continue guiding the whole selection, and they can continue independently. The procedure moves along slowly, but it is a strategy rich with opportunities for students who are learning to comprehend. It is also an enjoyable time because students are not struggling with text they cannot understand.

Sometimes groups close with two to five minutes of word work if the teacher has noticed several children having difficulty with a certain word. Intermediate and upper-grade groups might close with vocabulary practice, with concept development for the following day, or with reminders of what students should be doing during independent time.

TEACHING COMPREHENSION ■
DURING GUIDED READING

Teaching comprehension is difficult because it means teaching thinking skills, which are invisible. Teaching long division is easy because the teacher can see where students' problems or errors in reasoning or procedure occur. Guided reading helps to make thinking visible through modeling, instruction, practice, and discussion.

Modeling With Think-Alouds

One of the best ways to demonstrate thinking about comprehension (metacognition) is think-alouds. The teacher reads a passage and thinks aloud while reading, thus modeling the thinking of an expert reader who is identifying the specific strategies being used (Kucan & Beck, 1997). Beth Davey (1983), a pioneer in think-alouds, suggested that the five most important strategies to model with think-alouds were predicting, visualizing, making analogies, expressing confusion, and demonstrating fix-up strategies such as rereading.

Teachers may wonder aloud about what will happen next and make a prediction. As they read farther in the passage, they can identify when a prediction is confirmed or rejected ("That's not what I thought Colin would do!"). Monitoring of comprehension can be demonstrated when something is "misread" or a thought is lost. Modeling makes comprehension strategies more explicit and visible. Students see and hear strategies for self-correction and learn that even expert readers may have to redirect, reread, or reconsider. After demonstrating these techniques, teachers can have students try think-alouds with partners and then independently. By marking stopping points in the text, teachers can help the readers stop and think.

> Students' understanding and recall can be readily shaped by the types of questions to which they become accustomed.

QUESTIONING ■

All the techniques in Chapter 8, on comprehension, can be used in guided reading groups; here just one of them, questioning, will be discussed. How can teachers be sure they are working with all types of comprehension during guided reading? Since students' understanding and recall can be readily shaped by the types of questions to which they become accustomed (Duke & Pearson, 2002), the teacher should ask questions at all levels: literal, inferential, and critical. Naming and discussing the types of questions help students identify the strategy to use, and they will be able to consciously use each strategy again. Winicki (2004) suggests reading the text twice to develop questions, once with a reader's eye, to pick out the kinds of things students should notice, and once with a teacher's eye, to pick out aspects kids would miss on their own, such as theme, sensory images, or language use.

Literal, or "Right There," Questions

Literal comprehension questions ask what the author said, that is, the explicit meaning. A question of this type is sometimes called "reading the lines" because the answer can often be found in a single line of the text. These are the *who, what, when,* and *where* questions. Taffy Raphael (1986), who developed Question Answer Relationships (QAR), called these types of questions "right there questions" because the answers are right there in the text. They can be underlined or copied. Often the same words that make up the answer are found in the question, and there is usually a single right answer. QAR delineates how questions and answer-finding techniques are related and uses student-friendly labels.

For example, if the class were reading the children's classic *The Tale of Peter Rabbit,* by Beatrix Potter, the questions might be, Who were Peter's brothers and sisters? or Where did Mrs. Rabbit tell her children not to go?

> "How did you know that?" . . . is the number one metacognition question for getting children to discuss the process of reading and to identify the strategies they used to solve problems.

During guided reading, the teacher not only asks questions and receives answers but also asks, "How did you know that?" It is the number one metacognition question for getting children to discuss the process of reading and to identify the strategies they used to solve problems.

Think and Search Questions

The second tier of literal comprehension questions is think and search questions. The entire answer is in the text but not all in one location. These types of questions show relationships such as cause and effect, sequence, comparison and contrast, or topic and subtopic. Not each type of relationship is in every passage, of course. Returning to *Peter Rabbit,* the questions might be, Why did Mrs. Rabbit tell her children not to go into Mr. McGregor's garden? or What were all the places that Peter hid from Mr. McGregor? The student has to think about what is being asked, such as the sequence, and then search for all the events. Think and search questions are more difficult than literal recall questions. Children whose strategy is to scan the text to find words that are similar to the question and copy down the sentence are now stumped because that technique will no longer work. They soon realize that the entire text must be read to find all the pieces of information and then figure out how they are related to each other.

Inferential, or "Author and You," Questions

Inferential or interpretive questions require that students base their answers on the text, but they must also use past experience or common sense to find a reasonable answer. Because children must use both the text and personal experience, the inferential answer is not a wild guess. The answer must be probable, not just possible, and partially based on the text. Making inferences or interpretations is a higher and more difficult level of comprehension than just looking for the answers in the text because students must use two elements intertwined with each other. The teacher might ask, "Why do you think Peter was so curious?" or "When the old mouse could not tell Peter where the gate was, why do you think Peter started to cry?" Raphael (1986) called these types of questions "author and you questions" because the answers are not solely in the text. Readers must interact with the text and draw on their own experiences in order to arrive at an answer.

Texts require that the reader make inferences because authors cannot tell the reader every little detail. They expect that the reader will be able to fill in missing information or "read between the lines." Consider the line "While Jenny got ready for school, she thought about her big presentation." The author expects that the reader can fill in the details, imagining Jenny reflecting on her presentation while brushing her teeth, combing her hair, and getting dressed. Some children approach reading in a straightforward manner and think their only task is to parrot what the text says, and so they miss all the information "between the lines."

Authors also expect readers to understand basic emotional reactions and apply what they know to the characters in the story. In *The Sign of the Beaver* (Speare, 1983), Matt will not use his new crutch until after the Indians have left his cabin. The author expects that the reader knows Matt was embarrassed to try out something new and possibly difficult while strangers were watching him, so the author never directly says that Matt was embarrassed.

Inferential or interpretive tasks also include identifying the theme or moral, generalizing, and drawing conclusions. Another inferential task might be imagining how the story would be different if it were told from another character's point of view. Because these questions are abstract and require interpretation, many children will not be able to answer inferential questions without instruction and modeling by the teacher. A cue for *Peter Rabbit* might be, How have you acted when you were really, really afraid? Guided reading groups also give students a chance to hear not just the teacher's instruction but also other students' processes of inferring or assembling information from two sources into one answer. Some readers do well with inferential questions because they always think and relate to their own experiences as they read, prefer the big picture, and cannot be bothered with small details, such as the answers to those picky literal questions.

Activating prior knowledge, or in some cases supplying background knowledge if students lack background to interpret the text, can help students become inferential readers. The teacher should choose concepts that are likely to be obstacles to comprehension. Concepts are more helpful than vocabulary. For example, a class was reading *The Cay*, by Theodore Taylor (1969), in which a small blind boy and an old man are marooned on a Caribbean island surrounded by coral. To the young students, coral was a lacy, delicate object sometimes found in fish tanks or jewelry but certainly nothing that could rip out the bottom of a boat. When the teacher supplied information about different Caribbean corals, the class then understood why local fishing boats, which may have been capable of rescuing the characters, would not be sailing near the island. Being taught a concept directly, listening to other children's relevant experiences, or searching one's own memory all bring background knowledge to the foreground so that when a passage is read, the text and the background can be woven together for making inferences and for deeper comprehension.

Another strategy to encourage inferential thinking is **visualization**, which requires knowledge of the text and background knowledge. Young readers need to realize that good readers develop pictures in their heads about what the characters look like, how the setting appears, and whether a character walks with mincing steps or long strides. Visualization becomes more important when children move beyond the picture book stage. Good readers start to build images in their minds and adjust their visualizations as additional information is given by the author. When students recall information, some of it is attached to the picture they visualized.

In a dramatic scene in *Roll of Thunder, Hear My Cry*, by Mildred Taylor (1977), the father, Mr. Logan, is run over by his own wagon while trying to change a wheel during a storm. When a group of students in one of my classes was asked about what happened, a big debate ensued over where the father was standing and if the wagon rolled forward or backward when the horse reared up. The imagery attached to that scene enhanced the readers' memories until they were absolutely positive that the author had stated the facts exactly as they "saw" them.

Children who are not visualizing are totally startled when asked, What kind of flowers do you think were in the pots that Peter knocked over? or What color was the wheelbarrow on which Peter climbed? The reader's first response is always that the text didn't say, but as students begin to build an image in their mind's eye, the entire event is redrawn, as well as the color of the wheelbarrow. The facts, the sequence, and the images are all strengthened.

Critical, or "On My Own," Questions

Critical questions go beyond the text, asking questions of opinion, significance, or judgment. Critical comprehension can be thought of as "reading beyond the lines." Raphael (1986) called them "on my own questions" because the answers are not found in the book at all. These questions ask readers to think about and use their own experiences. The text material provides a jumping-off spot and can contribute to the reader's confirming, altering, or rejecting previous beliefs. Concerning *Peter Rabbit*, the teacher might ask, What kind of problems might happen if you went into a garden without the owner's permission? Was Peter naughty or just curious? or Should children be punished when they disobey their parents? These types of questions can prompt interesting and lively classroom discussions. They are often too complex, too abstract, or just too long for younger children to write out answers to, but what a shame if children did not have an opportunity to discuss questions that required a critical response. If the

Figure 6.5   Guided reading planner

GUIDED READING PLANNER

Prediction before reading:

Text features to notice: _____

First section p. _____ to p. _____

Prediction question: _____

Literal question: _____

Prove it. How did you know?

Think and search question: _____

Where did you find the two parts? How do they fit together?

Inferential question: _____

How did you know that? Why is that a likely answer?

Second section p. _____ to p. _____

Prediction question: _____

Literal question: _____

Prove it. How did you know?

Think and search question: _____

Where did you find the two parts? How do they fit together?

Inferential question: _____

How did you know that? Why is that a likely answer?

Critical question: _____

Why do you think so?

Last section p. _____ to p. _____

Prediction question: _____

Literal question: _____

Prove it. How did you know?

Think and search question: _____

Where did you find the two parts? How do they fit together?

Inferential question: _____

How did you know that? Why is that a likely answer?

Critical question: _____

Why do you think so?

teacher does not give students an opportunity to extend reading beyond the stated text, how will they come to the realization that written text can provide the impetus for examining one's own beliefs? Teachers can use the guided reading planner, Figure 6.5, to help them plan a variety of questions for a reading selection.

Using the Levels of Questioning During Guided Reading

A good place to start guided reading is with a "fat" question, that is, a critical query, such as, What happened when you were someplace you shouldn't have been? Encourage personal stories (at least a few of them) and guide the children to some of the concepts that will be encountered, such as the feeling of fright, hiding to avoid being caught, disobeying a parent who had the child's safety in mind, and getting out of the fix.

Next, the teacher needs to set a purpose and a length for the passage to be read. For example, "Read the first column on page 46 and find out what the rabbit family was going to do for the day." When the class has finished reading silently, it is time to ask questions:

What was all the rabbit family going to do that day?

Who were Peter's brothers and sisters?

Where did Mrs. Rabbit tell her children not to go?

Why did Mrs. Rabbit tell her children not to go into Mr. McGregor's garden?

Be sure to ask how students found the answers, what information they used to reach their conclusions, what they knew that was similar, and how they knew what a sand-bank was. Reflecting on and naming the comprehension strategies make guided reading powerful. Otherwise, it is just a question-and-answer period led by the teacher. Remember that the final objective is to develop independent readers who pose questions to themselves while reading.

Move on to the next section and have the children read the remainder of the page to find out what Peter did.

What did Peter do?

Was Peter naughty or just curious?

What part seemed confusing? (This is a metacognition question.)

Why did Mr. McGregor want to chase nice little Peter out of his garden?

What kind of problems might happen if you went into someone's garden without permission?

Answers can be oral, or some of the answers can be written down. Proceed in this manner to the end of the book or the day's selection. Intensive word work should not interrupt the flow of the story.

Metacognition questions are different from any of the previously discussed question types. They are not about the content of the story but about the reading process. Asking what was confusing or whether anyone reread a section for clarification helps children consciously think about their reading behaviors.

Once the students have finished the story of Peter Rabbit, do not stop there. The critical questions remind children that they should think about what they read in a larger context than just the story, such as transferring new knowledge to their own lives. Also, critical questions can be the most intriguing to ask and answer; for example, Should children be punished when they disobey their parents?

This question could lead to quite a discussion, with all kinds of provisos and opinions. Guide students to explore in detail the similarities and differences between their lives and the story. Children who kick each other as they leave the classroom after reading a story about respect and human kindness did not have a teacher who encouraged transfer!

VARIATIONS ■

Several other teaching activities share many of the objectives of guided reading. They are discussed in the following sections.

Directed Reading Thinking Activity

When prediction is a central feature of guided reading, the process becomes the Directed Reading Thinking Activity (DRTA), originally developed by Russell Stauffer in 1969. It has never gone out of use. The teacher starts by asking the students to speculate what a story or a passage might be about. Many possible answers are given before the students read to support or refute their predictions. Predicting transfers the role of purpose setting to the students and encourages metacognition as they think through their lines of reasoning (Roe, Smith, & Burns, 2005).

Predicting is a very powerful motivational and thinking tool. Children love to predict and then read to find out if they were right. They typically approach story predictions as a puzzle, trying out different solutions and hoping their favorite prediction will be the one chosen by the author. Sometimes their predictions are much more interesting than the author's story!

Predicting requires that students think logically about the direction of the story and then use their own experiences in conjunction with the text to hypothesize. They can call on their memories of similar stories, personal experiences, and plots of movies to justify their predictions. Once students understand that a single "right" answer is not required and any reasonable, justifiable answer will be accepted, they will volunteer and support or challenge other predictions with enthusiasm. After the students complete reading the next passage, the teacher asks if they want to stay with their original prediction or change their minds.

Multiple literal recall questions are usually not necessary because children must justify their opinions by recalling important points. After finishing a DRTA lesson, the teacher may decide to use the story again to teach or refine other skills or strategies. This second reading may be a more opportune time for noticing multiple meanings of words, common suffixes, or text features. To do all this on the first reading interrupts the flow of the story and thus disrupts reading for meaning. This extending and refining of skills was originally recommended by Stauffer to encourage accuracy in reading in addition to speculation, but the second step sometimes falls by the wayside.

For *Peter Rabbit*, the teacher might ask, "What do you think Mr. McGregor will do to Peter?" Some will predict capture, some will imagine a great chase, and some will recall that Mrs. McGregor baked Peter's father into a pie and predict a similar demise for Peter. Encourage several predictions, and have the children explain what brought them to their conclusions. Then let the students read to find out what actually happened to Peter. The enthusiasm of the students will be surprising.

Predicting and Visualizing on the Overhead

Predicting and visualizing can be done with the whole class by means of an overhead projector and a story printed on a transparency. If the school has new technology, an interactive whiteboard would be even better. Choose a short story, preferably one that is unpredictable or that could have several possible twists. Divide it into sections, sometimes stopping in the middle of a sentence: "And then he saw a. . . ."

Uncover the sections one at a time and invite the class to read along as you ask for predictions and justifications, visualizations, and inferences. Be sure to ask at what point students changed their minds and their predictions. For students who are timid about guessing, you can ask, "Do you think that Claire is right, or do you agree with Jason?" because it is important that everyone be involved. Everyone participates in predicting because no one can read ahead. Everyone can listen to the reasoning. All will have a guess and be eager to read the author's ending.

> When students learn to pose question for themselves while reading, they have gained a very powerful technique.

Question Generation

Why should the teacher be the only one asking questions? Independent readers must learn to develop and ask questions of themselves as they read. This takes a great deal of practice and modeling because children tend to flock to the trivia questions. However, when students learn to pose question for themselves while reading, they have gained a very powerful technique. The National Reading Panel (2000) summarizes the research: "There is strong empirical and scientific evidence that instruction of question generation during reading benefits reading comprehension in terms of memory and answering questions based on text as well as integrating and identifying main ideas through summarization" (4-88).

To model question generation, have students read a small section of text. Then ask them some questions and draw their attention to the types of questions you asked. Then have the students develop questions for the next section. Younger students do not have to understand the underlying levels of comprehension in order to form good questions; they can usually do quite well by thinking up "skinny questions" and "fat questions," that is, fact questions and discussion questions. Knowing the difference takes some time; skinny questions answer who, what, when, or where, and fat questions answer why or how. Another simple definition is that skinny questions can be answered in one sentence and have only one answer, but fat questions require more than one sentence and may have several reasonable answers. The teacher can guide question development by prompting, "What would you like to know about what happens next?" A student might respond, "What does the monster do after the fog horn is turned off?"

Cooperative group work follows as students ask and answer each other's questions. In small groups, everyone gets to have a turn more often, so greater proficiency at developing questions is attained, and participation is more active. Peer-led discussions are very powerful. Peers set their own agendas, and the content focuses on topics that will help them understand the text better. Richer and more complex interaction occurs among peers than during teacher-led discussions (Almasi, 2003). Perhaps students are more willing to share with peers because they do not have to worry about teacher approval.

Students can progress to working in pairs and finally to reading independently as they ask themselves questions. The higher-level questions, those that integrate information, are the best. Students can also evaluate whether the questions covered important material or whether they were "in-the-lines" or "beyond-the-lines" questions. Feedback from the teacher about the quality of the questions leads toward improvement in questioning skills.

For variety, try two interesting permutations. For a written assignment in response to reading, ask the children to write questions instead of answers. The questions by themselves will give the teacher a good indication of comprehension. A team challenge might follow. The other variation, for teachers willing to put themselves in the learner's role, is to ask the students to develop questions that the teacher has to answer. By reading the relevant parts of the text or by explaining the reasoning process, the teacher again models what good readers do.

A summary of research on effective teaching said, "Effective teachers provide more personalized and small group instruction, more contextualized skills teaching [not isolated workbooks], substantially more reading and writing opportunities, and more interactive lessons than their less able peers" (Allington, 2002a, p. 276). Sounds a lot like guided reading to me!

7

Grouping for Reading and Choosing Books

O for a Booke and a shadie nooke, eyther inadoore or out:
With the grene leaves whisp'ring overhede, or the Streete cries all about.
Where I maie Reade all at my ease, both of the Newe and Olde;
For a jollie goode Booke whereon to looke is better to me than Golde.

—John Wilson

This chapter combines two topics: grouping students for instruction and choosing books. They really are related! When a teacher chooses a grouping format, the next questions are, What should they be reading? Do different grouping formats require different criteria for choosing texts? and How can appropriate texts be located? This chapter provides some answers to these questions.

■ READING GROUPS

In a balanced reading program, teachers use three basic patterns for reading instruction: whole-group instruction, small-group instruction, and independent reading. This is true whether teaching reading with a basal or with literature. Each format serves somewhat different purposes and offers different levels of support and intensity of instruction.

Whole-group instruction is easier to plan and manage than small-group instruction is, and the teacher is always present to guide, answer questions, or give feedback. Strong support for students is available as the teacher provides explanations, does think-alouds, and models a variety of strategies during lessons. Furthermore, a student can listen to classmates of all abilities as they provide insights into how to accomplish a task or interpret the text (Almasi, 2003). The disadvantage is that there is always a range of reading levels within a class, and whole-group instruction will be frustrating for some and not challenging for others.

Small-group instruction has been the most consistent pattern for teaching reading because it allows children to be grouped by instructional level. Small-group work can be done with today's basals, which are designed for both whole-class work and leveled-group work. Literature circles and book clubs can also be used for reading literature in a small-group format. Students have the opportunity to take leadership roles in small groups and have the support of five to eight others as they hear multiple and varied ways in which the teacher and peers use strategies to process text. However, students must be able to work independently while the teacher is occupied with a group, and the teacher must provide directions or activities for them.

Individualized reading allows for the most choice and the best match between student and text, both in reading level and in interest. The disadvantage of this format is that there is little or no time for instruction, and students must be able to work without teacher assistance for the majority of the time.

When a teacher uses all three formats for grouping, a balance is struck between the teacher and the students in terms of instruction, support, social interaction, choice, and leadership.

WHOLE-GROUP INSTRUCTION ■

Whole-group instruction is a standard format with advantages and disadvantages. Some of the disadvantages can be ameliorated with scaffolding.

Whole-Group Instruction With a Basal Program

Today's basals, which all use units coordinated around a theme, have been developed for whole-group and leveled instruction. The whole class participates in some instruction related to the theme. Whole-group instruction allows everyone to hear the reasoning used to construct meaning and provides struggling students with role models.

Literature Focus Units and Novel Units

Generally designed for younger students, a literature focus unit highlights one main piece of literature but uses a set of related texts, such as books by the same author, books with the same theme, or versions of the same story. For older students, the novel unit, in which the whole class reads a single novel, allows for substantial direct instruction. With one text, it is easy to integrate language arts instruction so that reading, writing, listening, and speaking are all taught and practiced together in a thoughtful manner, with each skill enriching the others.

Because the teacher provides whole-class instruction and guided reading throughout the process, the book chosen can be at the general instructional level of the class. The teacher cycles through prereading, reading, and responding activities daily with younger students and on a longer cycle with older students. The novel needs to be rich enough in content and theme to be worth spending two to three weeks with.

Scaffolded Reading

No matter what the book, it will not be at everyone's instructional level, which is why the teacher uses whole-group guided reading and then various structured activities to help students during independent reading. Jody Brown Podl (1995) calls this guided independent reading, which she admits is an oxymoron—but one that every teacher will understand. The more academic term is *scaffolding*. "Scaffolding—providing support to help learners bridge the gap between what they know and can do and the intended goal—is frequently singled out as one of the most effective instructional techniques available" (Graves, Graves, & Braaten, 1996, p. 14). Scaffolding allows students to carry out a task (in this case, comprehending a novel) that would be beyond them if they were unassisted.

When everyone in the room is included in a lesson, psychological and social advantages accrue. With scaffolding, all students can participate in the class novel at some level, which suggests to the students that everyone belongs in this class and is able to participate in the class. When students with learning disabilities and English language learners are part of the class, scaffolding becomes even more important.

The teacher plans all the normal activities for prereading, during reading, and postreading but also plans alternate or additional activities—called differentiated scaffolded reading experiences—for students who need greater assistance.

The usual problem is that when the teacher pulls aside, offers extra support to, or does guided reading with a targeted portion of the class, the reading assignment takes about twice as long as independent silent reading. Though the lessons the small group does with the teacher are worthwhile and instructive, the targeted group, which sometimes struggles the most and takes the longest to read a passage, ends up with a reading assignment that the rest of the class finished during their independent silent reading. Graves, Graves, and Braaten (1996) suggest "modifying the text," or providing a summary of the remainder of the chapter, so the small-group students can start even with their classmates on the following day. This can be done occasionally, especially with very difficult sections. One of the reasons students struggle is that they lack extensive reading practice, so if they are not required to read the whole novel, they need to be assigned other substantial reading to do in small groups or independently.

An alternative is that while the teacher does guided reading with the targeted group, other groups can participate in oral shared reading and discussion, an arrangement that deemphasizes the longer instructional time spent with one group. Students who have learned literature circle techniques can handle this system quite independently once they understand the expectations. The teacher can also suggest that anyone who wants to read in the guided group can join the teacher. Good readers, poor readers, and those who simply feel in a more social mood that day can join the guided group.

Study Guides as Scaffolding

Teachers can also give selected students a study guide that will act as a virtual teacher while the students read silently. Embedded questions and stop-and-go questions work well for study guides. See Chapter 8 for explanations and more ideas. Study guides can provide definitions of vocabulary words, briefly explain concepts that may be beyond a student's experience, or draw a student's attention to a character's motivation in a narrative. It is preferable to put these questions in the order of the story so students have a purpose for reading. For example, if students read three to five pages without finding an answer, they know they need to backtrack because they have not closely monitored their comprehension and have missed a crucial point.

Study guides can also be offered to other students who prefer a little extra guidance for finding and interpreting the most important parts. The guides can be based on the needs of the students or on special difficulties presented by the text. Either way, they remove obstacles before the obstacles become problems. Students who need the extra prompting and scaffolding will probably be able to participate successfully in all the postreading activities.

Essential Questions and Grand Conversations

Guided discussions with the whole group, conducted while the book is under way and after it is completed, can help students explore a novel in depth, make connections, clarify their thoughts, and test their ideas against their classmates' ideas. This is the time when children can explore what the Great Books Foundation calls essential questions or what Gail Tompkins (1997) calls grand conversations.

Essential questions are inference questions that could have more than one answer. The students must combine facts from the book with their own knowledge to interpret the story. Students sit in a circle so they can discuss their interpretations with each other while the teacher facilitates the conversation but gives no answers. The text is used by students to prove their points or highlight which clues brought them to a certain conclusion. Everyone must participate at some time during the discussion.

> Essential questions are more than questions essential to the story; they are questions essential to life.

The teacher starts with the essential question. For example, for the story "The Parsley Garden," by William Saroyan, the essential question could be, "Why did Al react so strongly after he was caught stealing the hammer?" For "The Veldt," by Ray Bradbury, "Why aren't the children upset when the psychologist comes back to see them in the nursery?" For "Through the Tunnel," by Doris Lessing, "Was it an act of independence or immaturity for the boy to swim through the underwater tunnel?" These questions may seem straightforward, but they are not. They are critical or essential to the story. Students must use the text, infer motivations, make judgments, and evaluate the circumstances. The questions are not just about the characters in the story. They are about prejudice, retribution, pride, selfishness, being spoiled, growing up, independence, and risk taking, which are useful and interesting topics for students. Essential questions are more than questions essential to the story; they are questions essential to life.

Children learn to analyze, interpret, and synthesize as they have an opportunity to hear someone else's reasoning and compare their answers with their classmates'. My favorite example is Marjory. Near the end of a Great Books circle, I asked everyone to offer a final opinion. Marjory was the last. Later, I asked her if it was difficult or easy to be the last to give her opinion. She said at first, when she realized she would be the last respondent, she thought it would be easy because she could hear everyone else's opinion first, but when there were so many contradictory but good interpretations and such sound reasoning, it was difficult. She changed her mind four times before it was her turn and learned that making judgments takes time, thought, and consideration of multiple viewpoints. Not a bad lesson to learn.

Grand conversations are similar to essential questions. Sometimes students start with a quickwrite, an unstructured three-to-five-minute response, to recall the story or to rehearse answers. Grand conversations are broader and may focus on illustrations, authors, comparisons, or literary elements as well as an interpretation of the story. It would be a great waste to spend a whole-group discussion on literal recitation of answers when the students could be having a conversation!

Integrated Language Arts

The novel unit is a good vehicle for teaching all the aspects of literacy in an integrated manner, which is one of the principles of balanced reading. Students can write about what they are reading, discuss it, and listen to the observations of other students. Is there any novel for which a teacher could not dream up a dozen connected writing opportunities?

Two teachers who taught the same grade but lived in different states developed a clever idea for integrating reading and writing. They arranged to teach the same novel at the same time. Students in each class were assigned e-mail pen pals from the other class. As they proceeded through the book, they wrote to their pen pals, explaining what they thought of the book, and recounted various activities their class had done. Next time you are at a conference, see if you can find a colleague who teaches the same book and might be willing to teach it at the same time you do.

■ SMALL-GROUP INSTRUCTION

Especially in the lower grades, small groups are where differentiated, or leveled, instruction takes place. Since the range of abilities only expands as students get older, more upper-grade teachers ought to consider grouping. Guided reading groups (discussed in Chapter 6) are organized for children with the same needs and approximately the same reading levels. The materials most often used with small groups are basals and leveled books.

Although three reading groups has been the dominant pattern since the 1950s (Otto, Wolf, & Eldridge, 2002), the number of groups depends on the range within the class, the students' ability to work independently, and the teacher's ability to plan for multiple guided and independent groups. Teachers also have options in scheduling groups. The children who have the greatest needs may meet for a longer time or more often for intensity of instruction. In a study of schools with a high proportion of students living in poverty, the most effective schools included more small-group instruction. Other elements at work in the most effective schools were more scaffolding, phonics instruction applied during reading, more high-level questions, greater parent outreach, and more independent reading (Taylor, Pearson, Clark, & Walpole, 2000).

One of the challenges of small-group work is that teachers must plan for activities that children can do without adult assistance. Effective teachers spend considerable time teaching students literacy routines that they can do independently or with other children. The tasks they plan are productive literacy activities that involve reading and writing rather than cutting and drawing. Allington's study of effective elementary teachers (2002b, p. 742) found that they maintained a higher "reading and writing versus stuff ratio" than less-effective teachers did. The effective teachers' students were reading and writing in various content areas for 50% of the day.

Small groups do not always have to be leveled, guided reading groups. Students can be grouped flexibly, temporarily, randomly, heterogeneously, cooperatively, or in pairs (Caldwell & Ford, 2002). Each arrangement serves a slightly different purpose.

Literature Circles

Literature circles are a little different from most small-group work. They are a structured small-group activity that uses novels. They allow for greater choice, for student-directed activities, and for extended periods of uninterrupted reading. They provide a time for social interaction and the exchange of ideas and give students a chance to discuss and listen in a real conversation about a book as opposed to a question-and-answer session.

In literature circles, groups of four to eight students read and study a single book together. There are many possible variations, but two key features are constant: students choose their own books, and the groups are heterogeneous. Teachers offer a limited selection of books so that groups will not be too small and numerous.

Reading is done independently, but study and discussion are collaborative. The groups can be led by the teacher or by the students, but either way, the students must take substantial responsibility because the teacher will have to monitor four to six groups. Some teachers alternate days for literature circles with days of more direct instruction, but continuity is a real advantage. Have you ever read for several days straight during the summer or while on vacation and thought it was absolutely luxurious not to have to read piecemeal? Reading literature nonstop and then having a good chat about what you read is a great enjoyment.

The following account of initiating literature circles is an adaptation from "Changing the Classroom Climate with Literature Circles," from the *Journal of Adolescent and Adult Literature* (Burns, October 1998, pp. 124–129; reprinted with permission). It describes a sixth-grade class in which students were given as much choice and control as possible. It describes one version of literature circles.

Changing the Classroom Climate With Literature Circles

Kenneth is leading a discussion using questions that he developed himself. Four other students in his group are answering his questions, giving their opinions or predictions, and finding proof. Suzanne is silently reading *Island of the Blue Dolphins*, Libby is reading *The Light in the Forest*, and Evan is reading *Julie of the Wolves*. After 20 minutes, Kenneth's small discussion group is finished, and soon Suzanne is sharing some of her favorite passages from *Blue Dolphins* with four of her classmates, while Evan and Libby continue reading their own books. The class is using literature circles to strengthen literacy skills and change the climate of the classroom.

Literature circles incorporate several features that can make the classroom climate more cooperative, responsible, and pleasurable while encouraging growth in reading. These features include student choice, groups of students with mixed ability, student management of small interactive groups, and substantial time to read during the school day.

Literature circles offer students a limited selection of books on a central theme, not just a random offering of novels. Six titles seems to be a perfect number. The sixth-grade unit described above was based on a survival theme, using *Sign of the Beaver, Sarah Bishop, Hatchet, Julie of the Wolves, The Light in the Forest*, and *Island of the Blue Dolphins*. The entire class had already read *The Cay* and was familiar with the survival theme.

The students in this class, located in a suburban area, were all able to read near or above grade level. In a classroom with a wider range of reading abilities, books of diverse reading levels should be offered.

The **power of choice** was one of Linda Gambrell's most consistent findings about reading motivation. "The research related to self-selection of reading materials supports the notion that the books and stories that children find 'most interesting' are those they have selected for their own reasons and purposes" (1996, p. 21). With literature circles, students are able to make several of their own decisions, which is motivating to reluctant readers and gives students a feeling of control over part of their learning.

The teacher began with short book talks that included information about the characters and plots and the length and complexity of the books. The class was familiar with *Sarah Bishop* and *Sign of the Beaver* because they had previously read excerpts. After a few students who had read some of the books gave testimonials, students each chose two books to read. For middle school students, it seemed to work better to have them make rapid choices so that they picked a book that really interested them rather than waiting to see what their friends had chosen.

The next step was for the teacher to determine groups and balance them with a mix whenever possible. Because each child had made two initial choices, it was relatively easy to honor choices and establish groups of four or five students. Gender of the main character seemed to have only a moderate effect on choice, so each literature circle was composed of roughly equal numbers of boys and girls. With heterogeneous groups, when a section was challenging, there was always someone who could help. The exciting, can't-wait-to-see-what-happens-next plots also helped. Strong interest can transcend reading levels (Hunt, 1997).

Elbaum, Schumm, and Vaughn (1997) concluded that middle-grade students, both good readers and poor readers, preferred working in mixed-ability groups or mixed-ability pairs to either whole-class instruction or individual work. The students perceived that in mixed-ability groups, students helped each other more, learned more, and enjoyed being in the group more.

When groups met for the first time, their job was to determine their own homework assignments for the next two weeks. Some groups chose to read shorter amounts each day for the full 14 days, but other groups chose to read more daily so that they did not have homework over the weekends or a holiday that occurred during this time. Some groups divided by pages, and some divided by chapters. The students then copied the agreed-on schedule into their assignment notebook and gave a copy to the teacher.

To **choose roles**, each group received a packet of five different role assignments: Discussion Director, Vocabulary Enricher, Passage Picker, Illustrator, and Creative Connector. The Discussion Director had to develop four discussion questions, which could not be answered just by finding the "right" passage in the book. They had to be "Why did. . . . ," "What do you think . . . ," or "Predict how or what . . ." questions. Although the class had practiced developing higher-level questions with a previous story, formulating them was not a skill that came easily to many students; instruction and practice were necessary.

The Vocabulary Enricher chose five words in the story that students were unlikely to know, found the definitions, and taught them to the group. Four interesting, surprising, or significant passages were chosen by the Passage Picker, who could share them with the group in a variety of ways. The Illustrator drew a favorite scene (no form required), and the Creative Connector helped the group see similarities between the text and other texts or personal experiences. See examples of role sheets for upper-grade students in Figures 7.1 through 7.4.

After roles were chosen, the teacher laid out a schedule for the days the groups would meet with their discussion circles. On a typical day, everyone read silently for the first five minutes. This was really a necessity to allow for transition, for everyone to settle in, for minor problems to be solved, and for establishing a quiet atmosphere in the room. Then Group A met with the teacher for 20 minutes while the other five groups read silently. Group A returned to reading while Group B met with the teacher. Groups C, D, E, and F read silently for the entire period. The next day, groups C and D met with the teacher while everyone else read silently. On the third day, groups E and F had their turns with the teacher, and the pattern continued for two weeks.

The **power of social interaction** that arises in a literature circle is a key component of this strategy's success. Verbalizing the content, listening to other modes of thinking, and hearing other perspectives all contribute to deepening comprehension. Literature study moved from an individual act of creating

(Text continues on page 108)

Figure 7.1   Role sheet for a literature circle: Discussion Director

---

DISCUSSION DIRECTOR

Name:_____   Book:_____

Tomorrow's Assignment: p._____ to p._____

Your job is to develop a list of questions that your group will discuss about this part of the book. Usually the best questions come from your own reactions and concerns. Develop questions that require a discussion, <u>not just a detail</u>. Use the sample questions below to help you.

Discussion Questions for Tomorrow's Assignment:

1. _____

   _____

2. _____

   _____

3. _____

   _____

4. _____

   _____

Sample Questions:

How did you feel while reading this part?

Did this section remind anyone of similar experiences of their own?

What do you think caused_____?

What questions did you have when you finished this section?

Did anything in this section surprise you or turn out differently than you expected?

Why do you think the author had _____ happen in the story?

How would the story have changed if the author had not let_____ happen?

If you had been _____, how would you have _____?

How are the characters developing or changing?

How is _____ different from _____?

Predict what you think will happen next.

What part did you like best? Least?

Summarize what happened in this part of the book.

Figure 7.2   Role sheet for a literature circle: Vocabulary Enricher

---

VOCABULARY ENRICHER

Name: _____   Book: _____

Assignment: p. _____ to p. _____

Find four words in the reading assignment that you don't know or you think an average student wouldn't know. Look up a definition that would make sense in that sentence. You may make up your own sentence or write the sentence that was in the book.

1. Word: _____   p. _____

Definition: _____

Did you use a _____ dictionary or guess from _____ context clues? (check one)

Sentence: _____

2. Word: _____   p. _____

Definition: _____

Did you use a _____ dictionary or guess from _____ context clues?

Sentence: _____

3. Word: _____   p. _____

Definition: _____

Did you use a _____ dictionary or guess from _____ context clues?

Sentence: _____

4. Word: _____   p. _____

Definition: _____

Did you use a _____ dictionary or guess from _____ context clues?

Sentence: _____

Now teach these words to your group members or have them guess the meanings from the context.

Figure 7.3   Role sheet for a literature circle: Passage Picker

---

PASSAGE PICKER

Name:_____

Tomorrow's assignment: p._____ to p._____

Passage Picker: Pick three paragraphs or passages from the assigned reading and choose a plan for the paragraphs to be shared with the group.

	Reason for Picking	**Reading Plan**

1. Page _____
 	
    Passage begins with these words:
 	
    _____		

2. Page _____
 	
    Passage begins with these words:
 	
    _____		

3. Page _____
 	
    Passage begins with these words:
 	
    _____		

Reasons for picking a passage

Exciting

Surprising

Funny

Scary

Significant

Vivid with details

Good dialogue

Reading/sharing plan

1. Passage picker reads aloud

2. Picker has someone else read aloud

3. Everyone reads silently

4. Then everyone comments on the passage

Figure 7.4   Role sheet for a literature circle: Creative Connector

---

CREATIVE CONNECTOR

Name:_____

Tomorrow's assignment: p._____ to p._____

Of what does this reading assignment remind you? It might be something else we have done in this class, something from another class, a story or a book you have read, or a movie you have seen.

My Connections

1. _____   What's the connection?   _____

_____

2. _____   What's the connection?   _____

_____

3. _____   What's the connection?   _____

_____

Questions to Ask Your Literature Circle

Ask your group to make connections also. Help them to think by asking them two questions.

Samples:

Does this remind you of something else we've done in class?

Do any of these ideas connect to something you've studied in another class?

Do you recall a time when _____?

Has something similar happened in your life?

Questions:

1. _____

_____

2. _____

_____

meaning to a social act of students' negotiating meaning together. The main character in *The Light in the Forest* elicited the most discussion because his acts were interpreted as everything from bratty to an attempt to adapt to changing cultural expectations.

The students liked the intimacy of the small reading group because it allowed more opportunity to participate and be actively involved, which also changes the classroom climate. Students enjoy the relaxed atmosphere of belonging to a "book club" and working in a congenial setting where discussion is allowed and even encouraged. Because relationship goals are very important to preadolescents, a program designed to attend to both social and academic goals can be very engaging (Hicks, 1997).

As each group finished its discussion, the students received a packet for the next round, and each student had to pick a new role. Students were reminded of their next meeting date, and they wrote down their new assignments. Much to the teacher's surprise, many students completed their books in six school days, and several started another book that their classmates were reading.

Finding time for a pleasurable book, appreciating literature, and having time to read in school appear often in curriculum guides but seldom in lesson plans. If teachers really want to develop lifelong readers, then they need to allow students to have an opportunity to experience reading interesting books just for the pleasure of it. One of my favorite moments of teaching occurred when one of my students was called to the office over the intercom. She got up, took her book, and continued reading all the way down the hall.

> If teachers really want to develop lifelong readers, then they need to allow students to have an opportunity to experience reading interesting books just for the pleasure of it.

The students were able to read the books in this unit independently. They were not the kinds of books that involved heavy symbolism or those that required extensive background knowledge. Those types of books need mediated reading with a teacher activating prior knowledge and guiding interpretation. Literature circles work best when the books are meant to be enjoyed.

The **teacher's role** is to prepare materials, establish guidelines, and then be a group member. Because this was the class's first encounter with literature circles, the teacher was a part of each circle. She kept the group on task, established a pattern for taking turns, encouraged students to talk with each other rather than to her alone, and sometimes answered when called on by the Discussion Director, who generally took charge of the group. If students are not taught the patterns and the responsibilities of literature circles, they tend to lose focus and wander off task. It is important that an adult be present as groups learn the process. Ann Brown (1997) suggests that even with experienced groups, the teacher should hold a short debriefing at the end of each session for students to assess listening behaviors, interactions, and the types of questions that were asked.

For literature circles to run smoothly, much preparation is needed. Six sets of related books must be available in sufficient quantities, role sheets must be ready, and expectations for students' responsibilities must be clarified. The process also works best when the teacher has read all the books. Although there are experts who say the teacher need not read the books to be able to facilitate a good discussion, assessment of the comments and facilitation of the conversation proceed with much greater grace and accuracy when the teacher knows the books well.

Literature circles should be one of the organizational patterns in a teacher's repertoire because many aspects of building a positive classroom climate are incorporated into this method of sharing literature. When students are allowed to make their own choices about what to read, to prepare their own lessons, and to take charge of discussions with their peers, the climate of the classroom changes. The teacher is no longer the sole commander of the students' fates. [End of "Changing the Classroom Climate with Literature Circles."]

But did they get it? "Changing the Classroom Climate with Literature Circles" does not address evaluation. The whole process might feel a little slippery to teachers who are used to keeping their thumb on the pulse of every student. I always wanted to slip in a worksheet or at least one set of individually answered questions, despite the fact that the kids were self-directed and were actually excited about reading.

Remember thinking about the joy of reading without interruption? Could you imagine having to stop and answer a dozen questions or make a story map before being able to go on to the next chapter? Perhaps, at least once in a while, we should let our students enjoy reading the way adults do if we really want them to spend a lifetime taking pleasure in reading.

However, if after meeting with a group, the teacher thinks that the students need to probe for greater depth or that some students are not fulfilling their responsibilities, students can be given a specific assignment to prepare by the next group meeting.

Guided reading of challenging materials and direct instruction in strategies can be done when literature circles have concluded as it is exceedingly difficult to teach lessons from four to six different books simultaneously. This small-group format is only one part of a balanced reading program, but it provides benefits that neither whole-class nor independent reading can.

> Allocating time to read in school confers validity to the idea that reading is important.

INDEPENDENT READING ■

Independent reading allows for the greatest choice and the best match in reading level and interest but has limited peer interaction and the least direct instruction. Allocating time to read in school confers validity to the idea that reading is important, and the volume of reading done by a child correlates highly with reading proficiency. Books for independent reading should be easy, that is, at the students' independent reading level, and highly engaging. With the number of amazing new trade books available, finding appropriate materials should be no problem—unless your school library was last restocked in 1974. If Allington's recommendations (2001) were followed, every classroom would have 500 different books, evenly split between narratives and informational books and between books at or near grade level and books below grade level. When children are allowed to read books of their own choosing, positive attitudes and motivation are increased.

For students with learning disabilities, the effect of silent independent reading may not be as strong. Students experiencing comprehension difficulties may be more engaged by oral reading (Wilkinson, cited in Allington, 2001). Direct instruction with cognitively oriented strategy instruction produced the largest gains in these students (Swanson, 1999).

Silent Sustained Reading, Drop Everything and Read, and Incentive Programs

Silent Sustained Reading (SSR) and Drop Everything and Read (widely known as DEAR) can address the need for uninterrupted reading time, usually 20 minutes daily, as well as the extensive differences in reading abilities and interests found in every classroom. Children choose their own books, so motivation is high. To add a social component and encourage comprehension, some teachers have a two-minute partner share at the close of the session. Usually children keep a log of their reading for accountability. Gay Ivey and Douglas Fisher (2005) recommend that SSR of interesting trade books at diverse reading levels be included in content area classes to help students increase their motivation, background knowledge, and vocabulary in the subject.

Although 20 minutes used to be the recommendation, the correlation between time spent reading and reading proficiency is so strong that many teachers have set aside a much longer time for silent reading. Some of it may be assigned reading, and some may be free choice.

Incentive programs, such as Accelerated Reader (Renaissance Learning) and Reading Counts! (Scholastic), encourage independent reading in and out of the classroom. However, independent reading is a time for practice with little or no opportunity for instruction, so incentive programs should not be confused with instructional programs.

Readers' Workshop

A more structured version of SSR is called readers' workshop. Nancie Atwell (1987) popularized this format. In a readers' workshop, students are allowed to read books of their own choice and at their own pace. Atwell wanted kids to read the way adults do, making their own choices and learning to love what they read, and she also wanted her students to experience modeling, so often she read when they did and discussed her own reading experiences with her students. Modeling the value of reading may be especially important in diverse classrooms with students who do not see themselves as readers (Au, 2002).

Atwell's rules for using readers' workshop help explain how the procedure works. Students must read for the entire period. They cannot do homework or read material for another course because reading workshop is not a study hall. They must read a book (no magazines or newspapers, in which text competes with pictures), preferably one that tells a story. In other words, they must read novels, histories, or biographies, as opposed to books of lists or facts, with which readers cannot sustain attention, build up speed and fluency, or grow to love good stories. Coming prepared to class means the students must have a book in their possession when the bell rings. Students who need help finding a book or who finish a book during the workshop are obvious exceptions. They may not talk to or disturb others. They may sit or recline wherever they like as long as feet do not go up on furniture. There are no lavatory or water fountain sign-outs to disturb the teacher or other readers. In an emergency, they may simply slip out and slip back in again as quietly as possible. A student who is absent can make up time and receive points by reading at home, during study hall, or afterschool (Atwell, 1987). If this seems idealistic to you because some students do not choose a book or will not become engaged, wait them out. Provide them with a choice of two books, and almost certainly they will decide eventually that reading is better than sitting silently for 20 minutes. They might discover they like it.

For Atwell, the reading of books was the central activity of her classroom. It was what she wanted students to value most, so she made time for it in school and did not relegate it to homework. She said, "Periods of silent independent reading are perhaps the strongest experience I can provide students to demonstrate the value of literacy" (1987, p. 157).

I changed my practices a few years ago. Reading is now done in school. The responses and assignments are done as homework. I was not as philosophical as Atwell; I just noticed that kids demonstrated better comprehension when reading was done at school. Making a Venn diagram, drawing a story map, or devising a time line is more reasonable homework against a background of screaming siblings or a blaring television than reading is, and Venn diagrams, story maps, and time lines can be sandwiched between soccer practice and dinner more easily than reading can. Reading with comprehension takes sustained attention and quiet.

For readers' workshop, Atwell started with a ten-minute minilesson. It might be an introduction to an author or a genre. All students might read and discuss an opening of a chapter or book, or they might talk about a reading process. Once everyone was settled, the teacher settled into a quiet corner of the room for in-depth conferences with students.

Responding to readers is done through conferences or journals. Some teachers confer with students during the workshop time, asking open-ended questions. This is a good choice for younger students. However, for older students, dialogue journals can be used as well. Atwell speculated that written responses in a dialogue journal might help her students respond at deeper, more critical levels because they would have more time to consider their responses. She modeled her answers and encouraged students to respond at an interpretive level rather than at a recall level.

Some teachers respond to the journals of only a portion of their students each day, rotating the sections. Some have students write back and forth to each other, and some teachers combine teacher and student responses to make responding more manageable. To encourage reflectiveness or to calm their own anxieties about comprehension, some teachers end the day with an open-ended exit slip, requiring students to answer a question or two before going to their next class.

1. What is the biggest problem the main character has encountered so far?

2. What is the best part of the book up to this point?

3. What questions would you like to ask the author?

4. Describe the setting of the section you read today.

5. Which character are you most like? How have you felt or acted the same?

6. Find the paragraph you wish you had written. Copy the first three sentences.

7. Make a prediction about what is going to happen next.

■ RESPONDING TO LITERATURE

After reading, whether in whole-group, small-group, or individual format, students can respond in writing to what they have read. They can write responses in the form of letters, diaries, journals, newspaper articles, postcards, retellings, summaries, or poetry. Or they can critique in the form of recommendations, advice columns, and book reviews. They might also think of questions they would like to ask the author or each other. Younger students can make an ABC book, a time line, or a chart, or they can play with the language by making riddles, hinky pinkies (see Chapter 10), or analogies.

Students can also respond orally to what they have read, through a variety of creative presentations, from puppet shows to news shows. They can turn a portion of the text into a script for Readers' Theatre, write a song, or stage a tableau. In a tableau, several children stand frozen in a scene from the book and then unfreeze one at a time to explain something about their character.

Finally, students can respond visually with a project requiring artwork. They can draw the sequence of the plot in a cartoon format, make a collage, or create a pop-up book. Other art-related activities include inventing a board game, developing a CD or book cover, creating a six-sided cube with scenes or story elements, producing a scrapbook of a character, or making masks of the characters. More complicated projects might include making a story wheel, constructing a weaving (story strips woven together), or creating a quilt of the story as a group project. Though these activities are great fun and give students an opportunity to think about and interpret the story, our ultimate purpose is to teach reading. The extension activities, such as puppet shows, board games, field trips, bulletin boards, and movies, are appropriate and supportive, but reading is the primary objective. That is where the bulk of the students' time needs to be spent.

■ CHILDREN NEED TO READ EXTENSIVELY

It comes as no surprise to teachers that good readers read more than poor readers. The 1998 National Assessment of Educational Progress (NAEP) (cited in Allington, 2001) reported a consistent relationship between amount of reading done and students' NAEP reading scores. Only 28% of the students who reported reading 5 or fewer pages each day achieved the Proficient level, compared with 51% who read 11 or more pages daily. The 2003 NAEP results show the same relationship between pages read daily and reading scores at ages 9, 13, and 17. A positive note is that over the past 20 years, both 9- and 13-year-olds increased the number of pages read for school and homework, but 17-year-olds made no significant increase. Twenty-five percent of the 9-year-olds and 21% of the 13-year-olds read 20 or more pages daily, compared with 13% and 11%, respectively, in 1984 (Donahue, Daane, & Jin, 2005). Home environments and the emphasis in school on real reading rather than workbook pages may account for some of these changes. Multiple studies confirm the strong correlation between amount of reading and reading proficiency.

The types of reading activities in a classroom also make a difference. Direct reading (reading actual texts) produced more gains than indirect reading (phonics drill, copying, circling). Silent reading increased reading volume much more than round-robin oral reading did. Even small increases in teacher modeling and demonstration of strategies (as opposed to providing directions) made a difference (Allington, 2001). Children clearly need an opportunity to spend significant time reading whole texts.

> Children clearly need an opportunity to spend significant time reading whole texts.

CHOOSING BOOKS ■

We teachers know we can vary the organizational patterns among whole-group, small-group, and individual reading. We also know that the amount of reading matters, but neither of these factors addresses what to read when moving beyond the basal program. Readability and content are the two issues to consider when choosing books.

Determining Readability and Leveling Books

Children need books they can actually read. Success rate has a substantial impact on student learning. Easy books for independent reading are just fine. To determine what books are at a child's reading level, the teacher needs to know the readability level (the difficulty of the text).

The traditional method of determining readability was to count the number of syllables and sentence length and find the reading level on the Fry Readability Graph (see Chapter 12). Although the Fry gives a good indication, using it is a chore. Internet sites provide easier ways to find the readability or the level of a book, and as a bonus, these sites offer a host of additional information.

Microsoft Word can be set to give a Flesch-Kincaid readability score after completing a spell-check. To obtain the readability of any passage that has been typed in, go to the Tools menu in the top menu bar. Click on Options. Then click on the Spelling and Grammar tab. Check both "Check grammar with spelling" and "Show readability statistics." Every time spelling is checked, a readability score will appear. On a Macintosh, go to the Tools menu. Click on Preferences, and then select the Spelling and Grammar tab. Under Grammar, check "Show readability statistics." All the readability formulas depend on word difficulty, determined by length, syllable count, or frequency, and on sentence length. They provide a good estimate of difficulty.

Another way to find readability is to visit http://www.interventioncentral.org. On the right, under online tools, click on OKAPI Reading Probe Generator. Paste or type a passage into the Text to Be Analyzed box. If you think the passage is for Grades 1–3, leave the Spache formula in the pull-down menu. If you think the passage is for Grades 4–12, use the pull-down menu under the Spache box to get the Dale-Chall formula. Click Run Readability Analysis. The next screen will give the readability score and even underline the hard words.

Accelerated Reader levels can be found at http://www.renlearn.com/store. Click on Order Quizzes and type in the author or title. The readability appears as a grade level equivalent, and an interest level is also given. This data bank covers 40,000 trade books.

Lexile units do not use grade level for readability, but the Lexile units can be converted, more or less, with the chart in Figure 7.5. At http://www.lexile.com, click on Educators, then on Lexile Book Database. Search by title, author, Lexile range, key words, or International Standard Book Number (ISBN). The search can also be limited to Spanish language books or textbooks. If you are searching for an assortment of books at a particular level, the site gives ISBN, titles, authors, and readability in Lexile units. Each title may be clicked for additional information. This database covers 26,000 books, including informational trade books.

The leveling systems, Reading Recovery and Fountas and Pinnell's Guided Reading (1996), rely on human judgment, not just mathematical formulas. Fountas and Pinnell use qualitative factors such as age-appropriate content, illustrations, layout, curriculum support, language structure, judgment about prior knowledge, and format—the type size and spacing (Fry, 2002). Fountas and Pinnell (2006) recently published a book of K–8 titles, all organized by level, and all under one cover. A pay-per-visit Web site at http://www.FountasandPinnellLeveledBooks.com is available from Heinemann for finding the levels of books. For additional leveled books, visit Reading A-Z at http://www.readinga-z.com, where a series of books at levels A to Z can be downloaded without charge; 300 more are available for a small fee. Although not a book-finding site, Sites for Teachers (http:www.sitesforteachers.com) is a portal to 900 different Web sites for materials and activities of all kinds.

Unfortunately, the systems for reporting reading levels differ and are incompatible. Although it may not satisfy any system developer completely, the chart in Figure 7.5 gives an approximation of comparability. The chart is averaged and extrapolated from several sources, including Gunning (2003), the Lexile Framework Map (Metametrics, 2005), Fountas & Pinnell (1996), Developmental Reading Assessment (Pearson, 2005), and the National Geographic catalog (2005).

Choosing Children's Literature

While learning to read, students should have access to a wide variety of books, including books with patterns, books with decodable print, nonfiction, books coordinated with content areas, books with captivating artwork, and especially books with great stories for extended periods of independent reading.

Figure 7.5 Conversion chart for readability systems

Fountas & Pinnell	Grade level & basals	Reading Recovery	DRP	Lexile	DRA	National Geographic Windows on Literacy
A emergent	K	1			1	1
B caption	K, PP @ 1.0	2			2	2
C	PP1 @ 1.1	3–4			3–4	3–4
D	PP2 @ 1.2	5–6			5–6	5–6
E	PP3 @ 1.3	7–8	34–35		7–8	7
F	P @ 1.4	9–10	36–37		9–10	8–9
G	1^1 @ 1.5	11–12	37–39	200	12	10
H	1^2 @ 1.6	13–14	39–40	250	14	11
I	1^2–2 @ 1.8	15–17	40–41	300	16	12–13
J	2 @ 2.0	18–19	42–43	350	18–20	14–15
K	2 @ 2.3	20	44–45	400	24	16
L	2^2–3 @ 2.5		46–47	450	28	17–19
M	2^2–3 @ 2.8		46–47	475	30	19–20
N	3 @ 3.2		48–49	500	32	20–21
O	3–4 @ 3.6		48–49	550	34–36	21–22
P	3–4 @ 3.8		48–49	650	38	22–23
Q, R, S	4		50	700	40–48	24
T	4, 5		51–52	750		
U–V	5		52–54	800		
W–X	6		54–55	900		
Y	7		56–57	1000		
Z	8		58–59	1075		

Source: Burns, B., "I Don't Have to Count Syllables on My Fingers Anymore: Easier Ways to Find Readability and Level Books," *Illinois Reading Council Journal,* December-January 2005-2006.

Note: DRP = Degrees of Reading Power; DRA = Developmental Reading Assessment.

Internet sites are a tremendous help for finding books. Scholastic's Reading Counts! is an incentive-practice program similar to Accelerated Reader (Renaissance Learning), but the site can also be used to find an amazing variety of books using multiple search terms. At http://teacher.scholastic.com/products/readingcounts, click on "Shop Books & Quizzes in e-Catalog" in the right column and then "Search Titles" in the blue column on the left. The listing of 34,000 books can be narrowed by broad interest levels; reading level in grade level equivalent, guided reading level, or Lexile units; English or Spanish titles; and fiction or nonfiction. The user may also choose from a long list of topics and themes, genres, cultures and diversity, reading skills, popular series, awards, and programs. Multiple search boxes can be checked. On a trial search, 102 science titles came up with a reading level of 2.0–2.5. Clicking on a title gives additional information, including a specific reading level, a word count, and a rating on a five-star system.

■ THE ADVANTAGE OF GREAT LITERATURE

Teaching with literature has many advantages. The language is more natural, the stories are wonderful, and students who read literature in the primary grades are not so perplexed when they encounter increasingly complex narratives at the intermediate level.

Best of all, literature provides models of ethical responsibility, inspiration, aesthetic experiences, and social cohesion (May, 1998). Literature offers a look at characters of depth whom we can admire or despise with a passion. It takes us away to times and places we are not able to go and allows us to vicariously explore adventurous situations we might be afraid to try on our own. It gives us insight into our own character and the character of others so that we can understand how other cultures function when our own experiences are limited or restricted. Children need different role models from those they see daily in the media!

A last advantage of literature is the exquisite language and artwork found in special books. The plot of *The Secret Garden*, by Frances Hodgson Burnett, could be summarized in a paragraph, but children love to listen to the lyrical language. They eagerly visualize the coming of spring, and they come to love the characters. It is a terrific book to read aloud.

The Newbery Medal is given yearly for the most distinguished contribution to American literature for children. This award has been given by the American Library Association since 1922. The most distinguished American picture book for children receives the Caldecott Award. It is also awarded by the American Library Association and has been given since 1938.

Teaching Strategies With Literature

Any skill or strategy taught with a basal can be taught with a novel. However, when extensive novel study is used, teachers must be aware of the variety of comprehension strategies that need to be learned and must make sure that balanced instruction accompanies the literature. Beginning teachers might want to consult a teacher's manual of a basal series, a scope and sequence chart, or their state standards to make sure that students are participating in the breadth and depth of experiences embodied in a successful reading program.

Teaching literature, whether with a whole class, with literature circles, or with independent reading, offers excellent opportunities to incorporate all the aspects of a balanced literacy program. Skills and strategies can be taught and applied within the context of engaging reading materials, students are grouped both homogeneously and heterogeneously, children benefit from discussion with others, the language arts can be integrated, choice provides motivation, and there is an opportunity to balance teacher and student leadership.

8

Instruction for Comprehension

The sagacious reader who is capable of reading between these lines what does not stand written in them, but nevertheless implied, will be able to form some conception.

—Johann Wolfgang von Goethe

Comprehending meaning is the heart and soul of reading, and learning to fully comprehend written text is complex. It is a task so intricate that it takes several years to become a mature reader who can handle simultaneously and almost automatically the multitude of tasks involved in reading comprehension.

There are two key problems in teaching comprehension. One is that it all happens in the child's head, and so the teacher cannot see what the child is doing. (Fortunately, research has led to teaching techniques to help make thinking more visible.) The other problem is that we sometimes fail to make it clear to the students what comprehension is. I scrapped the introduction from the first edition of this book to include a 1979 study by Canney and Winograd (cited in Baker & Brown, 2002). The researchers prepared four types of passages: one with correct grammar but some words that did not make sense, one with grammar and word violations but some resemblance to connected discourse, one consisting of strings of random words, and one of only strings of random letters. Children in Grades 2, 4, 6, and 8 were presented with the passages and asked if each

> Capable readers are active rather than passive.

could be read and why. Children identified as poor comprehenders in second, fourth, and even sixth grade focused on the decoding aspect and reported that all but the letter string passage could be "read." Some kids just don't understand that reading is supposed to make sense.

CAPABLE AND LESS-CAPABLE READERS ■

Capable readers are active rather than passive. They know that reading means making sense of a text. They create goals, preview the structure, predict, evaluate, select which parts to read carefully, and integrate their prior knowledge. They pay close attention to the setting and characters in fiction, and they summarize in nonfiction. They monitor their reading, take breaks to consider as they read, and consider the process after reading (Duke & Pearson, 2002). They know they have to work at comprehending.

Less-capable readers are more likely to focus on decoding rather than meaning, and as they get older, they are more likely to focus on a single detail rather than on the whole. Some students are just "doing school," gliding through the text without constructing meaning—in other words, without actually thinking about what they are reading. Sometimes they just do not know what it is they are supposed to do when reading. They use the same procedures, no matter what the task.

> [Less-capable readers] seem reluctant to use unfamiliar strategies or those that require much effort. They do not seem to be motivated or to expect that they will be successful. Less capable readers and writers don't understand or use all the stages of the reading and writing processes effectively. They do not monitor their reading and writing. Or, if they do use strategies, they remain dependent on primitive strategies. For example, as they read, less successful readers seldom look ahead or back into the text to clarify misunderstandings or make plans. Or, when they come to an unfamiliar word, they often stop reading, unsure of what to do. They may try to sound out an unfamiliar word, but if that is unsuccessful they give up. In contrast, capable readers know several strategies, and if one strategy isn't successful they try another. (Tompkins, 1997, p. 137)

■ AN INSTRUCTIONAL MODEL FOR TEACHING COMPREHENSION

Numerous studies from the past 25 years of research show that comprehension strategies can be taught. Poor readers can learn the habits and strategies of good readers. This model for teaching any of the comprehension strategies should look familiar to anyone who has studied Madilyn Hunter's lesson planning; in reading it is called transactional strategies instruction because of the abundant interaction among the teacher, the students, and the text. It is explicit instruction and includes the following elements (Duke & Pearson, 2002; Pressley & Wharton-McDonald, 2002):

1. Explicit description of the strategy and when, why, and how it should be used (Instruction is more explicit and detailed when a strategy is first introduced, but effective teachers continue to instruct and review.)

2. Teacher modeling of how the strategy is used

3. Collaborative use of the strategy (The content is used in interactive discussions as a vehicle to stimulate discussion and application of the strategy.)

4. Guided practice (The teacher provides scaffolding and feedback, with students gradually assuming more independence. Teacher responses are

determined by the reactions of the students, and reinstruction may occur if needed. Groups of students often problem solve together with teacher assistance. As students become more competent, assistance is reduced.)

5. Independent practice (Teachers still cue and prompt about which strategies may be profitably applied.)

Teaching comprehension strategies takes considerable instruction, modeling, talking through, thinking aloud, and applying, with lots of practice in text. It requires asking "How did you know that?" "What clues did you use?" "What were you thinking about?" and "How did you connect that?" If a comprehension strategy is not consciously known, then the student will not be able to transfer that skill to a future task. In other words, the student not only has to be able to do "it," but also has to know what "it" is, and when to do "it" again. This is all part of metacognition, which includes readers' being aware of how they handle the reading process, what the task requires, and if it is making sense. For the teacher, perhaps the most difficult part of teaching strategic reading is remembering that the content of the story is not really what is being taught. The content of the story is only the vehicle for learning the process.

Explicit explanations and intensity of instruction while mastering a strategy are key for struggling learners. They have no strategies to use when what they have read seems meaningless, or if they have learned isolated strategies, they do not know when to apply them. English language learners need clear directions so they can be comfortable knowing what to do. Handling vaguely understood directions and text and at the same time handling a second language is an overload. The same is true for struggling readers who do the best when they know what to do and why it is useful. One difficulty in basal instruction is that instruction moves from one skill to another relatively rapidly. In contrast, the most successful reading interventions taught a single strategy and followed it up with repeated application activity over a four- to ten-week period (Allington, 2001).

Learning how to comprehend is also enhanced when there is social interaction. As students hear the teacher explaining how she came to an understanding or listen to other students explaining how they reached a conclusion, they begin to understand the process. Vygotsky (1978) is famous for this reasoning: With guided practice and observing the thinking of others, individual students will then be able to do a task by themselves.

Teaching comprehension, just as all other aspects of reading, needs to be balanced. It includes both giving explicit instruction in specific strategies and spending a great deal of time actually reading, discussing, and writing about what was read. Neither instruction nor practice is sufficient by itself. Richard Allington (2001), past president of the International Reading Association, says American schools need a lot more comprehension instruction and lots and lots of independent reading.

FACTORS AFFECTING COMPREHENSION ■

Even when children know that reading is supposed to make sense, comprehension is affected by a number of other factors. They include the ability to recognize words quickly and automatically, the background knowledge and vocabulary that the reader brings to the task, the difficulty and complexity of the style in which the text is written, and the motivation of the reader. Fortunately, there are ways to control or to strengthen these factors when they are missing.

Fluency and Automaticity in Word Recognition

To comprehend material, students must be able to decode fast enough and automatically enough to keep the content in working memory so that meaning can be constructed. If readers are not fluent and automatic in decoding skills, they use all their cognitive attention for decoding and fail to comprehend. Fluency does not ensure comprehension, but comprehension is difficult without fluency.

> Fluency does not ensure comprehension, but comprehension is difficult without fluency.

Background, Prior Knowledge, and Schema

Another factor that affects comprehension is the reader's prior knowledge. If the reader can recognize nearly every word on the page but does not have a clue as to the meaning, there is often a mismatch between the reader's schema and the text. A schema is composed of organized personal background knowledge, and it acts as a filing system that has been set up to organize past experiences and interpret future experiences. For example, a restaurant schema includes tablecloths, menus, waiters, price ranges, favorite dishes, and so on, so as we read, "Elena walked into the restaurant and was escorted to a table," we do not expect that the escort is going to sit down with her. Readers' schemas help them understand new text, make connections, and conjure up pictures while reading. Schemas also include attitudes that will influence judgments about what is read. When a student has a fully formed schema, just a few clues in the text will trigger it, and the reader will understand the entire situation, even with an incomplete explanation by the author.

When the schema is missing, the situation is not comprehensible. Trying to order a computer part is always an exercise in humility for me. "With two dozen legacy computers running 10/100 Fast Ethernet, the GX5 is the switch you'll want. . . . You'll appreciate how easily you can add newer Gigabit-equipped workstations, servers and backbone uplinks. At the heart of the GX5 is a sophisticated chipset that forms an impressive 12.8 Gbps wire-speed switch fabric" (MacMall, 2005). I can read every word, but my schema does not match. There is even a picture to help me, but I still have no idea. Having no idea what I am reading about is a major block to my comprehension.

When a schema is missing, the student is reduced to recalling the information on a rote basis and cannot make any judgment about the material being read because it is not really understood. Vocabulary falls into the prior knowledge category, too. When students have strong oral vocabularies or are native English speakers, reading is easier. Words that are sounded out, even if not quite correctly, can often be recognized. Students who know words that represent concepts have an entire schema with which to work. Readers with limited background knowledge or limited vocabulary have a harder time reading because they cannot make those intuitive leaps to fill in the gaps where information is incomplete.

Lack of prior knowledge is usually not as severe as mine with computer parts, but even small gaps can produce unexpected results. One of my students who wrote about *Sarah Bishop* (O'Dell, 1980) discussed putting a jacket on a deer because the book said that Sarah had dressed a deer. Another student mentioned that an Indian visitor of Sarah's was sick because the text said he was ill at ease. Another, in a retelling, said that Ulysses poked out the eye of the Cyclops with a spear dipped in oregano because she had read the spear was of seasoned wood. Based on their past knowledge, these students formed images, and in remembering the passages, swore there were jackets, flu symptoms, and herbs.

Some missing schemas totally block comprehension, and other mismatches just change the details. Because readers construct meaning based on what they already know and try to integrate new ideas into their schemas, the same text can have different interpretations for different readers. Existing schemas are hard to change, and readers have to be willing to abandon, alter, or replace their preconceived notions as new information is added. Time used building background prior to reading is time well spent.

Difficulty of the Text

The difficulty of the text also affects comprehension. Many students are confronted daily, especially in the content areas, with texts that are too complex for optimum learning (Allington, 2001). For young students, five unknown words on a single page may mean the book is too difficult for independent reading. Although readability is usually determined by syllable count and sentence length, text structure, style, and unfamiliar concepts affect comprehension, too.

When you are teaching a new comprehension strategy, consider choosing a text that is easy—one that does not pose too many barriers to comprehension, such as unfamiliar vocabulary or concepts. Texts should be selected that are well suited to the strategy being learned, but more likely the reverse will occur; the strategy being taught will be determined by the demands of the text.

Motivation

"Teachers have long recognized that motivation is at the heart of many of the pervasive problems we face in educating today's children" (Gambrell, 1996, p. 17). The determination of readers to be problem solvers when the going gets tough is a factor in comprehension. Ways to

> Most readers who are not taught comprehension strategies explicitly are unlikely to learn them or use them spontaneously.

increase motivation are presented at the end of this chapter.

COMPREHENSION STRATEGIES ■

Comprehension strategies are specific, learned procedures that foster active, competent, self-regulated, and intentional reading. Most readers who are not taught comprehension strategies explicitly are unlikely to learn them or use them spontaneously (Trabasso & Bouchard, 2002). However, proficient readers may not even be aware they are using strategies until something goes awry with meaning. Strategic readers have a variety of techniques at their disposal and can intentionally select which ones to use and determine when to use them.

Which strategies do good readers need and use? The first group of strategies includes the basic problem-solving strategies that good readers use to construct meaning from text:

1. Linking one's background knowledge to the text

2. Figuring out unknown words

3. Visualizing

4. Predicting and then confirming or rejecting the prediction

5. Monitoring and thinking aloud

6. Generating questions

7. Using fix-up strategies when the text does not make sense

8. Using story and text structure

9. Summarizing

The second group of strategies includes those that readers use for higher level thinking:

1. Inferring

2. Generalizing and synthesizing

3. Evaluating

The last group involves attitudes and dispositions held by good readers:

1. Understanding that reading is meaningful communication

2. Seeing the need to read and choosing to do so

3. Having the willingness to expend considerable time and effort to become proficient

(Allington, 2001; Pressley & Wharton-McDonald, 2002; Duke & Pearson, 2002)

■ COMPREHENSION ACTIVITIES FOR BEFORE READING

Teaching or activating concepts and background knowledge, teaching unfamiliar vocabulary, and visualizing will all enhance comprehension. These strategies are crucial for readers in Grades 4–12.

Teaching Unfamiliar Concepts and Content

Providing background knowledge or concepts can supply the big picture for readers so that ideas from the text comfortably fit into a comprehensible whole. People are able to learn the most when they already know 90% of what they are reading. Think of this background information as a hook on which to hang new information or a file folder into which new information can be integrated. This is obviously important for reading textbooks in which entirely new content is encountered, but it is also important in fiction, especially with stories that are set in other times and cultures or stories that use concepts from an unfamiliar adult realm. Concepts that are not well known to children, such as mortgages, organic fertilizers, or patents, need to be pretaught. When the author does not explain these ideas but the teacher explains them before reading begins, comprehension is improved, and readers actually give more time and attention to the sections dealing with the highlighted concepts. A teacher needs to be cognizant of which content, setting, or concept might block understanding. Not everything needs to be pretaught.

Linking Background to New Content

Children need to develop the strategy of searching their own schemas when encountering new material. To teach this strategy, teachers need to take a slightly different tack from providing the background. They need to probe the experiences of the class and help students make their own connections.

To prepare for reading about Hermes in Greek mythology, students were asked to recall where they had seen Hermes' symbols. Their responses included the following: The winged feet are the symbol of a tire company; the Detroit Red Wings use a logo of a shoe with wings; Hermes is in a Saturn car commercial; his staff is on the Blue Cross logo; and a staff with intertwined snakes is used on a sign at a drugstore. The students' responses helped them realize that this mythological character was somewhat familiar and that they could make connections to aid their comprehension and to improve recall.

Prereading discussion is one of the most useful activities for activating prior knowledge or developing concepts. Artifacts, pictures, and video or CD clips all help. References to a film always work because students seem to know every movie ever produced. One student will say, "Have you ever seen this movie? Well, it's like that," and a chorus of now-understanding heads will nod in unison. Calling on every student during a discussion validates everyone's experiences as well as keeping everyone involved. For those who do not wish or are unable to offer connections of their own, the teacher can offer choice questions, such as, "Do you think Tony's example or Kaitlyn's example is better? How does her story relate to our discussion?"

> Calling on every student during a discussion validates everyone's experiences as well as keeping everyone involved.

The difficulty with whole-class discussion is that it is all verbal interchange, and those students with something else on their minds or those who have auditory deficits may still miss the connections. The following activities offer greater opportunity for student participation.

KWL is a three-part activity in which students describe what they already know about a subject, what they want to know, and then what they learned. It is perfect for nonfiction material, but it can also be used for unfamiliar concepts or settings in fiction. Its best use seems to be in small groups, in which plenty of discussion and interchange can occur, ensuring more active participation. See Chapter 12 for a full description.

Used prior to reading, an **anticipation guide** alerts students to the issues or facts in an upcoming reading selection. It consists of a list of statements with which the reader agrees or disagrees. The statements are usually written in an ambiguous fashion or in a true-or-false format. They are meant to encourage discussion, not to function as a pretest. Each student responds to the statements independently and then works with a group to develop consensus answers if possible. Selected issues can be discussed with the whole class, or a poll can be taken to ascertain opinions. "Children who are orphaned are best left in the care of a family member" could be an anticipation guide statement for an upcoming selection about a child who becomes the responsibility of an uncaring relative.

Unknown Vocabulary Words

It is a great aid to comprehension to understand vocabulary such as *disdainfully*, but if the word can be skipped over without affecting comprehension of the story, then it is not a critical word for preteaching. The greater the importance of a word to understanding the story, the more it needs to be explained and connected prior to reading. Without understanding the concept of a juvenile work camp in *Holes* (Sachar, 1998), the reader might not understand where Stanley is. Chapter 9 gives many ideas for teaching vocabulary, including the strategy of using context clues.

Visualizing, or Mental Imagery

Unfamiliar settings and times can be imagined easily when the teacher provides pictures before reading. When reading about a story set in Japan, when trying to imagine Kublai Khan's court, or when reading about rural Mississippi in the 1930s, it helps readers to have a picture in their head so they can see the characters moving through the setting rather than on an empty stage or in a setting that looks more like the readers' own neighborhood. Pictures and maps provide the framework for visualizing the text. These pictures are not always easy to find, but they are well worth the search. An excellent source is the American Memory Web site (http://memory.loc.gov/ammem). This is a collection of more than nine million items from the collections of the Library of Congress and other institutions.

Visualizing increases memory for the text that was imagined and improves the reader's detection of text inconsistencies (Trabasso & Bouchard, 2002). Visual images seem to last longer than verbal ones. Do you better remember people's names or their faces?

Although the teacher may initially supply pictures, students need to continue envisioning the characters and actions, adding new details as the story progresses. To help students make visualization a strategy, the teacher can explain how it aids memory, can model it, and can prompt students to imagine and share the images they see. Their images will be unique because they are drawn from personal experiences.

Discussion provides mental rehearsal and helps students remember an image for an extended period of time (Sousa, 2005). The following example is a response by a sixth grader to "Which scene in the chapter could you visualize the best?" Notice how the writer added homes that look more like his own than like the homes of ancient Greece, but there is also no doubt that the student could imagine Ulysses' longing to reach home as he saw the distant, familiar sights.

> In Keeper of the Winds, I could visualize Ulysses and his crew almost reaching their hometown. I saw Ulysses' castle on the top of the mountain. I also saw the large red brick houses with the smoke coming out. Along with that I saw people walking on the dirt road. You could see the port with ships lined all around and the mates were working hard on them. In the distance you could see people farming their land.

Drawing scenes also helps students deepen the images because the students return to the text to get the details they want to include. A single scene can be drawn, or a series of scenes can be depicted, which helps to firm up the sequence of events.

COMPREHENSION SKILLS AND ■ STRATEGIES DURING READING

Guided reading allows for strategy instruction and constant interchange among teacher and students, but what about providing scaffolding or support during silent reading? Independent reading is perhaps the most difficult time to try to scaffold (provide support for) reading strategies because the entire complex process is happening silently and without many outward signs. Following are ideas for aiding comprehension during both guided and independent reading.

Predicting and Confirming or Rejecting the Prediction

Predicting is about connecting: connecting a text to prior personal knowledge or to other texts that have been read and also about connecting information within the text. The research on predicting has its roots in the 1980s, with schema theory (Anderson & Pearson, 1984). Predicting is never wild guessing, for it must be probable, not just possible. Because it must be probable, teachers must explicitly teach students what the process is and how to find clues within the text that support a prediction (Almasi, 2003).

Predicting functions at two levels: predicting the next word or phrase in a sentence and predicting the next event in a story. Predicting at the sentence level helps confirm word recognition; for example, Alejandro had smooth black hair reaching to his _____. The reader who is monitoring can predict ears, shoulders, collar, waist, or any noun that could act as a marker for hair length. Successful prediction requires being aware of the meaning (semantic cues) and of regular English sentence patterns (syntactic cues). As the first letter comes into view, *Alejandro had smooth black hair reaching to his s_____,* the reader also adds graphophonemic cues and within a microsecond confirms *shoulders*.

Predicting at the story level has long been used to stimulate readers' interest before they start a story. During reading, students who predict are more likely to monitor their own comprehension because they wonder if their prediction is going to be the choice made by the author. Some predicting is more like self-questioning; for example: "I wonder why he did that? That seems strange. I bet he doesn't have any friends." Various studies have demonstrated that when students predicted what a character might do based on their own experiences, they showed superior comprehension of that story and future stories.

Interestingly, predicting is more powerful if the predictions are explicitly compared with the text during reading (Duke & Pearson, 2002). Prediction works far better in narratives. Introductions can sometimes give clues to upcoming topics in expository text, but there is often no predictable order in which subtopics will be discussed.

One method for practicing prediction is to reproduce a story and cut it into sections, distributing only one section at a time. Another method is to reproduce a story on an overhead transparency or a projected computer image and show only one section at a time.

A prediction tree can be used for responses (Figure 8.1). After reading a section, a student or a small group must make a prediction and provide the clues from the text that make the prediction probable. Requiring students to write it down ensures that everyone will actually predict and encourages more active participation. The probability of the prediction can be discussed, as well as the clues used to draw that conclusion, and these discussions will act as a model for those students still making off-the-wall predictions that have no basis.

Story Chains use both predicting and vocabulary introduction. The teacher selects words from the story (phrases are even better) in the order that they appear. The students predict a story, using the words in the same order. Schemas are activated, new terms are used in context, and perhaps the actual plot is revealed.

Monitoring Comprehension and Thinking Aloud

Good readers monitor as they read, recognizing when they understand and when they do not. Monitoring comprehension is one type of metacognition (thinking about our own thinking). Good readers also notice when the text is internally inconsistent, as in the following paragraph.

Fish must have light in order to see. There is absolutely no light at the bottom of the ocean. It is pitch black down there. When it is that dark the fish cannot see anything. They cannot even see colors. Some fish that live at the bottom of the ocean can see the color of their food; that is how they know what to eat. (E. M. Markman, cited in Baker & Brown, 2002, p. 361)

Figure 8.1 Prediction tree

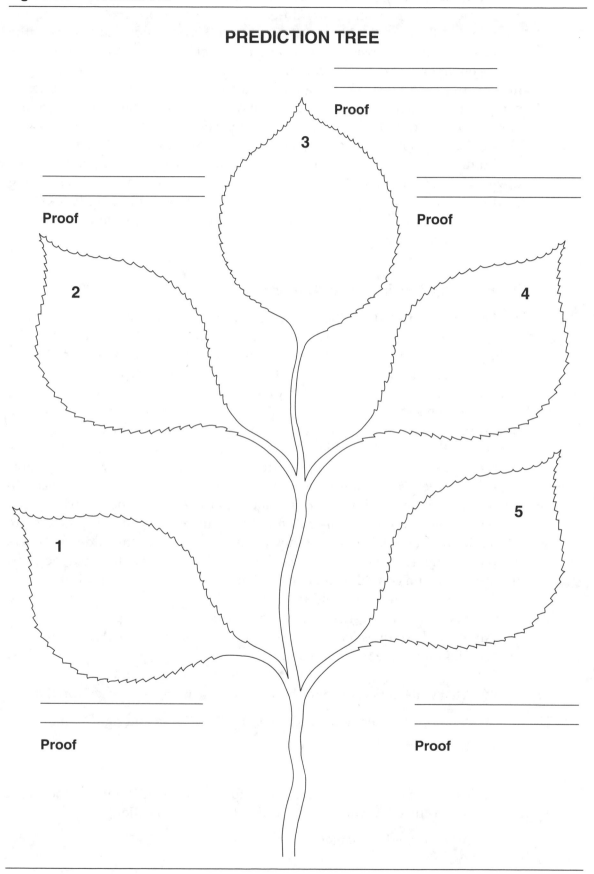

PREDICTION TREE

Thinking aloud (see Chapter 6) is a metacognitive strategy that can be used as the prelude to teaching many different comprehension strategies. Teachers model what they are thinking while reading a passage and how to handle the "clunks" in comprehension. It will certainly be enlightening to some students that even an expert reader gets stumped or confused and has to find a way to make sense of the text. Thinking aloud has been shown to improve students' comprehension when the students read and also when teachers routinely think aloud while reading to students (Duke & Pearson, 2002). When students think aloud, their thinking and strategy use are more visible to the teacher.

Thinking aloud and the following techniques for monitoring help to slow down students and make thinking while reading a habit. Those pauses during reading are a hallmark of capable readers. When those "thinking breaks" are included, students comprehend better and are better able to summarize information (Silven & Vauras, 1992).

Monitoring During Independent Reading

During silent reading, the teacher can provide a virtual teacher, that is, a study guide, a set of questions, or specific times to stop and think. These can be thought of as written prompts or reminders, similar to questions or directions a teacher might provide during guided reading, so that students can never read too long without checking their comprehension.

For students who read just to get to the end, the teacher can place **embedded questions** in the middle of the text, rather than at the end of the passage, to encourage the students to stop and monitor comprehension. The advantage is that the questions are "asked" just after children have read a relatively short passage. If they cannot respond to a question, they immediately go back to what they just read and find or formulate the answer. Since there is no room to actually write questions in a text, numbers similar to footnote numbers are placed in the students' books. To show students where the embedded numbers are placed, the teacher can reproduce the text on an overhead transparency, and the students then copy the numbers into their own texts where indicated. Or a teacher with infinite time could insert the numbers into all the students' texts. The numbers match questions written on a separate piece of paper.

An example of questions for a section of Sharon Creech's *Walk Two Moons* (1994) might look like the following:

1. What will happen when the branch Sal is swinging on breaks? (prediction)

2. What did happen to Sal and to her mother? Were you right? (confirm or reject prediction)

3. How do you see the scene in the hospital corridor? (visualize)

4. What do you think Sal is feeling? How would you feel if this sad event had occurred in your family? (inference and connection)

5. Summarize this chapter.

If students are more independent, the teacher can simply use questions and directions that are more generic.

1. Make a prediction.

2. Was your prediction right?

3. Visualize the scene.

4. How would you feel?

5. Summarize.

Teach students who are more likely to spot the answers without paragraph-specific prompting to use **stop-and-go questions**. A student stops to read a question and then "goes" until the answer is found or a clue for a response is encountered. When students are aware of the purpose, they find themselves reading with a reason rather than just aimlessly wandering through the text. And reading with a reason aids comprehension considerably.

> Reading with a reason aids comprehension considerably.

The questions should be in the same order as the text and should not have page numbers. Providing page numbers encourages students to scan or skip pages on which no answers are to be found. A child who reads several pages without finding the answer has to use a fix-up strategy such as rereading or reconsidering (discussed below).

When I have asked students whether they prefer using the stop-and-go style or reading straight through and answering questions at the end, the response is always split about 50–50. However, the weakest readers almost always prefer the stop-and-go style because it nudges them to continually monitor what they are reading. They know they will get all the important parts and be ready to participate in a classroom discussion.

The teacher can also use all the formats simultaneously, distributing the complete questions to students who need greater prompting and giving the more independent version to students who are able to read with less prompting. The students might not even notice there are different versions.

As students come to need less guidance to identify strategies they should be using during silent reading, they can determine their own responses. **Say Something** and **Write Something** make excellent bridges. Say Something is done with partner reading. As students finish an entire page, each partner must turn to the other and say something. Write Something requires students to write a single sentence after reading each page and is done independently. The bottom of the page may not be the most desirable stopping spot, but it is logistically manageable for everyone. This technique also serves to help students monitor their comprehension so that they do not get too far before realizing that they have not understood.

At first, the "somethings" are summaries of the plot. The more practice students have in reacting to text rather than just summarizing, the more they will respond with a question, a reaction, or an interpretation. This example is from *Roll of Thunder, Hear My Cry* (Taylor, 1977):

> p. 42. It was raining hard and the kids had to walk to school.
>
> p. 43. I would have been mad when that bus came by and I got all soaked in the gully.
>
> p. 44. I wonder why Little Man is so fussy about his clothes.
>
> p. 45. Big Ma tries to comfort Little Man.

Good readers will have relatively complex responses, but less-mature readers will at least have the literal plot and will be able to fully participate in a guided discussion with higher level questioning. Write something provides an excellent assessment of comprehension and is easily checked by the teacher. As an added benefit, it makes a good foundation for learning to write a summary.

The teacher can extend this activity by having children compare and evaluate their summaries. Children's work is often more interesting than teacher modeling, and students can explicitly explain and demonstrate how they came to their answers.

Students who are used to monitoring their comprehension can simply place a check (I understand), exclamation mark (this is important), or question mark (I don't understand) at the end of each paragraph or page. These will act as reminders of important parts or difficult parts when the class reconvenes to discuss the text.

More-independent readers can choose what information they write and can respond with **reading logs**, the most open-ended type of response to reading. Teachers can encourage higher level responses by replying to the logs with higher level responses or by asking students to use starter stems, such as "The most interesting part was . . . ," "This reminds me of another story where . . . ," "The scene that I see most vividly in my mind is . . . ," or "The main character must have been feeling . . . because. . . ."

Generating Questions

Both answering and generating questions enhance comprehension. Learning to generate questions benefits comprehension in terms of improved memory, accuracy in answering questions, and better integration and identification of main ideas (Trabasso & Bouchard, 2002). See Chapter 6 for a more thorough discussion.

Using Fix-Up Strategies

Read the following paragraph aloud as an experiment:

The Boat

A man was building a boat in his cellar. As soon as he

had finished the boot, he tried to take it through the

the cellar door. It would not go though the door. So he

had to take it a part. He should of planed better (Schwartz, 1997, p. 41).

Did you notice the conflicting word and meaning cues in the passage? Did you detect *boot* for *boat,* the double *the, though* for *through, a part* for *apart, should of* for *should've,* and *planed* for *planned?* You probably unconsciously fixed the errors as you read for meaning.

Good readers who are monitoring their comprehension use fix-up strategies, or compensatory strategies, when the text does not make sense. This is usually because the reader has miscued rather than because the text contained errors, as in the preceding passage. Corrective action may mean rereading a section; skipping the part or word that is unclear, hoping that future information will clarify the problem; or just rethinking. Good readers go back and read more carefully, consider everything they know about the topic or root words, look at the pictures, get help from another source, or ask someone. These behaviors can be seen easily when a reader self-corrects during oral reading.

Poor readers are not aware that the text is not making sense, or they believe they comprehend when they do not. When they realize they have a problem, they are unsure what action to take. Often they just keep going. Being questioned frequently, through guided reading or the virtual teacher, can help poor readers realize they did not understand. Explicit teaching of fix-up strategies is necessary for these students. The teacher can help students learn to apply fix-up strategies by questioning rather than correcting, as shown in the following example:

Student: One of the chefs hailed the other captains.

Teacher: Was he calling them for dinner in the middle of the battle?

Student: (Puzzled, then rereads.) One of the chiefs hailed the other captains.

For those students who want to jump in and correct their classmates, the teacher can ask them to offer a problem-solving clue instead. R. M. Schwartz (1997, p. 47) suggests posting the following list in the classroom to remind students that the ultimate task is to obtain meaning, not get every word correct the first time: Readers know that

1. Good readers think about meaning.

2. All readers make mistakes.

3. Good readers notice and fix some mistakes.

A **cloze exercise** is an excellent way to practice fix-up strategies using semantic and syntactic cues. Cloze passages (from the word *closure*) omit every eighth word and substitute a blank. The entire first and last sentences are left intact, and any answer that makes sense is acceptable. It is a good exercise for partners because of the social interaction as they discuss choices and help each other notice when a word does or does not fit with the meaning, with the syntax of the sentence, or with the previous paragraph.

When preparing a cloze exercise, do not provide a word bank at the bottom of the page except with very young readers because a word bank will prevent students from using several fix-up strategies and will reinforce the idea of "one correct answer."

■ COMPREHENSION STRATEGIES FOR AFTER READING

Most strategies can be taught or practiced before, during, or after reading a selection, but some seem best after reading, as students go back and analyze in greater depth what they have read.

Using Story and Text Structure

Understanding the elements in a story and the organizational pattern in expository text helps students comprehend the structure. The research results are not strong, indicating that teaching structure works best for the text in which the instruction occurred. Nevertheless, identifying structure does help students notice all the elements.

Story mapping, or story grammar, asks students to identify the elements of the story. It can be taught with modeling, guided practice, and independent practice with a series of stories. It looks like an outline, as shown in Figure 8.2. David Sousa (2005) recommends using the story map with English language learners as a foundation for retelling. The most useful function of story maps may be to help students develop adequate summaries (Allington, 2001).

A story map can also take the form of pictures of the major events of the story, connected by arrows, as in a flow chart. Pictures can also be arranged in a tic-tac-toe grid, with the first line for the beginning of the story, the middle

Figure 8.2   Story map

STORY MAP
Title: _____
Setting: _____
Characters: _____
Problem: _____
Event 1: _____
Event 2: _____
Event 3: _____
Resolution: _____

line for the middle, and the bottom line for the ending. As children visualize the scenes, they also unscramble the sequence and determine cause and effect.

Good readers use **text structures** or notice relationships such as cause and effect or comparison and contrast. These structures help the reader relate ideas to each other in ways that make them more understandable and memorable (Duke & Pearson, 2002).

The Venn diagram (see Figure 11.6 in Chapter 11 for an example) can be used for **comparing and contrasting**. Students use it to see the similarities and differences between characters, settings, and even stories. It is a set of overlapping circles, with the similarities listed in the overlap.

Analyzing **cause and effect** is a more difficult task than sequencing or comparing and contrasting because it often involves inference. Younger students who are not accustomed to thinking in this pattern may simply list adjoining events, whether they have any relationship to each other or not. Once you have explicitly taught what is meant by cause and effect relationships, try a two-column worksheet that lists causes in one column and effects in the other. Leave one side of each pair blank so that the student fills in sometimes the cause and sometimes the effect. This arrangement fulfills the same function as written questions but draws students' attention to the cause and effect relationship. The key word in cause and effect is *why*. Children in Grades 4–8 made impressive gains when taught to ask and answer *why* questions because *why* questions seemed to make the facts of a dense text become more comprehensible and memorable (Pressley & Wharton-McDonald, 2002).

Summarizing

Summarizing is a difficult task that asks readers to sort the important from the unimportant and reorganize it in a new, paraphrased form. Research suggests that instruction and practice in summarizing improve not only summarization but also the overall comprehension of content (Duke & Pearson, 2002). An interesting finding that applies to summarization and all the comprehension strategies is that when students have metacognitive knowledge—that is, they consciously know that summarizing will help them retain more of what they read—they then know how to proceed with future texts and are more likely to use the strategy. Teachers always tell students what to do and usually how to do it, but I think that as a profession, we consistently fail to explain why what we teach is important.

> Research suggests that instruction and practice in summarizing improve not only summarization but also the overall comprehension of content.

Young readers start by retelling the story, which improves comprehension, sense of story structure, and oral language. James Baumann, Helene Hooten, and Patricia White (1996) suggest using a retelling instructional chart, illustrated in Figure 8.3.

The next step is to state the main idea. This is more difficult than retelling because it requires combining, evaluating, and sometimes inferring. Poor readers have a difficult time relating everything and deciding what the main idea is. They can tell you several of the details but not combine them into a

Figure 8.3   Retelling instructional chart

RETELLING INSTRUCTIONAL CHART

To RETELL part of a story, try . . .

Putting the story into your own words.

Saying the ideas in the order they happened in the story.

Including all the most important events and ideas.

Using the book to help you remember events or ideas.

---

meaningful whole. To help them connect the bits of information into a main-idea sentence, try this summary format:

Summary Format: Somebody? Wanted? But? So? (Beers, 2003)

Example: Goldilocks wanted to see what was in the house, but the bears returned and frightened her so she ran away.

The write something technique can also provide good practice for identifying main ideas, especially when the "something" is a one-sentence summary less than one written line in length. To make ideas this short, students must paraphrase, which is another way to manipulate information and improve recall. Whole-class processing and evaluation of the "somethings" help students understand why one piece of information or one event may be more critical than others. Retelling and summarizing the events of a story are important methods of assessing comprehension.

■ STRATEGIES FOR HIGHER LEVEL THINKING: INFERRING, GENERALIZING, EVALUATING

Mature readers go beyond the printed lines; they infer, generalize, and evaluate. These abilities often depend on the reader's schemata and general knowledge. Younger children may not have developed the capacities for these skills fully, or they simply may not have accumulated enough background knowledge to bring into play when attempting to use higher order thinking. Both explicit teaching and background building help with higher order skills.

Inferring

To infer, readers must combine what is in the text with their own knowledge to answer questions such as, How do you think Maya felt when . . . ? Good readers use their prior knowledge to fill in the gaps an author has left out. Students need to be explicitly taught what an inference is and that readers are supposed to make inferences while reading. Young readers assume that everything that needs to be known has been said by the author, and in order to answer the teacher's questions, they need only look back to find the relevant section in the text. It comes as a revelation that authors expect readers to infer.

Gunning (2005) suggests the following model:

1. Explain the skill.

2. Model.

3. Share the task by asking and answering inference questions, with the students supplying the clues used for the inference from the text or prior knowledge.

4. Ask an inference question, and after the students supply the inference, point out the support.

5. Ask an inference question and have students give the inference and the support.

Students who do not think beyond the concrete level benefit greatly from hearing how other students used their own knowledge—knowledge the concrete thinker may also possess—to put together two or more pieces of information to form an inference.

Character motivation is an area that requires making inferences because authors often choose to show motivation through action rather than through direct explanation. When teachers ask, "Why did the character do that?" students may appear stymied until the teacher asks, "If you were in that situation, what would you do?" Tim Shanahan's Character Perspective Chart (Shanahan & Shanahan, 1997), shown in Figure 8.4, helps make inferring from another point of view more structured and visible. This chart is used to retell important aspects of the story from two different points of view.

Generalizing and Evaluating

Good readers also generalize and evaluate. A whole flock of skills, including distinguishing fact and opinion, detecting bias, understanding connotations, and identifying the author's purpose fall here. The research is relatively silent on this aspect of reading (Rosenshine & Stevens, 2002). Learning to critically evaluate and judge by using standards, logic, and analysis are goals shared by the content areas as well as reading instruction. It is a difficult area to assess, but logical thinking can never start too early. The decision-making chart is a graphic organizer that makes critical thinking visible. Not only must differing points of view be identified, but students must also make a personal choice and identify the best reason for their decision. In Figure 8.5, the student must decide whether Ulysses should stay with Calypso or continue his journey home.

Figure 8.4 Character perspective chart

CHARACTER PERSPECTIVE CHART	
The Big Orange Splot, by Daniel Pinkwater	
Main character: Who is the main character? Mr. Plumbean	Main character: Who is the main character? Mr. Plumbean's Neighbor
Setting: Where and when does the story take place? Plumbean's Neighborhood	Setting: Where and when does the story take place? Plumbean's Neighborhood
Problem: What is the main character's problem? Plumbean's neighbors pester him	Problem: What is the main character's problem? Bird drops paint on Plumbean's house
Goal: What is the main character's goal? What does the character want? To decorate his house and get neighbors to leave him alone	Goal: What is the main character's goal? What does the character want? To make neighborhood all the same again
Attempt: What does the main character do to solve the problem or get the goal? Decorates house and talks to each neighbor	Attempt: What does the main character do to solve the problem or get the goal? Try to convince him to change then each changes to be like him
Outcome: What does the main character do to solve the problem or get the goal? Plumbean's house looks like his dreams and neighbors accept it	Outcome: What does the main character do to solve the problem or get the goal? All houses in neighborhood are decorated in same way
Reaction: How does the main character feel about the outcome? Happy	Reaction: How does the main character feel about the outcome? Happy
Theme: What point did the author want to make? Follow your dreams	Theme: What point did the author want to make? It is important to be the same

Source: Shanahan, T., and Shanahan, S., "Character Perspective Charting: Helping Children to Develop a More Complete Conception of Story." *The Reading Teacher*, 50(8), 668–677, May 1997. Reprinted with permission of Timothy Shanahan and the International Reading Association. All rights reserved.

Figure 8.5 Graphic organizer: Decision-making chart

DECISION-MAKING CHART: ULYSSES

Ulysses should stay with Calypso because . . .

Calypso

Should Ulysses Return Home?

Ulysses should return home because . . .

1. He would not grow old. (immortal)

2. At home he would live on memories.

3. He would be kicked out of his castle.

4. She'd make him her eternal consort.

5. His home will be wherever Titan's rule.

6. His other son would kill him.

1. He should see his son.

2. His wife is being faithful.

3. He could be turned into an animal by Calypso.

4. His things are being taken.

5. He has been gone for 20 years.

6. He has paid for blinding Polyphemous, Poseidon's son.

Your conclusion:

Return home.

Best reason:

His wife is being faithful to him.

Maggie

The Internet has added a new demand for critical reading and thinking skills. Evaluating sites can be difficult even for adults. Many texts are not carefully edited, some are hoaxes, and some are just weird. Students need to learn to read file extensions such as .gov and to locate source information about sites to determine credibility. Readers unknowingly follow links from the home page of a trusted source, naively thinking all the linked information is endorsed by the home page organization (Coiro, 2005). Evaluating a list of search-engine results is not yet on most reading scope and sequence charts, but it is a skill often needed and can result in considerable savings of time and effort. Coiro suggests Internet skills need to be taught for searching, navigating, evaluating, and synthesizing information. Synthesizing is especially important if teachers want students to produce research that is more than a cut-and-paste composite.

■ PUTTING IT ALL TOGETHER

Eventually, the reader orchestrates all the strategies for simultaneous use, and the teacher can help by using comprehension routines. Several techniques use groups of strategies as integrated routines, but research has found that these work better after students have a working competency with individual strategies. Reciprocal Reading (Palincsar & Brown, 1986) uses questioning, summarizing, clarifying, and predicting. Students Achieving Independent Learning (Pressley et al., 1994) uses predicting, visualizing, questioning, clarifying, making associations, and summarizing. These are good methods for moving the student from working with a single strategy to considering multiple strategies.

■ INFLUENCING THE ATTITUDE AND MOTIVATION OF READERS

Reading requires the skill and the will to read. It is a complex task that requires years of sustained attention and practice in order for one to become proficient, but for children who love to read, it is a pleasure every step of the way. Attitude and motivation contribute to the success or lack of success of the reader. Although attitudes cannot be taught, they can be influenced.

The most critical attitude or realization is knowing that reading is meaningful. This attitude is enhanced by observing expert modeling; by being encouraged to constantly seek meaning, both in guided and independent reading; and by discussion and social interaction about reading.

Successful students understand that they can learn by reading and will work hard to achieve a personal goal. They realize that school is not an isolated set of events unconnected to the outside world and that what they are learning about is of personal, real use. Teachers who connect the content that is read by the class to their students' daily events, experiences, and future lives can influence those students who seem to think the entire extent of their job is to fill in all the blanks on a worksheet.

Although the strongest motivation is intrinsic, a teacher can set up a climate that makes motivation likely to develop.

Interest

Choose the most interesting books and stories for instruction. "Research findings indicate that both good and poor readers perform significantly better on high interest as compared with low interest materials" (Asher, cited in Fink, 1998, p. 389). Great stories foster the love of reading, and many children first became hooked on reading when their teacher read aloud to them. Interest enhanced comprehension with fifth-grade readers, even with materials that were difficult (Renninger, cited in Wigfield and Guthrie, 1997). Rosalie Fink (1998) interviewed adult dyslexics who became very successful in their fields. They all became avid readers, usually between the ages of 10 and 12, because they became interested in a particular genre.

Long materials—books—are usually better than short materials because the flow of ideas is continuous and interest is already present at the start of each day's lesson. Background has been developed, so the concepts, settings, and characters are easy to understand. With a series of unrelated short stories, interest, schema, and concepts have to be rebuilt every day. This may be the best reason for not using a lot of worksheets; they are not interesting, and the class has to start from scratch each time. Duke and Pearson (2002) suggest that independent practice materials be as motivating as possible. High-interest texts, reading for real reasons, and opportunity for discussion all contribute to enthusiasm.

Choice

Another way to encourage interest is to allow students to have some choice about the materials they read. Students consider the most interesting books to be those they choose by themselves. Self-choice is one of the strongest components in literature circles, readers' workshops, and silent sustained reading. Biancarosa (2005) considers choice a powerful way to engage students and urges that independent reading time be built into the school day. School may be the only place where lower-income students can find a book of their choice, so classrooms need to be well supplied.

Success

Motivation is influenced by success. Allan Wigfield and John T. Guthrie (1997) found several factors of motivation that correlated with reading achievement. Several were related to success—a feeling of efficacy (positive self-evaluation of competence), challenge (satisfaction of mastering material), a desire for competition, and social recognition. Motivation and success enhance each other, but it is difficult to maintain motivation if a reader is not successful.

Students' self-concepts as readers are linked to reading achievement (Gambrell, 1996), so reading tasks need to be within the students' reach. Students should be taught at their instructional levels with scaffolded or supported instruction. A particularly good first question for struggling readers is, Tell me something about the story. Even struggling readers can answer successfully in front of the class or reading group, and the teacher is able to ascertain something about the strategies the student is using.

What about when failure occurs, as it inevitably does when one is learning a new skill? Pressley (2006, p. 443) recommends three messages for every classroom:

1. Trying hard fosters achievement and intelligence.

2. Failure is a natural part of learning.

3. School is more about getting better than being best.

Since some students attribute success to luck or ability, it is important to show the connection between effort and success.

Providing Time

Many children really do like reading, and they are willing to spend time and effort to learn to read. However, they are not willing to give up basketball, phone calls, video games, friends, and Internet chat rooms. Family scheduling conflicts or just plain family conflicts also make it difficult for many students to read at home. The teacher who schedules uninterrupted, extended periods of reading in school gives students opportunities that they may not be able to arrange for themselves.

Social Opportunity to Discuss Books

Reading is an individual and isolated activity, and this is one of the reasons it is so unappealing to many children. If given an opportunity to talk about texts they are reading, students become motivated (Wigfield & Guthrie, 1997), and comprehension improves. Literature circles and classroom discussions (as opposed to recitations) present this opportunity. Outside of school, we do not quiz each other on what we have read. We offer responses, reactions, and evaluations of the ideas and information offered (Allington, 2001), so it makes sense to structure discussions along the same lines in school, especially if we want children to be engaged in the discussion.

Cooperative learning and reciprocal reading are both powerful techniques that are collaborative and social. Biancarosa (2005) cites several research studies of cooperative learning that improved reading comprehension and achievement across the content areas for students in the upper elementary grades through high school as well as for English language learners and students with learning disabilities in inclusive settings.

The teacher's enthusiasm when sharing thoughts about the class text or personal reading can be infectious. Providing motivating situations and interesting content and tasks may be the most challenging and important responsibilities of any teacher.

The Teacher

The teacher really does make a difference, more than the materials used and more than the philosophy adopted. The classes of teachers who are businesslike and have a high task orientation show significant correlations with achievement (Rosenshine & Stevens, 2002). Teachers who understand the complexity of the reading process, teach strategies, and foster a love of reading will make a difference in the success of their students.

9

Vocabulary Instruction

Words are the soul's ambassadors, who go
Abroad upon her errands to and fro.

—J. Howell, "Of Words"

Substantial knowledge of vocabulary provides many benefits to the speaker, listener, reader, and writer. It is the single most powerful predictor of how well a reader understands text, with a correlation factor of .71 (Thorndike, cited in May, 1998). This figure means that seven of every ten good readers also have good vocabularies.

Thus it might seem reasonable to teach list after list of vocabulary words in order to improve reading comprehension. However, it is a correlation, not a cause. Both vocabulary and reading comprehension depend on verbal abilities, yet readers can miss the whole point of a passage if they do not understand key vocabulary, and they certainly can miss the nuances if they do not understand certain words. Vocabulary is important.

Reading and vocabulary study provide mutual benefits. Wide reading increases vocabulary, and vocabulary knowledge increases reading comprehension. Linking vocabulary with reading is a strong strategy because new words are encountered in meaningful context and responses to reading provide many opportunities for working with those words. The National Reading Panel report (2000) supports the idea that a large portion of vocabulary words should come from content learning materials.

> Linking vocabulary with reading is a strong strategy because new words are encountered in meaningful context.

The idea of teaching vocabulary for its own sake, outside of any context, does not match anything that is known about long-term learning and worthwhile use of class time. "To separate word knowledge from reading . . . is in essence weakening a natural bond" (Laflamme, 1997), meaning that vocabulary is one of the parts in the whole-part-whole model of balanced reading, and to teach or learn isolated vocabulary words violates the entire idea. Teacher direct instruction, opportunities for students to practice and apply their word knowledge, and wide reading in both fiction and nonfiction constitute balanced vocabulary instruction (Rupley, Logan, & Nichols, 1999). Out-of-context learning of vocabulary seems best suited for calendars featuring a word of the day.

In this chapter, the word *vocabulary* will refer to reading vocabulary, or the meanings of words in print that are not in the student's oral vocabulary. Identifying known words in print should be thought of as word recognition. This chapter will focus on how definitions and new-word usage are learned, how vocabulary is learned from reading, and how vocabulary can be learned for reading.

■ VOCABULARY DEVELOPMENT

Having a substantial oral meaning vocabulary provides a solid foundation for reading. To reduce the complexity of learning to read, early literacy texts are generally written so that the words encountered are part of students' oral meaning vocabulary. They just have to be decoded, not learned. Second language learners, students with limited oral vocabularies, and students with limited background knowledge do not have this advantage, so they especially will benefit from vocabulary development.

Jeanne Chall (cited in Irvin, 1990) estimated that typical first graders understand and use about 6,000 different words. An average child will learn an additional 3,000–4,000 words per year, according to various research studies, but only about 400 are formally taught in school. How are the remainder learned? Some come from direct experience. Students who play sports learn *dribble, offensive, bunt,* and *clutch.* Some words are discovered by watching television. Every child in the United States is familiar with the word *morph* from watching cartoons and one day may even learn *metamorphosis.* Also, many new words come from daily conversation: "Billy, you're just *exasperating!*"

However, most vocabulary is learned through reading. Almost without exception, people who read widely have large vocabularies. The use of multiple modalities provides one of the advantages of learning words from reading: The word is seen, it is read in meaningful context, and it is heard (because most readers mentally pronounce new words to decide if the words are already in their meaning vocabulary). William Nagy (1988) provides fascinating statistics about vocabulary acquisition. Readers learn only about one word in 20 through context, but an average fifth grader who reads for about 25 minutes a day will encounter 20,000 unfamiliar words a year. That accounts for 1,000 new words learned each year through reading. By the end of elementary school, an average student knows about 25,000 words, and 50,000 by the end of high school (Graves & Watts-Taffe, 2002).

■ DEPTH OF WORD KNOWLEDGE

There are several levels of word knowledge. There are words we have never seen or heard before, words we remember having seen or heard but whose meaning we are unsure of, words we have a general idea about, words we are fairly sure about, and words we know well and can use correctly. It is only through many exposures in varying contexts that we thoroughly learn words. Between 10 and 24 exposures may be required before we gain comprehensive knowledge of a word.

Encountering words in a variety of contexts helps us learn connotative meanings or multiple meanings of words; for example, run fast, a run in my stocking, the blood ran through his veins, home run, run away, run to the store, my horse ran last, the car ran over the nail, the car ran out of gas, the rain ran down the window, the colors ran into each other, run a red light, ran late, ran low, the running board on the Dodge, run the blockade, run for election, ran me ragged, rum runner, ran into difficulties, and so on. The more one encounters a word, the greater the depth of understanding.

> Between 10 and 24 exposures may be required before we gain comprehensive knowledge of a word.

Which Words Are Learned Most Easily?

Warwick Elley (1996) found that the words learned most easily were those that were repeated often, accompanied by illustrations, or accompanied by meaning clues. Words that were connected to a plot, that were vivid, or that were associated with a familiar concept were also learned easily. For example, the posttest scores from Elley's studies showed a 40% learning gain for *parasol*, but little gain in learning was shown for *anguish*.

One reason *parasol* was learned easily is that it is a synonym for the more common word *umbrella*. Synonyms are easy to learn because the concept is already known. Words that are already known but that have different and new meanings, such as *acute* in *acute angle* and *acute pain*, are more difficult. Concept words, such as *integrity*, *epidemic*, or *glorify*, either do not have single-word synonyms or require readers to have background knowledge to understand them, and they are thus more difficult to learn. Some words are used only in certain contexts. *Balmy* means warm, but please don't put your chicken in the microwave to make it a little *balmier*. Some words require much explanation, repetition, and usage in varied contexts.

IS IT WORTHWHILE TO TEACH VOCABULARY? ■

If so much vocabulary is learned through wide reading, is it worthwhile to teach vocabulary at all? Yes, it is worthwhile, especially since reluctant readers are the ones least likely to be reading independently. It is worthwhile because students study literature and content areas and encounter words that are critical to comprehending the text. Meaning vocabulary used to be considered the domain of the intermediate and upper grades, but with the introduction of trade books in primary grades, reading vocabulary is no longer as tightly controlled. Words outside students' speaking vocabulary are now encountered more frequently in the lower grades, and English language learners are in every grade. Being taught those crucial words helps students understand the text.

■ INDIRECT TEACHING OF VOCABULARY

Indirect teaching of vocabulary is elusive to define or measure. For example, primary students learn many new words when their teacher reads aloud to them (Robbins & Ehri, cited in the National Reading Panel report, 2000). They also learn new vocabulary as they discuss the story events. The effect of indirect teaching of vocabulary is not as deep as the effect of direct teaching, but it is still significant.

The studies by Elley (1996) illustrate the differences between direct and indirect teaching. A short story was read aloud to seven-year-olds. The story took about ten minutes to read, contained 20 unfamiliar words, and was read three times over a period of seven days. There was some discussion of the story, but no explanation of the unfamiliar vocabulary was provided. Nonetheless, classroom gains from pretest to posttest scores for vocabulary ranged from 13% to 21% and averaged about 15%. When the scores were analyzed by the children's ability levels, the top 75% averaged a 15% gain while the lowest-ability children averaged about a 23% gain.

The study was repeated with eight-year-olds but with a twist. In this study, half the students listened to a book read aloud three times. The other half also heard the story, but the teacher stopped to explain unfamiliar words. Students who participated in the indirect lesson again averaged a 15% gain, but those who heard explanations of the unfamiliar words gained 40% on the posttest.

Frank May (1998) presents an interesting study by Edward Maher that deals with vocabulary gain and various study methods, such as reading aloud to older students (fifth graders). For each group, vocabulary words were listed on the board before a selection was read. The control group looked up the words in the dictionary and read the selection silently. The experimental group had the story read to them by the teacher. As the vocabulary words were encountered in reading, the teacher asked if any of the students knew the word. If they did not, she simply told them the meaning, reread the sentence, and continued. Brief pretests and posttests were administered. On the posttest, the control group retained less than 50% of the words, but the experimental group retained more than 90%.

Many words are learned through guided reading and discussion rather than through formal teaching. Very often the teacher just mentions a detail: "The *fronds* are the leaves on a palm tree." Or a student gives a vocabulary clue or a definition in a response: "The monster took so long to surface because he had to *depressurize*. If he came up too soon, he would have burst."

■ CHOOSING WORDS FOR DIRECT TEACHING

There are several guidelines for choosing which vocabulary words to teach. May (1998) suggests choosing only two or three words from the day's reading and teaching those words in depth. He considers that teaching a few words well is far superior to superficially teaching many words, most of which will not be remembered.

Lack of Clues by the Author

If a word in the book being read by the class is critical but the author gives few or no clues to its meaning, teach the word. If the author has provided direct explanations or sufficient context clues or if the words can be skipped without affecting the meaning of the story, then there is little reason for the teacher to provide instruction.

Words Important in General Usage

Some words may not be critical to the story but will be encountered over and over again in general usage. These words are worthwhile choices for instruction.

Concept Words

Words that represent new concepts need to be taught. Concept words need considerable explanation and a whole background of connected ideas and examples, not just a definition. *Accomplice* is not synonymous with *friend* or *helper.* It does not seem to have a single-word synonym. In the content areas, new concepts abound, such as *superconductor* or "changing to a democratic form of leadership." Several related vocabulary words can be grouped around a concept for efficiency and for the natural connections that occur.

Words Used Inappropriately

On-the-spot minilessons can be used to clear up confusion caused by words used inappropriately, as in the following examples: The *pheasants* lived on feudal lands under the rule of the lord of the *manner*; the sail was tied to the mast with ox hide *tongs*; it was *funner* to work in groups than to work alone.

Words Critical to the Story Line

Camille Blachowicz and Peter Fisher (1996) offer useful suggestions for choosing vocabulary. For an upcoming story, map the story line, choosing vocabulary words that are critical to the story elements. This vocabulary should be used multiple times in discussing, explaining, summarizing, and responding to the story. Figure 9.1 is an example of a vocabulary story map at the high school level.

The Possible Big Ideas section includes words that may not be in the story but are needed for effective discussion. These are exactly the kind of words that students often lack, such as words describing character traits or precise concepts and description (*haughtiness* and *destitute*). Without those words, a summary usually reads pretty much like this:

> Mathilde felt sad because she was sort of poor. To cheer her up, her husband got an invitation to a fancy dance, which made her happy. She bought a dress that cost a lot and borrowed a diamond necklace from a friend. She was sad when she lost it. They worked for ten years to pay for a new necklace. After they finished paying for it, she found out the necklace was fake, which made her mad.

The story map could be shared with the students prior to reading or used by the teacher to select vocabulary that is integral to understanding, discussing, and writing about the story. Certainly in "The Necklace," the teacher would omit the word *paste* in prereading vocabulary so as to avoid giving away the story.

Figure 9.1   Story map for "The Necklace," by Guy de Maupassant

---

VOCABULARY STORY MAP: "THE NECKLACE"

Characters

Mathilde, who believes there is nothing more **humiliating** than to look poor among women who are rich.

M. Loisel, who gives his wife 400 **francs** for a ball gown.

She suffered **ceaselessly** from the ugliness of her curtains.

Setting

The **vestibule** of the palace

The **ministerial** ball

A rented **garret**

Problem

Mathilde loses a borrowed diamond necklace and is sick with **chagrin** and **anguish**.

M. Loisel borrows money and accepts **ruinous obligations**.

They are **impoverished** by the debt.

Resolution

M. and Mme. pay the accumulation of debt and interest for ten years.

After the debt is paid, Mathilde sees the friend from whom she borrowed the necklace and finds out it was only **paste**.

Possible Big Ideas

Putting on airs, **humiliation**, egotism, arrogance, conceit, vanity, **disdain**, haughtiness, destitute, indigent, irony, false pride, image, deprivation, poverty, **calamity**, **compromised**, **luxuries**

■ PREREADING ACTIVITIES FOR TEACHING VOCABULARY DIRECTLY

An analysis of vocabulary research indicates the most successful methods use richness of context, active engagement, a large number of exposures, and a variety of responses and techniques, including group activities (Kamil, 2004).

There are not many strategies for initial teaching of vocabulary. The most direct method is to tell the meaning to the students. The real work is making connections and using the word enough times so that it will be integrated into a student's schema or prior experiences and accessible and memorable. If a word is used in multiple contexts with several examples of appropriate usage, one of them usually makes a connection with the student and broadens the student's ideas about how the word is used. Active engagement and multiple exposures can be provided through reading, discussion, visualization, and writing as students manipulate the words in context. For English language learners, visualization, group activities, and physical response are especially effective. Various activities for direct instruction in vocabulary use these principles in different combinations and degrees.

> The most successful methods [of teaching vocabulary] use richness of context, active engagement, a large number of exposures, and a variety of responses and techniques.

Using the Dictionary

The most common vocabulary exercise is to look up meanings in the dictionary and write a sentence for the targeted vocabulary words. The frustration that teachers feel with the amount of time this takes for such meager results is validated by researchers. Miller and Gildea (cited in May, 1998, pp. 211–212) conclude, "The errors children made [using dictionary definitions] were so serious and frequent as to make the task instructionally useless." Copying definitions from the dictionary lacks richness of context, integration with prior experiences, meaningful usage, and the opportunity to discuss usage and meaning with others. Besides, kids just pick the first or the shortest definition.

The dictionaries themselves are usually less than helpful. Classroom dictionaries are constrained by space, so definitions are compacted, technical, or impossible to understand unless the meaning of the word is already known. Every part of the entry is fraught with problems. Words are defined by their roots; for example, *glandular*: of or like a gland; having glands; made up of glands. Correct usage depends on the child's knowing the parts of speech, which are rather abstract and often not truly conquered until seventh or eighth grade. Every teacher has seen sentences similar to "He luminoused the room with the candle." Pronunciation keys are undecipherable.

Nonetheless, dictionaries are occasionally needed, and at some time in their education, students need to be taught how to use them. They need to know how to locate a word, how to identify and use the parts of the entry, and how to choose among multiple meanings. On the last day of revising this chapter, a clinician told me a tale of her attempt to model dictionary usage with the word *Conestoga*. Her students initially wanted her to Google the word! They really need to learn the efficiency of using a dictionary. It works best to teach dictionary skills with words that are needed for a content lesson or a story so that the task is authentic and integrated.

Enhanced Dictionary Assignments

Dictionary usage can be made more successful by supplying additional clues, such as using a word in context. Seeing the actual whole sentence from the

Figure 9.2   Context to dictionary

	Guess	Dictionary
In one or two corners there were **alcoves** of evergreen with stone seats or tall moss-covered flower urns in them.		

story will trigger greater recognition of the vocabulary word during reading than will studying the word in an unrelated sentence or phrase. Teachers may have to add a context clue to the sentence if the author was not helpful in the original text. Students should first make a guess about the meaning based on the context. Having a preliminary general idea aids students in then choosing the correct definition and understanding what the definition means. An example of a context-to-dictionary exercise is shown in Figure 9.2. This technique works very well as a partner activity, and the students' definitions are often better than the ones in the dictionary.

Fourth- and sixth-grade students could better assess whether vocabulary usage was consistent with the definition if words were taught with sample sentences rather than with sample phrases (Scott & Nagy, 1997).

Another helpful cooperative activity is to assign a group of four or eight words in context to a team of four students. They must share the dictionary search, teach the words to each other, and develop sentences cooperatively. The discussion and self-correction that occur make this a surprisingly effective activity, and it actually takes less time than having students do it independently.

Presenting Vocabulary in Context

Learning vocabulary in context is effective because syntactic (grammatical) and semantic (meaning) clues are present. If a word is studied out of context, students can use only graphophonemic clues, roots, and affixes. Context can help students develop a theory about the meaning of a word, although the theory is usually general.

Imagine a student who is unfamiliar with *artichoke*. It could be anything, and *choke* is quite misleading. Add *hearts of* to *artichoke*. Although it sounds like the cardiovascular system of some beast, it can at least be identified as a noun by the syntactic clue. Add "Donna dipped the light green hearts of artichoke into butter and ate the delicacy with delight," and the students have far better clues to work with, although they may still interpret Donna's action as rather barbaric. Semantically, *light green hearts* does not make sense, so the students probably reconsider the beast theory and propose a vegetable theory.

More activities for direct teaching of vocabulary follow. Some activities include formal use of context, but mostly, rich context and active engagement develop from modeling and discussion within the activity. Most of these pre-reading activities aim to integrate the new vocabulary with students' schemas and backgrounds, but the principles of multiple exposures and meaningful usage must be carried out through responses to reading.

Word Splash

Word splash is a versatile technique. A variety of words, usually five to ten, are splashed (written randomly) across a paper, a transparency, or the chalkboard. Most of the words are unknown vocabulary words, but a few might be more common words that will give clues about the content, characters, or setting of the story. A student chooses any word from the set and then offers a sentence or definition. The teacher expands with an example, steering the conversation to the word's usage in the story. The procedure continues with supportive conversation until all the words have been defined or used in context. Students are called on to combine two of the words in a sentence, and the teacher checks off words as they are used. Students tend to volunteer promptly so that they will be able to choose those words with which they are most comfortable. The technique sounds very simple, and it is, but an amazing amount of connected information is shared in a relatively short amount of time. An example of word splash is shown in Chapter 12.

The next step can be to predict the story based on the vocabulary words. These predictions should be reasonably on target if the teacher has chosen words that apply to the setting, the plot, and the characters, although any predictions that can be justified are acceptable. Students cannot wait to read the selection to see whose predictions will come the closest.

Concept Wheel

A simple but effective technique is the concept wheel (Rupley, Logan, & Nichols, 1999). A vocabulary word from the selection is listed in one quarter of a "wheel" or circle (Figure 9.3). The teacher asks, "What words come to mind when you think of _____?" Students activate their prior knowledge, and the teacher can help them expand the relationships for the benefit of others in the class who may think they have no experience with the word. Several students contribute as the teacher lists the connections on the board. Finally the teacher gives the definition, or the class reads it from the glossary. The key element comes when the teacher asks the students to find three words that will personally help them remember the vocabulary word. These are written in the remaining three quarters of the wheel. One of them might be a sketch or picture clue. This technique provides multiple exposures, active participation, and a variety of contexts and connections.

Figure 9.3 Concept wheel

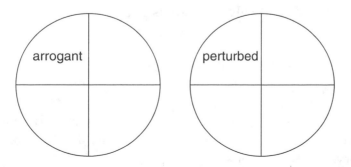

Story Chain

With a story chain, students are presented with a list of words in the order in which they appear in a story. A list of phrases works even better. The words are defined, illustrated, used in context, related to other stories, matched to other concepts, or elucidated in any other useful way. Students are then asked to predict sentences that might be in the story and eventually to tell a short story using the words in order. A single student can tell the entire story, or it can be a class effort in which each student builds on the preceding student's sentence. It is great fun, and the words are used in meaningful and sometimes inventive context. When the real story is finally read, the students have not only worked with the vocabulary, but they have predicted the story, both of which enrich comprehension.

Vocab-o-Gram

Vocab-o-Gram (Blachowicz & Fisher, 1996, 2006) is another activity that relates vocabulary and story prediction. This time, students are asked to predict how a list of vocabulary words might fit into a story structure. Working in teams allows students to share their knowledge and make better predictions. Figure 9.4 shows one child's initial predictions for *Greyling* (Yolen, 1991). In this case, the predictions are inaccurate.

After reading the selection, students can reject or verify their predictions. In the example, the students moved *wail* from being a character to being a sound made by the wind. The mystery words (unknown words) were solved; a *selchie* is a seal-child, and *slough off* is what the seal-child did with his skin.

Possible Sentences

This activity is appealing to children, produces much discussion, and often spurs the children to pull out their dictionaries to settle disputes. In Possible Sentences, the teacher provides sentences that may or may not use all the words correctly. In other words, the sentences could make sense but may not. Figuring out the definitions is essential for finding out whether a sentence makes sense (Blachowicz & Fisher, 1996). Possible Sentences can also be used for discriminating nuances of meaning. In the last sample below, the characteristics of a virtuoso must be compared with those of a rival to determine whether the definitions could be inclusive or whether they are opposites.

The staunchly built house collapsed during the heavy shower.

The heat was oppressive in the closed-up house.

The canary breathed slowly through its gills.

The borscht was blue and supported by steel rods.

Could a philanthropist be a miser?

Could a virtuoso be a rival?

Though the possible sentences themselves are not included in any book the class is reading, the vocabulary used in the sentences should be associated with a subject, story, or book under study.

Figure 9.4   Vocab-o-Gram: *Greyling*

VOCAB-O-GRAM: *GREYLING*	
Use vocabulary to make predictions about . . .	
(May be used more than once)	
The setting Townsfolk roiling seas sandbar	What will the setting be like? little town by the sea
The characters Fisherman Greyling Baby Wail townsfolk	Any ideas about the characters? There's a big wail. Maybe the fisherman is related To baby. Greyling is a Fish
The problem or goal	What might it be? Somebody gets stranded on sandbar
The actions	What might happen? Fisherman saves baby. Fisherman is saved.
The resolution	How might it end? Joyously or sad (grief) both sad and happy; bittersweet
What question(s) do you have?	What happens to the baby?
Mystery Words selchie, slough off	

Source: Vocab-o-Gram for *Greyling* by J. Yolen. Blachowicz, Camille; Fisher, Peter J., *Teaching Vocabulary in All Classrooms,* 3rd edition, © 2006, p. 50. Reprinted by permission of Pearson Education, Inc., Upper Saddle River, NJ.

Word Sorts

Word sorts can be used before reading to get general ideas about the categories in which words fit, or they can be used after reading to consolidate meanings. If the teacher chooses the categories, the activity is a closed sort; if students determine the categories, it is an open sort. Words can be sorted by story elements, by parts of speech, by sections of the story, by traits of specific characters, or in any other useful way. A sample word sort is provided in Chapter 12.

Drawing and Labeling Pictures

When the vocabulary consists of mostly nouns, children enjoy drawing representations of the words and assembling them into a picture. Teams of students pool their knowledge and then divide the task of looking up the remaining unfamiliar words. Pictures are completed by each student independently. Because visual images have such staying power, pictures are great memory cues to use on vocabulary note cards, in vocabulary books, or any time words are learned.

■ EXTENSION ACTIVITIES FOR DIRECTLY TEACHING VOCABULARY

The following activities, which range in scale and complexity, are useful for extension activities.

Character Trait Maps

Words for labeling character traits are often missing in students' vocabularies. Even if the words are known, students are unable to distinguish the subtle differences among *smart, witty, cunning, perceptive, wise,* and *clever,* for example. These vocabulary words and their connotations are learned easily through discussion of characters in literature.

Some experts suggest teaching the words prior to reading, but students may not yet have examples in their schemas, so the words do not "stay put." It works better to label character trait maps after reading. The students will be able to relate the incidents and verbalize the character trait in some general way. The students or the teacher can then provide the word that exactly describes the trait. Using these words in a written response after developing the map will cement the words in place more firmly. Figure 9.5 is an example of a character trait map for the character of Brian from *Hatchet* (Paulsen, 1987).

Semantic Gradient Scales

When working on the subtle differences in the character trait map, it may be useful to establish words differentiated by degrees in a semantic gradient scale (Blachowicz & Fisher, 1996). For example, in Figure 9.6, several words are arranged from *hottest* to *coldest.* This scale helps students see how new words fit into a pattern of known words. The weather-related words offer a clear example to emulate. Developing words that fit between *courageous* and *cowardly* might coordinate with a literature lesson, while the freedom list might fit either social studies or a science fiction story.

Semantic Mapping

Semantic mapping, or webbing, is meant to extend the meaning of a concept word or to activate related concepts that would be useful for understanding a story, as illustrated in Figure 9.7. Semantic maps go far beyond just learning the definition and usage of a word. The targeted word is placed in the middle of the web, and related, categorized terms are contributed by the class for the spokes of the web. Semantic webbing helps students see relationships between ideas and connect known information with new information.

Semantic webbing is most useful for either a complex idea that the students are not familiar with, such as *communism,* or for a simple word that the teacher

Figure 9.5 Character trait map: *Hatchet*

CHARACTER TRAIT MAP: *HATCHET*

Brian in *Hatchet*

Insightful
- Uses windbreaker to carry raspberries
- Realizes he can create fire from the sparks of his hatchet

Defeated
- Let fire go out, didn't eat, and wanted to die when a plane didn't see him
- Sobbed after porcupine attack

Tenacious
- Builds a door for his shelter despite hurt back muscles, swollen eyelids from mosquito bites, sunburn, a swollen forehead, and cramped legs

Realistic
- Knows he will not be rescued easily because they were off the flight path

Clever
- Followed the birds to find berries

Perceptive
- Connects tracks on sand to turtle eggs, connects water refraction to spearing fish

Inventive
- Devises bow and arrow, a fish spear, a raft, and a fish pen

Determined
- Rips himself free from the submerged plane

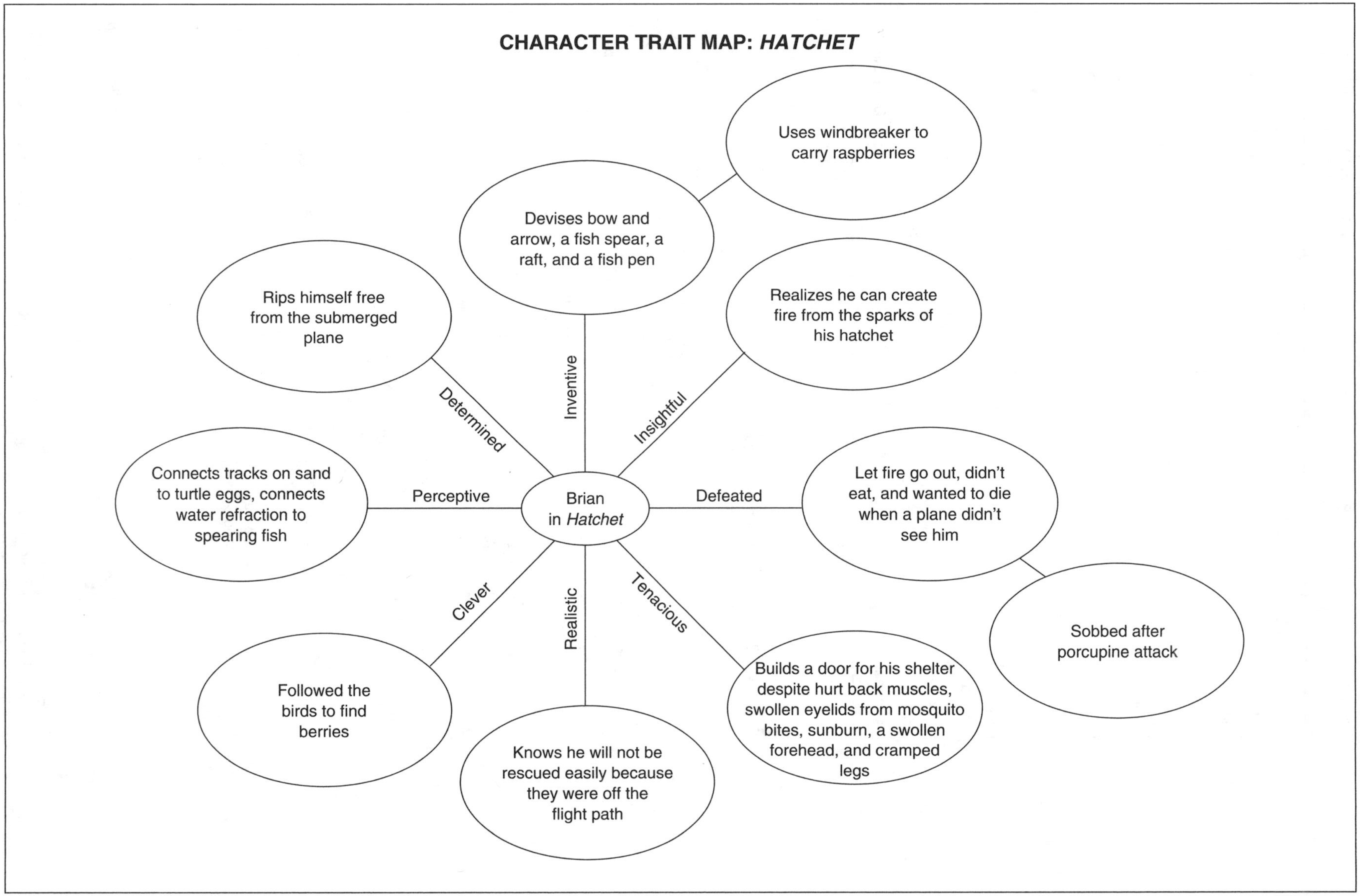

Figure 9.6 A semantic gradient scale helps students see how new words fit into a pattern of known words.

Hottest	Courageous	Free to Do as You Please
scorching		
sultry		
steamy		
tropical		
balmy		
sunny		
cool		
nippy		
raw		
freezing		
frigid		
glacial		
Coldest	**Cowardly**	**Totally Controlled**

Figure 9.7 Semantic map for *Fear*

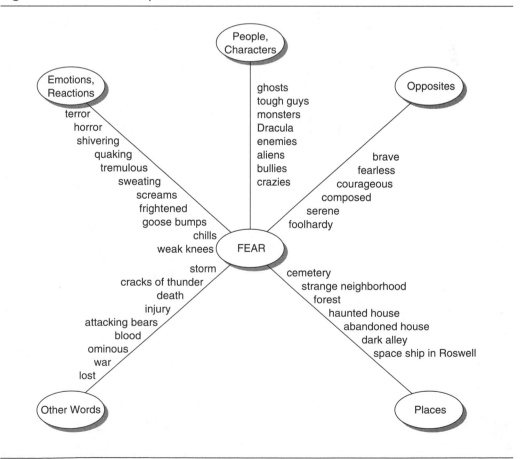

Source: Adapted from Nagy, W., *Teaching Vocabulary to Improve Reading Comprehension,* Urbana, IL: National Council of Teachers of English, 1988.

can use to activate associated ideas for an upcoming story, such as *fear*. The teacher can add items to the web in terms of more precise vocabulary or nudge the discussion toward ideas in the impending story. Semantic maps can also be used to review information after reading or to gather information while reading if the categories are predetermined or the students know how to group by topics.

Semantic mapping can be done individually by students, with the results combined on the board or overhead projector, or as a class activity. The advantages of semantic mapping include being able to see the relationships visually and to determine the categories. Most importantly, the students can participate in the discussion that will accompany the construction of the map.

Word Wall

Word walls are usually displays of high-frequency words above or below an alphabet and are used in the primary grades, but the idea can be adapted for vocabulary words. In this adaptation, word walls provide a growing list of vocabulary words that is visible throughout the year. My friend Mary Conrad, an eighth-grade teacher, gives extra credit points to students who use words from the word wall appropriately in their daily assignments.

Frayer Model

A strategy for deep vocabulary development is the Frayer Model (Frayer, Frederick, & Klausmeier, 1969), which is time consuming but suitable for developing very important concept words. The procedure has seven steps, listed below on the left and illustrated in the right-hand column with *guided reading* as the term to be defined:

Frayer Model Example Defining Guided Reading

1. Define the new concept, discriminating the attributes relevant to all instances of the concept.	1. Guided reading: The teacher and the student read the same text together and discuss it as they proceed.
2. Discriminate the relevant from irrelevant properties of instances of the concept.	2. It is irrelevant whether the text is fiction or nonfiction or how many students are in the group.
3. Provide an example of the concept.	3. The teacher and the class or group discuss an implied cause in a passage.
4. Provide a nonexample of the concept.	4. Silent reading from beginning to end with questions at the end is a nonexample.
5. Relate the concept to a subordinate concept.	5. Reading for a purpose is a subordinate concept.
6. Relate the concept to a superordinate concept.	6. Reading instruction is a larger concept.
7. Relate the concept to a coordinate term.	7. Transactional reading and Directed Reading Thinking Activity are similar.

Word Play

Sometimes it is just fun to play with words, especially when there are five or ten minutes left before taking the class to music or before dismissal. Several activities are suitable in these short segments of time.

Figurative language, such as idioms, poses obstacles for young students. Consider the following phrases: *stealing his thunder, raining cats and dogs, head over heels, once in a blue moon, top drawer, dressed to kill,* and *middle of the road.* Students tend to interpret the words literally, resulting in much confusion. Since it is hard to find a story in which several examples of figurative language are used in meaningful context, teaching figurative language can be done out of context. Illustrations of the figurative and literal meanings can be quite inventive.

Analogy study develops precision in word relationships and increases vocabulary. Students can also develop their own analogies. The analogies in Figure 9.8 were devised by a sixth-grade class working on a science fiction unit. It was hard to tell which they enjoyed more—making up analogies or solving their classmates' analogies.

Figure 9.8   Analogies provide an example of word play

_____ : Milky Way :: Planet : Earth	galaxy
Dark : _____ :: light : star	black hole
sphere: moon :: _____ : orbit	oval
space ship : escape pod :: _____ : parachute	airplane
Martian : Mars :: _____ : Earth	Earthling
Star Wars : movie :: Deep Space Nine : _____	TV show
Godzilla : Tokyo :: King Kong : _____	New York
20,000 Leagues Under the Sea : Jules Verne :: Sphere : _____	Michael Crichton
Darth Vader : _____ :: Luke Skywalker : rebels	Empire
Spock : _____ :: Data : Cyborg	Vulcan

Acronyms, palindromes (words or phrases that read the same forward and backward, such as *kayak* and *Madam, I'm Adam*), metaphors, mixed or otherwise, homophone pairs, riddles, and games are all enjoyed by children. What do you call a dog's feet when they stop? Paws pause. *The King Who Rained*, by Fred Gwynne, is filled with many more funny homophone riddles. In *Teaching Vocabulary in All Classrooms* (1996), Blachowicz and Fisher included several word-play activities that exploit these word games, as well as 13 commercially published vocabulary-word games.

■ TEACHING STUDENTS STRATEGIES FOR LEARNING NEW WORDS

Students need to be consciously aware of vocabulary strategies in order to use them to determine the meaning of unknown words while reading independently.

Scaffolding

Teachers can provide scaffolding for students who are struggling to learn new words. One of the best types of scaffolding is modeling during guided reading. The teacher demonstrates, omitting the target word; reads to the end of the sentence; and makes guesses about what the unknown word must mean. The teacher might use the root or affixes, a picture, or the structure of the sentence to speculate on the possible meaning. Then the teacher reads on and finds clues to confirm or reject the guess, perhaps trying additional strategies, demonstrating that readers often have to try several strategies before finding one that provides the necessary information. After modeling, the teacher asks students to try the same procedures on another word.

> Students need to be consciously aware of vocabulary strategies.

Students can practice the fill-in-the-blank procedure by doing **cloze exercises,** which provide practice in using both semantic and syntactic clues. Chapter 8 provides a detailed explanation.

Zip Cloze

Zip cloze can be used with young students who are just learning about vocabulary strategies. Blachowicz and Fisher (1996) suggest putting a story on an overhead transparency and blocking out words with masking tape or a sticky note. (Choosing selected vocabulary words seems more useful in this exercise than deleting every eighth word, as is done in traditional cloze passages.) Students use all the strategies they know to guess the missing words. When a word is guessed, the tape is "zipped" off, and students can compare their choice with the author's. The increasing number of visible words provides additional context.

Context Clues

Teaching students how to identify and use context clues provides a strategy for independently determining unfamiliar word meanings, but it is quite difficult to estimate how useful context clues really are. Whether the child notices the word and puts forth an effort to understand it is affected by age, ability level, text density, and the author's style. Grade 4 students have an 8% probability of learning a new word from context, but Grade 11 students have a 33% probability. Low-ability students will learn a new word from context 8% of the time, while medium- and high-ability students have a likelihood of 12% and 19%, respectively. If the text is dense, with one word in ten unknown, there is a 7% chance of learning new words, but the rate jumps to 14% for one new word in 74, and to 30% for one new word in 150 (Sousa, 2005). Some authors are more helpful than others, providing direct clues, appositives—words within commas or dashes—or synonyms to define words. Other texts provide very few context clues, either at the sentence level or in the selection as a whole.

Context clues are also more helpful for identifying synonyms of known words than for identifying new concepts. In the case of new concepts, context clues in combination with a definition are more effective than context alone (Allen, 1999).

When context clues do exist, students should learn how to recognize them. Modeling and examples always seem to work better than explaining, so here are several modeled formats. The varieties clearly overlap. Although some of these formats seem obvious, many students are unaware of how they work.

Print clues. On her head the prom queen wore a *tiara*, a circlet of silver and rhinestones, which sparkled in the spotlight.

The snake's new scales were *glistening*—shining in the sunlight—after he peeled off his old skin like a glove.

Piranha (small fish that eat meat and have sharp teeth) are so dangerous that Mr. Schroeder would not sell them in his pet store.

Definitions. When troupes are *quartered* for the night, they are provided with lodging.

Category. The Edwards' *whippet* won first prize in the dog show.

Visualization. Petite Mrs. Wiley could not see over the heads of the crowd.

*Opposite***s.** The kitten got tangled in the yarn but was quickly *extricated*.

Summary. Hydrangeas, bleeding hearts, irises, and *lilies of the valley* are flowers that grow in my yard.

Mood. The people dressed in black were in a *somber* mood as they watched the coffin being carried down the steps.

Experience. Mrs. Winton could not get a taxi during the thunderstorm, so when she reached home, she was *drenched*.

Words connected in a series. Oaks, elms, *catalpas,* and maples lined the shady streets.

Story or paragraph level. The meanings of many words do not become clear until later in the paragraph or story. Good readers keep checking back to clarify meaning.

Root and Affix Clues

Relating the root of a known word to an unknown word is often, but not always, useful. Relating words to their Greek and Latin ancestors is marginally useful except for scientific vocabulary. Endings can often identify the part of speech: *-ed* and *-ing* are usually verbs, and *-ist* and *-er* usually identify a person. The number prefixes, *uni-, bi-, tri-,* and so on, are usually consistent, but I did have a student tell me that *bird* was two "rds"! It is worthwhile to draw children's attention to root-word families and common affixes so they can unlock meanings by themselves.

REVIEWING VOCABULARY ■ WITH A MAGIC SQUARE

A quick self-checking review technique is the magic square. Students write the definition number in the box with the word, and if each row and column add up to 18, they know they are right. The square in Figure 9.9 will help with *Treasure Island.* (Item number one is missing on purpose; the magic square won't work if it is used.)

Figure 9.9   Magic square

Treasure Island

mutineer	rations	buccaneer
fatally injured	ablaze	ascertain
warily	dwindled	carousing

2. food

3. partying, drinking

4. dead

5. cautiously

6. brightly lit as if burning

7. a pirate

8. determine, figure out

9. a person who rebels or refuses orders from the captain of a ship

10. lessened

Teachers can make puzzles, matches, flashcards, cloze exercises, concentration games, word matching cards, and more on Quia Web (http://www.quia.com). This is a subscription site and requires a moderate fee, but teachers can customize the games with their own vocabulary words, and the students can access them and play the games online. Practice has never been such fun.

ASSESSING VOCABULARY ■

There must be something better than matching or multiple-choice vocabulary tests. Being able to respond to a multiple-choice test may or may not indicate deep knowledge. Here are a couple of quick ideas suitable for classroom testing that probe a little deeper. The teacher needs to choose certain response categories for certain words as one type will not fit all. An alternative is to ask students to choose among several response options, which will make them consider which option is the most suitable. Ask students to explain words in the following ways.

1. Use the word in an original sentence that is explanatory.

2. Use the application of a word. For example, a *radiologist* is most likely to use (a) a pitchfork (b) an x-ray machine (c) marketing research (d) a screwdriver.

3. Give a synonym or an antonym.

4. Give a larger classification category or an example.

5. Draw a picture.

6. Make a choice in context. For example, Because the farmers were poor, George Washington Carver taught them how to use (organ, organic, synthetic) fertilizers, which were made from natural materials.

Probably the best way to assess vocabulary knowledge is through written responses to the text from which the vocabulary was drawn. Readers know a word when it helps them understand a passage they have read and when they use the word to add precision to their answers.

Vocabulary study does not need to be the dull, superficial exercise most of us remember from our days as students. With careful selection of the words we teach, vocabulary study can improve our students' reading comprehension and have long-lasting effects.

10

Teaching and Learning Spelling

It is possible to spell a word correctly by chance, or because someone prompts
you, but you are a scholar only if you spell it correctly because you know how.

—Aristotle

After reading Bob Schlagal's work (2001), I realized why the current spelling research is such a revelation to me. Until the 1970s, the prevailing belief was that English spelling was "underprincipled and unpredictable" (p. 149). There had been some work in word frequency to determine the basal spelling lists, and work in memory research about the usefulness of distributed practice (small amounts throughout the week), but not until computer technology came along did we realize that English had a surprising degree of consistency that extended well beyond the high-frequency words. The more words that were included in an analysis, the more principled the orthography (spelling) seemed. The teaching of spelling has shifted from a memory task to a task of teaching hierarchically organized concepts about the written representation of English.

Spelling is a multifaceted system that includes alphabet knowledge, sound-symbol relationships, visual memory, knowledge about common and alternate orthographic patterns, rules, and the patterns that the system follows in doubling letters and maintaining sounds or meaning in derivative words. There are also words that defy any rational explanation, but fortunately not very many.

STAGES OF SPELLING DEVELOPMENT ■

The five successive stages of spelling development delineated by J. Richard Gentry (1982, 2000; Gentry & Gillet, 1993) have been used for many years. They help explain how spelling is developmental, how the stages are qualitatively different, and how each indicates a different mindset or cognitive awareness of how spelling works.

The Precommunicative Stage

Key word: At this stage, *eagle* may be spelled H ≥ O. Preschoolers start with scribble writing, which has no letters or symbols similar to letters, although several other aspects of literacy in English are included. The children know that the scribbles "say something," and the scribbles are written in horizontal lines that, after a while, are written in a left-to-right direction.

Soon, children add letters or letter-like symbols. Some children naturally acquire these basic conventions if they have been lucky enough to grow up in a print-rich environment and have seen their parents reading newspapers and books and writing grocery lists and letters. They notice the print on cereal boxes and the logos of their favorite fast-food restaurants and try to reproduce those letters. The luckiest of children have had stories read to them and have seen and heard how print and speech are related. For students who have not had these experiences, their teacher may be their only model, and their first purposeful exposure to print may be in kindergarten.

As children begin to learn the letters of the alphabet, their spelling and writing take on a new form. Symbols or numbers can be mixed in with uppercase and lowercase letters, often with little or no spacing. The writer can often read it back immediately after it is written, but there is no correspondence to words or sounds. Some children use many letters while others use just a few that they have learned. Some start with marks that are similar to letters but are not accurate in directionality or form. However, this is the beginning of spelling: the realization that meaning is conveyed and words are written with a standard set of characters—the alphabet. This stage is typical of preschoolers from ages three to five.

The Semiphonic Stage

Key word: At this stage, *eagle* may be spelled E. Semiphonic spellers make a huge leap in understanding when they grasp the alphabetic principle, the idea that a correspondence exists between letters and sounds. Children who receive phonemic awareness, especially in blending and segmenting in kindergarten and first grade, make significant spelling gains (National Reading Panel, 2000). Children begin to spell by using the initial sound, then the final sound, and finally the medial sound. An entire word may be represented with only one or two letters, as students cannot yet segment all the sounds. Second language learners may require additional assistance in recognizing and producing English sounds. Chinese children may have difficulty with /b/, /ch/, /d/, /g/, /sh/, /th/, and /v/ while Spanish speakers may have difficulty with /dj/ (*giant*, *badge*), /j/, /sh/, /th/, and /z/ (Snowball & Bolton, 1999).

Consonant sounds are much easier to spell because most of the sounds are similar to the letter names, though the letters *g*, *h*, *w*, and *y* do not provide much help. Letter names are also not helpful for diagraphs, so children often substitute *j* or *h* for *ch*.

Vowels, the bane of the English language, are usually not included at this stage. As students progress through this stage, more and more of the sounds are represented by letters. Spellers at this stage are usually five- and six-year-olds.

The Phonetic Stage

Key word: At this stage, *eagle* may be spelled EGL. In the phonetic stage, the sound-it-out strategy works best for children as they learn reasonably accurate letter representations of all the sounds. Because they can quickly and phonetically spell any word in their speaking vocabulary, children can become prolific writers. Phonetic spellers are usually six years old.

Their writing is quite readable. Ask first-grade teachers if they can read "primary," which is almost like a predictable foreign language. Any one of them will answer, "Ys, I kan red pri-mr-e." Although these substitutions may look peculiar to adult readers, the reasoning is developmental, systematic, and quite legitimate. In fact, primary teachers often use spelling to diagnose the phonetic understanding of their students. Figure 10.1 shows typical phonetic spelling patterns.

Figure 10.1 Developmental spelling patterns (typical patterns used by early readers when spelling phonetically)

Long vowels and short words are spelled by letter names.	oak	OK
	you	U
	are	R
Short vowels are spelled the closest to the letter names; thus, they seldom match conventional spelling.	bat	BUT
	bet	BAT
	bit	BET
	cot	CIT
	cut	COT
M or *n* before a consonant is dropped.	jump	JUP
	stamp	STAP
Vowels are dropped before *l, m, n,* or *r.*	atom	ATM
	open	OPN
	bird	BRD
The *-ed* endings are changed to *t* or just *d.*	stopped	STOPT
	timed	TIMD
Dr and *jr* sound the same.	dragon	JRAGON
Tr and *ch* sound the same.	truck	CHRUCK
D and *t* are confused as medial sounds.	ladder	LATER
	attitude	ADITUD

Consonant blends are challenging in both initial and final positions. Typically the *m* is dropped from words like *bump*; ,the *l* is missing from *l*-blends; *dr* and *tr* sound the same and are spelled *j*, *jr*, or *chr*; and *-ed* endings are spelled *t*, *d*, or *id*.

Vowels appear at this stage. Long vowels are usually accurate because they say their own names, but silent *e* and vowel doubling are not present. Short vowels are more problematic, and children choose a vowel letter that most closely fits with its name, as illustrated in Figure 10.1. Short vowels continue to be problematic for poor readers and spellers for many years (Schlagal, 2001). Teaching spelling through word families is helpful at this stage. Students will progress to the next stage when they learn that they must add other strategies besides sounding out in order to spell conventionally.

The Transitional Stage

Key word: At this stage, *eagle* may be spelled EGUL. In the transitional stage, vowels appear in every syllable; vowels are connected to *l*, *m*, *n*, and *r*; and long vowel alternative spellings (*ai*, *ee*, *a_e*) are learned even if not always correctly applied. Children also learn how *y* and *w* can be vowels, as in *-ay* and *-ow*. In some words all the letters may be present but in a rearranged order, as in *gril* for *girl* and *Jhon* for *John*. Transitional spellers use correctly spelled words in greater abundance in their writing, especially if they read and write regularly. Typically, seven-, eight-, and nine-year-old children are at the transitional stage.

Students advance in the transitional stage when they stop relying on sound mapping alone. While basic phonic knowledge is sufficient to spell cvc (consonant-vowel-consonant) words like *bed* or words with two or more consonants before or after the vowel (e.g., *slip*, *went*, and *blend*), progress in the transitional stage requires knowing the variations for representing sounds. Both consonants and vowels have alternate spellings, as shown in Figure 10.2. Partly this is due to the English language's having 40-some phoneme sounds and only 26 letters.

Which alternative is correct can depend on adjacent letters or position in the word, but some are just a matter of social convention, as in *go*, *know*, *load*, or *note*. Is the word *cake*, *caek*, or *kake*? The orthographic possibilities, however, are not endless. It is not likely to be *keik* (as in *weigh*) because that is uncommon. It is not going to be *cace*, *ceik*, or *kace* because *ce* sounds /s/, and it is not going to be *cayk* because *-ay* almost always occurs at the end of words. The diphthongs, *ou*, *ow*, *oi*, *aw*, and so forth, are also learned at this stage.

Children also learn the doubling rules. Words with long vowels, such as *hope*, drop the silent *e* and do not double the final consonant when adding *-ing* and *-ed*, as in *hoping*. Words with short vowels, such as *hop*, do double the final consonant, as in *hopping*. Words with an accented second syllable also double the consonant; compare *omitted* and *limited*. One-syllable words with a short vowel and ending with *f*, *l*, *s*, or *z* always double the final letter—the "floss + zz rule." Similarly, one-syllable words with short vowels and ending with /k/ are spelled with the ending *-ck*.

When children are ready to learn the rules for adding inflectional endings (*-ed*, *-ing*, *-s*), they are also ready to learn about open and closed syllables in two-syllable words. Open syllables are cv (*go*) and have a long vowel sound. Closed

Figure 10.2 Alternate spellings

Sound	Examples of spelling; infrequent patterns follow the double slash (//)
short a	c<u>a</u>t // pl<u>ai</u>d
long a	d<u>a</u>te, pl<u>ay</u>, r<u>ai</u>d, <u>a</u>ngel, cr<u>a</u>dle (open syllable) // w<u>eigh</u>, v<u>ei</u>n, gr<u>ea</u>t, surv<u>ey</u>
/aw/	s<u>aw</u>, dr<u>aw</u>n, l<u>au</u>ndry, <u>a</u>ll // fr<u>o</u>g, <u>o</u>ff, br<u>oa</u>d, g<u>o</u>ne, b<u>ou</u>ght, n<u>au</u>ghty *A* has this sound when followed by *w, l,* or *u*. The team *-au* is used within a syllable and *-aw* at the end and before final /n/ and /l/. Note: the *-og* words may have a short *o* sound in parts of the East Coast.
/b/	<u>b</u>at // e<u>bb</u>
/ch/	<u>ch</u>urch, wa<u>tch</u> // pic<u>t</u>ure, ques<u>ti</u>on (suffixes *-ture, -tion*)
/d/	<u>d</u>ime, stay<u>ed</u> // a<u>dd</u>
short e	b<u>e</u>d, h<u>ea</u>d // capt<u>ai</u>n
long e	th<u>e</u>se, f<u>ee</u>l, <u>ea</u>ch, h<u>e</u>, k<u>ey</u>, bab<u>y</u> // <u>e</u>vil, br<u>ea</u>the, rec<u>ei</u>ve, bel<u>ie</u>ve, b<u>e</u>fore (open syllable), trampol<u>i</u>ne
/ear/	d<u>ear</u>, st<u>eer</u>, h<u>ere</u> The letters *ea* have several sounds but are dependable in all rimes except for *-ear, -eaf,* and *-ead*.
/f/	<u>f</u>eet, sti<u>ff</u>, <u>ph</u>oto, lau<u>gh,</u> enou<u>gh</u> Use ff in one-syllable words with a single short vowel.
hard g	<u>g</u>o, <u>gh</u>ost, <u>g</u>uide // va<u>gu</u>e, e<u>gg</u> /g/ for ga, go, gu
/h/	<u>h</u>air, <u>wh</u>o
short i	p<u>i</u>n // g<u>y</u>m
long i	l<u>i</u>ke, cr<u>y</u>, fl<u>igh</u>t, p<u>ie</u>, p<u>i</u>lot (open syllable) // <u>eye</u>, t<u>y</u>pe, f<u>i</u>nd English words ending with a long *i* sound never spell the sound with the letter *i* alone. If the sound is spelled with a single letter, the letter is *y*.
/j/ /dj/	<u>j</u>ob, <u>g</u>iraffe, stran<u>ge</u>, bri<u>dge</u> // sol<u>di</u>er, indivi<u>du</u>al /j/ for ge, gi, gy Words ending in /j/ must be spelled -ge or -dge. The ending -dge occurs only after accented short vowels, usually in one-syllable words.
/k/	<u>k</u>eep, <u>c</u>all, bla<u>ck</u> // <u>ch</u>orus, anti<u>qu</u>e /k/ for ca, co, cu, ke, ki Use -ck for one-syllable words ending with /k/ after a short vowel.
/ks/	sin<u>ks</u>, so<u>cks</u>, bo<u>x</u>, a<u>xe</u>, e<u>x</u>it // pani<u>cs</u>
/kw/	<u>qu</u>een
/l/	<u>l</u>ast, ta<u>ll</u> Use ll for one-syllable words with a single vowel.
syllabic l	ab<u>le</u>, canc<u>el</u>, civ<u>il</u>, anim<u>al</u>
/m/	<u>m</u>at // co<u>mb</u>, autu<u>mn</u>
/n/	<u>n</u>o, do<u>ne</u>, <u>kn</u>ight, si<u>gn</u> // <u>pn</u>eumonia
syllabic n	writt<u>en</u>, less<u>on</u>, cous<u>in</u>, import<u>ant</u> (suffix -ant)
-ng, -nk	si<u>ng</u>, sa<u>nk</u>
short o	p<u>o</u>t, f<u>a</u>ther

(Continued)

Figure 10.2 (Continued)

long o	n<u>o</u>, n<u>ote</u>, b<u>oa</u>t, <u>ow</u>n, <u>o</u>ld // th<u>ough</u>, t<u>oe</u>, sh<u>ou</u>lder, s<u>ew</u>
/oi/	b<u>oi</u>l, b<u>oy</u> -oi is used in the middle of words and -oy at the end.
/ow/	c<u>ow</u>, cl<u>ou</u>d -ow is used at the end or in the middle, generally before n or l.
long oo	n<u>oo</u>n, cr<u>ue</u>l, bl<u>ue</u>, fl<u>ew</u>, r<u>u</u>le, s<u>ou</u>p // v<u>iew</u>, l<u>o</u>se, t<u>o</u>, tw<u>o</u>, fr<u>ui</u>t, tr<u>u</u>th, r<u>u</u>by
short oo	b<u>oo</u>k, p<u>u</u>t, c<u>ou</u>ld, // w<u>o</u>man
/p/	<u>p</u>ig
/r/	<u>r</u>un, <u>wr</u>ist // <u>rh</u>ythm, bu<u>rr</u>
r-controlled vowels	/ar/: c<u>ar</u> /er/: h<u>er</u>, f<u>ir</u>st, w<u>or</u>ld, f<u>ur</u>, h<u>ear</u>d // c<u>our</u>age, coll<u>ar</u> /or/: f<u>or</u>, d<u>oor</u>, m<u>ore</u> // w<u>ar</u> /air/: h<u>air</u>, c<u>are</u>, wh<u>ere</u>, st<u>air</u>, b<u>ear</u>
/s/	<u>s</u>ick, cla<u>ss</u>, el<u>s</u>e, offi<u>c</u>e, <u>c</u>ity, <u>c</u>ycle, <u>sc</u>ience // p<u>s</u>ychology /s/ for ce, ci, cy Use *ss* for ending one-syllable words with a single short vowel
/sh/	<u>sh</u>ip, <u>s</u>ure, <u>ch</u>ef, ac<u>ti</u>on, spe<u>ci</u>al, mi<u>ssi</u>on
/sk/	<u>sk</u>in, <u>sc</u>ary, <u>sch</u>ool, <u>squ</u>ash
/t/	<u>t</u>eacher, walk<u>ed</u>, a<u>tt</u>end, defini<u>t</u>e // ya<u>ch</u>t, dou<u>bt</u>
th: 2 sounds	<u>th</u>in, <u>th</u>en
short u	f<u>u</u>n, c<u>o</u>mpany, c<u>ou</u>ntry // fl<u>oo</u>d
long u	<u>u</u>nion, f<u>ew</u>, <u>u</u>se, val<u>ue</u>,
/v/	<u>v</u>iolin, lo<u>ve</u> // cal<u>ve</u>s No words end in *v*, so an *e* must be added.
/w/	<u>w</u>ant, <u>wh</u>istle // <u>o</u>ne
/y/	<u>y</u>es, <u>u</u>se, on<u>i</u>on, val<u>ue</u>
/z/	<u>z</u>oo, ja<u>zz</u>, pre<u>s</u>ent, applau<u>se</u>, gau<u>ze</u> // <u>X</u>erox Use zz for one-syllable words with a single short vowel.
/zh/	a<u>z</u>ure, ver<u>si</u>on, bei<u>ge</u>, re<u>g</u>ime
	Note: c, q, and x are redundant letters, meaning that the sounds these letters make are also represented by other letters. For example, the c spelling is listed with the /k/ and /s/ sounds.

syllables are cvc (*him*) and have a short vowel sound. Two-syllable words can be segmented by using the open and closed syllable rules: *so-lar, sol-vent*; if there is only one medial consonant, it usually goes with the second syllable. However, there are a significant number of exceptions. Learning the alternatives, the doubling rules, and syllabication takes a considerable amount of time and thoughtful teaching.

Here I must digress briefly from the stages of spelling to introduce an idea I have found helpful. As I was reading the spelling research, a pair of very nontechnical terms occurred to me: *noticers* and *nonnoticers*. Some students, as they read, notice all the patterns and all the irregularities. They seem intrigued by language and patterns and constantly compare their current notions with standard print. Others are nonnoticers, bright and talented students who never seem to notice the differences between their concepts and standard English conventions. Immersion in print-rich environments makes a difference, but they just do not pick up the nuances. Bringing the details to their attention makes a big difference.

I recently learned an excellent example of using a pattern to determine correct spelling. I have always struggled with words that end in *-able* and *-ible*, never knowing when to use which suffix. Diane Snowball and Faye Bolton (1999) taught me the difference in 20 seconds. Words that end in *-able* include the following: *workable, reliable, laughable,* and *remarkable*. Words that end in *-ible* include *visible, possible, edible,* and *legible*. Do you notice a pattern? Words ending with *-able* are usually those in which the root is "able" to stand on its own (although there are a few exceptions and some more rules). I have three college degrees, I read voraciously, and I have been immersed in print all my life, but this simple pattern escaped my notice. Direct and explicit teaching is a huge help for nonnoticers.

The Conventional Stage

Key word: At this stage, *eagle* is spelled EAGLE. Children who have learned to integrate and apply several strategies, including sound-symbol relationships, visual memory, and alternate patterns, are at the conventional stage. They are able to handle semantic demands, such as how to maintain the root word in word derivations. Although the meaning is constant, the sound changes in *sign, signal, design,* and *designate*. The real demons are those words in which the root changes, as in *wintry, forty,* and *curiosity.*

Conventional spellers know how to handle compounds, contractions, prefixes, suffixes, and double consonants. They know how sound is affected by the position of a letter in a word, and they can differentiate many homophones, such as *they're, their,* and *there*. Eventually children do learn the differences between those three.

As students progress toward expert spelling, they also learn historical or etymological demands, such as how to spell words derived from Latin or Greek (*psychology*) or words that keep their original foreign spelling (*llama, cello, trousseau*). Students continue to work on the exceptions and irregularities through eighth grade.

CHARACTERISTICS OF GOOD ■ AND POOR SPELLERS

Good spellers employ more strategies than poor spellers do. The most common spelling strategy of poor spellers in fourth to sixth grade is phonetic analysis, or sounding out, while better spellers use a variety of strategies, such as visual information, root words and affixes, and analogies to known words (Anderson, cited in Tompkins, 1997).

Good spellers are more likely to learn patterns than rules. Try these examples for pronunciation:

Metamere: Any of a longitudinal series of similar segments making up the body of a worm or crayfish

Orpiment: Arsenic trisulfide having a lemon-yellowish color and used as a pigment

Praenomen: In ancient Rome, a person's first name

If you are unfamiliar with these real words, you probably pronounced them automatically by using analogy and pattern, not by recalling rules of spelling.

> Teaching some [spelling] rules may be helpful, but children and adults remember patterns better than rules.

For example, "set-a-here" rhymes with *metamere*. The next word can be pronounced "or-pi(t)-meant" because the suffix *-ment* is familiar and *or* is a real word. It might also be "orp-i-ment" because in actual speech we blur syllable boundaries. Either way, it would be spelled the same. The prefix of *praenomen* can be pronounced to rhyme with the first syllable of *Caesar*, and *-nomen* recalls the word *nomenclature*. Thus teaching some rules may be helpful, but children and adults remember patterns better than rules.

Kathleen Brown, Gale Sinatra, and Janiel Wagstaff (1996) conducted a spelling study using pattern or analogy through word families. They also found that direct instruction helped the nonnoticers. Second-graders were taught dozens of common word families *(-ent, -at, -fight, -tion)* both explicitly and holistically throughout the school year. The researchers wanted to teach students to recognize and to spell particular words, but they also hoped that students would be able to notice patterns so that they could identify and spell unfamiliar words. Samples of students' writing were taken at the beginning, middle, and end of the year to ascertain how often students were using spelling patterns in unfamiliar words that followed patterns that had been taught.

High-achieving students were able to transfer the instructed pattern to new words 97% of the time by the end of the year. Low-achieving students were able to do it 87% of the time, nearly equaling their high-achieving peers. However, with rimes that had not been taught, it was a different story. High-achieving students were able to transfer spelling patterns of noninstructed rimes to new words 47% of the time by the end of the year, whereas low-achieving students were able to do it only 7% of the time. The nonnoticers always benefit the most from direct instruction.

Expert spellers have the ability to recall words visually. They can simply tell if a word looks right because they have the ability to retrieve a visual image of the word from their memory. Poor spellers do not seem to have the visual coding mechanism that allows them to retrieve it. Better visual recall may be related to the fact that better readers and writers simply read more text than their peers who have read less widely.

The errors that poor spellers make are not qualitatively different from the errors of spellers at earlier developmental levels although they persist with the sound-it-out strategy and are likely to lack skills of phonemic awareness. They have a much higher rate of omissions, insertions, and substitutions of *l*, *r*, *m*, *n*, and *ng* (Moats, 1995).

SPELLING SHOULD BE ■
TAUGHT DEVELOPMENTALLY

Teachers who understand the developmental nature of spelling can diagnose the work of their students and choose appropriate lessons. Teaching beyond students' instructional levels invites rote memorization of words, which is the main reason words learned for the Friday test cease to be used correctly the following week. In contrast, teaching students at their developmental level helps to clarify concepts within that level, so words continue to be spelled correctly because the principles are understood (Schlagal, 2001).

Morris and colleagues (cited in Schlagal, 2001) found that when students scored below 40% on their spelling tests (a surprisingly low number), they were not working at the correct developmental level. Not only were the scores low, but the quality of the errors deteriorated, not even coming close to the correct spelling of the words being studied. Apparently, they had not developed a sufficient orthographic foundation to make sense of and retain the words on the list. Morris, Blanton, Blanton, and Perney (1995) found that third and fifth graders who were working at their instructional level learned and retained approximately 85% of the words taught. Students working at their frustration level experienced small gains and retained only 45% of words taught. When students were moved to an appropriate level, they benefited from instruction and retained the words.

ACTIVITIES TO ENCOURAGE OR TEACH SPELLING ■

English has thousands of words. They cannot all be taught, but just 100 words account for 50% of the words used in children's writing, 1,000 words account for 89%, 2,000 words for 95%, and 3,000 for 97% (Hillrich, cited in Murphy, 1997). If students were taught just 1,000 words, they could spell correctly 89% of the time, which is a good return on the teacher's and child's investments in the study of spelling.

Semiphonic and Phonetic Strategies

In the semiphonic and phonetic stages, spelling instruction parallels instruction in phonics. In reading, students see letters and work out the sound; in spelling, students have the sound and work out the letters. One supports the other.

Teachers need to take advantage of regularities within the language. In the computer analysis mentioned at the opening of this chapter, Hanna, Hodges, and Hanna (cited in Schlagal, 2001, pp. 150–151) found "four fifths of the phonemes contained in the words comprising the traditional spelling vocabulary of the elementary school child approximate the alphabetic principle in their letter representations," which means 80% of the words in English are predictable. In Edward B. Fry's top 1,000 high-frequency words (2000), the spelling pattern of vowel/single consonant words (*rip*) predicts the word's sound 86% of the time, short vowel/two consonants (*risk*) 89% of the time, long vowel/silent e (*ripe*) 81%, double vowels (*rain*) 77%, and open syllable-consonant/long vowel (*go*) 77%. The irregulars, such as *come, said,* and *do,* get so much attention because they are high-frequency words.

One of the best ways for young students to learn beginning spelling is through writing. Writing also happens to be the sole reason anyone learns to spell. **Invented, inventive, developmental, or approximated spelling** frees young writers from being bound by absolute correctness. The words with which they practice are their words. S. S. Robinson (cited in May, 1998) found that children's invented spelling was the best predictor of subsequent early reading success, perhaps because spelling strengthens children's phonemic awareness as they listen closely for sounds to give them clues about which letters to write. They begin to generate hypotheses about how the whole spelling-reading-writing system works. Invented spelling also allows writers to write fast enough so that the content can be remembered. Invented spelling does not teach students how to spell correctly, but it does give them the underpinnings.

Young spellers need daily writing opportunities. They can write about their weekends, their families, or a class project. They can write birthday cards, messages to their classmates, or stories about seasons or holidays. Students can write about the content they are learning or about personal experiences. Since this type of writing is mostly practice and experimentation, it need not be graded.

The teacher provides encouragement as she moves around the room asking questions, helping a student relate a sound to a letter, or perhaps having the child listen for a medial sound (the one in the middle), which is harder to identify. As students become more proficient at the basic relationships, the teacher may identify a vowel, help children remember a high-frequency word they have seen in print, or compare a word in a child's writing to a word on a wall chart. It is an art to nudge children along the developmental scale at just the right time, adding to a child's spelling only those elements the child is ready for. This is why it is essential that teachers understand how spelling and phonetic knowledge develop.

> It is an art to nudge children along the developmental scale at just the right time, adding to a child's spelling only those elements the child is ready for.

Tapping phonemes is a standard phonemic awareness activity; it is also useful in spelling as students work to identify all the sounds in a word. An interesting variation is to ask them to tap one finger at a time, starting with their little finger and move in a left-to-right progression, thus establishing the sequence of sounds for spelling.

Voiced and voiceless pairs in spelling are sometimes hard to discriminate. At this stage, it is useful to help children discriminate between /p/ and /b/, /t/ and /d/, /k/ and /g/, /f/ and /v/, /s/ and /z/, /sh/ and /zh/, and /ch/ and /j/. The pairs are spoken in the same manner, but one is quiet and the other vocalized. These pairs are often confused in spelling, as in *efry* for *every.* Clear articulation, distinguishing between the pairs, and noticing mouth movement can clarify some of these spelling difficulties (Moats, 2005).

In **matching sounds to letters**, students can match words with the initial letter of the teacher's word, or the teacher can match the letter to a student's word. Sometimes, it is fun for the teacher to respond and allow the student to decide if the teacher's response matched or not. I have found that many clinic students do not have clear enunciation, making it difficult for them to determine the match. Samuel Orton, who worked with dyslexic readers starting in the 1930s, also found clear articulation to be a problem, especially with short vowels. He encouraged more-accurate spoken reproduction of words by students so their sounds might be more clearly recognized. This encouragement would be a help with spelling too.

Word sorting uses words written on individual cards or paper strips and then sorted or classified into categories. Word sorting is effective because it is manipulative and flexible (Zutell, 1998). Students can change their minds as they move the cards around and see patterns and contrasts. They are actively engaged in problem solving, making generalizations, and discovering relationships (Fresch & Wheaton, 1997). Schlagal (2001) recommends that all spelling words be in the students' sight vocabularies so that they concentrate on spelling patterns rather than word identification.

If students make their own categories, the sort is called open, but if the categories are provided by the teacher, the sort is closed. A set of cards may be developed to explore a single spelling issue, or a larger set of cards can be used for multiple sorts. A pocket chart works well so that all students can see the cards, which are securely held in place. Beginning readers can sort pictures by sound and then work on the spelling. When students reach the phonetic stage and are able to include all the sounds they hear, vowel sounds can be sorted. Sorting works well for contrasting patterns and for discriminating the usual sound from an alternate sound.

In each of the preceding activities, be sure to have children discuss their reasoning. Learning is a social process, and verbalization helps bring the concept to a conscious level. The correct spelling is just the end product. The process of generalizing the patterns is the real work.

Spelling by Analogy

Using analogies to spell (or read) vowel sounds and rhyming word segments is a very powerful technique that resurfaced in the 1930s, 1940s, 1970s, and 1990s, supported by practitioners' and researchers' beliefs. Some teachers may be more familiar with the terms *word families, onsets and rimes,* or *phonograms.* One can quibble about nuances in definitions, but they are all similar in classroom usage.

The idea is that when children learn one member of the family, they learn them all. Analogies are also highly efficient for learning vowel sounds because only the onset is segmented from the rime. Even beginning readers are able to make inferences between known and unknown words. To appreciate the effectiveness of learning vowel sounds through word families, try to pronounce the vowel sounds in the following syllables: *ma, ma, di, di, sa, soa.* Now try the following: *ad, ade, im, ime, ap, oap.* Which would be more helpful for reading or spelling the words *mad, made, dim, dime, sap,* and *soap?* Vowels, which are the scourge of spelling in English, are so difficult because there are 16 vowel sounds but only 5 vowel letters, with a little help from *y* and *w.* English language learners have an especially difficult time with English vowels. For example, Spanish vowels are much more consistent, and the Spanish letter *e* is pronounced long *a* (*café*), and *i* is pronounced as long *e* (*buenos dias*).

> Vowels, which are the scourge of spelling in English, are so difficult because there are 16 vowel sounds but only 5 vowel letters, with a little help from *y* and *w.*

In a famous 1970 study with 900 children, Wylie and Durrell found that only 37 rimes are needed to generate 500 words frequently used by children in first through third grade. These common rimes and other less common but useful rimes are found in Figure 4.3.

Phonograms, onsets and rimes, spelling by analogy, and word families are rich strategies for learning to spell ornery vowel sounds, for learning multiple words from a single lesson, and for developing a strategy that can be applied over and over again independently.

Hinky pinkies can be used when studying word families. Hink pinks are a pair of one-syllable words that rhyme, hinky pinkies are a pair of two-syllable words that rhyme, and hinkity pinkities are a pair of three-syllable words that rhyme. They are structured into riddles and can also provide an opportunity to study alternative spellings for rhyming words.

What do you put over a ship to keep it dry in storage? A boat coat.

What do you call a chubby cat? A flabby tabby.

What disease describes high school seniors as they apply to college? Admission condition.

Word Walls

Many teachers use word walls or large charts of words for references that can be accessed at a glance. The word wall might be organized either alphabetically, by word families, or by topic. No one at any age likes to pull out the dictionary constantly, but children will willingly check spelling from a chart that the teacher has prepared or that the class has developed. Some teachers like to prepare a laminated copy of the 100 most frequently used words (Fry, 2000) for students to keep at their desk (Figure 10.3). The more accessible the list, chart, or word wall, the greater the likelihood that it will be used. The 100 most frequently used words make up more than 50% of all the words children and adults write; therefore it is a very handy list.

Some charts include just the phonetically irregular sight words. The common but irregular words listed in Figure 10.4 are high-frequency words that continue to give students trouble through the middle grades. They may be learned by continuous exposure to reading because they are such high-frequency words, but explicit spelling instruction also helps.

Figure 10.3 The 100 most frequently used words

<u>a</u>	*about*	*all*	am	an
and	**are**	as	at	be
been	but	by	called	can
come	*could*	day	did	**do**
down	each	**find**	first	for
from	*get*	go	had	has
have	he	her	him	his
how	I	if	in	**into**
is	it	its	like	long
look	made	make	**many**	may
more	my	no	not	now
number	**of**	on	**one**	or
other	out	part	**people**	**said**
see	she	so	**some**	than
that	<u>the</u>	**their**	them	then
there	these	*they*	this	time
to	**two**	up	use	**was**
water	way	we	**were**	**what**
when	which	**who**	will	with
words	write	*would*	*you*	**your**

Source: Fry, E. B., *1000 Instant Words by Dr. Fry.* Westminster, CA: Teacher Created Materials Publishing, 2000.

Note: The **bold faced** words are irregulars that do not follow common decodable spelling patterns.

The ***bold faced and italicized*** words are predictable but follow patterns learned in late second or third grade.

The <u>underlined</u> words have different pronunciations in some cases.

Figure 10.4 Common but irregular words

of	they	one
some	could	people
great	because	does
know	again	own
come	though	answer
thought	said	many

Learning Spelling Through Reading and Writing

If children were exposed to a formal spelling program of 20 words every week from first grade to eighth grade, they would learn only 5,760 words. Wilde (1992) estimates that the average literate adult can spell 80,000 words. The remainder are learned by sight, through reading, or by analogy. At the end of an eight-year study, Hughes and Searle (1997) concluded that significant amounts of reading and writing are critical if students are to advance in spelling ability.

■ TECHNIQUES FOR TRANSITIONAL SPELLERS

Transitional spellers have conquered the basic sound-symbol relationships. Now they need to learn the alternate representations of the sounds and the orthographic regulations. This kind of work requires finer discrimination, greater visual memory, and more-specific instruction. A teacher is not offending a child's individuality when helping the child become a more proficient speller. Adding knowledge for the next stage of spelling is very different from marking every error in red and insisting on spelling perfection. Figure 10.2 listed the alternate spellings of all the consonant and vowel sounds. The list is considerable. Even in the middle grades, word families and spelling by analogy are useful.

Word Sorts

Word sorts allow for active manipulation rather than memorization. They are valuable at the transitional stage, which requires discrimination of a finer nature. Sets of words can be prepared on index cards, sticky notes, or small slips of paper. The sturdier varieties, once prepared, can be used from year to year if labeled and kept in zip-lock bags. The teacher can place category words at the top of each column, or students can decide on their own what the categories should be. The rule of "used but confused" is helpful for deciding on the words. If the categories are /ou/ in *ouch* and long *o*, the words might be *down, town, how, found, couch, sound, road, float, roast, rope, hole,* and *cone.* Adding *old, fold,* and *short* would make the activity more challenging for better spellers. Students must explain what the rule is, why each word fits or doesn't fit in a given category, or that some are irregular. Word sorts are not quite as effective as the Directed Spelling Thinking Activity (discussed next) because some children will sort by visual features unless they are required to pronounce the words and develop the rule. Word sorts are an excellent tool for noticing small differences or close alternatives.

Directed Spelling Thinking Activity

A particularly good activity for learning spelling alternatives is Jerry Zutell's Directed Spelling Thinking Activity (DSTA; 1996). It is patterned after Russell Stauffer's DRTA (see Chapter 6). In a DSTA, students who are using but confusing a word pattern are given a pretest of 16 to 20 words, including words from two or three contrasting patterns and a few exceptions. They might be consonant alternatives for /f/, such as *feet, laugh, sheriff,* and *graph,* or they could be vowel alternatives for long /a/, such as *raid*, *made*, and *say*. The words should all be in the students' speaking and reading vocabularies.

The group members then share their initial attempts and discuss their strategies and reasoning in attempting to spell the words. As students discuss the possible answers, they are actively engaged in discovering and thinking through the possibilities. Students may notice patterns or similarities and revise remaining words on the list. Only after discussion and a group prediction does the teacher present the correct spelling.

DSTA allows for active participation, concept development, and social learning, and it promotes attention to detail. It is also fun and a vivid contrast to many rote and dull spelling exercises.

Spelling Multisyllable Words

Learning syllable rules may not be necessary for most developmental spellers, but it can help struggling spellers. There are six types:

1. The closed syllable — cvc or vc — *fan, at*
2. The silent e syllable — cvce or vce — *gate, ace*
3. The open syllable — cv — *no*
4. The r-controlled syllable — vr — *dark*
5. The consonant-le syllable — cle — *little*
6. The diphthong or double vowel syllable — vv — *feet, cloud*

Many teachers have students practice only with real words, but nonsense words are effective because syllables are seldom complete, recognizable words. The one-vowel-sound-per-syllable rule is a useful place to start. Determining syllable boundaries is difficult for many spellers because boundaries in speech are not quite as fixed as boundaries in spelling. It is the boundaries between syllables that cause confusion rather than the number of syllables per word. Starting with multisyllable words that follow the rules will help.

Analogies can be valuable for multisyllable words too. Students start with known words such as *win*, *at*, *then*, *sit*, *car*, and *is*. They work on target words that have the same spelling patterns, such as *bitter*, *blister*, *begin*, *winter*, *batter*, *margin*, *flatten*, and *mister*.

Resources

Students need to know how to use the dictionary to check spellings. Dictionaries come in an assortment of levels of difficulty, from picture glossaries to college level. Having a selection of dictionaries helps to meet a variety of needs.

What about spell check on the computer? It is a fabulous tool, so students should learn how to use it. They need to be taught not to simply select the first alternative that appears and that proofreading still needs to be done, especially for homonyms. Turning off the automatic correction tool is a good idea because the automatically selected word may not be the right one, and the student is not alerted that there is an error.

Wide Reading and Writing

Reading and writing continue to be immensely important for providing the information to build word concepts. However, incidental learning may be temporary unless direct study of orthographic concepts fixes the word in memory. Presenting spelling words in context or through proofreading exercises seems to be more a distraction than a help (Schlagal, 2002).

Multisensory Techniques

A multisensory technique is visual, auditory, kinesthetic, and tactile (VAKT), and it includes saying, writing, checking, and tracing the word, and then writing the word from memory. The belief supporting this technique is that students learn best when information is presented in a variety of modalities. Originally developed by Grace Fernald in 1943, VAKT has been found to be successful with learning-disabled students (Murphy, 1997). Murphy's study of third graders showed an 11% increase in correct spelling by students using the VAKT method compared with students using traditional methods.

■ SPELLING RULES

Patterns are better than rules, but these four rules deserve teaching:

1. When a word ends in a single vowel and a single consonant, double the consonant before adding *-ed* or *-ing* if the word is monosyllabic or has stress on the final syllable.

2. When a word ends in a silent final *e*, drop the *e* before adding suffixes starting with a vowel. Dropping the *e* before *-ed* is intuitive and probably does not need to be taught.

3. When a word ends in a consonant and *y*, change the *y* to *i* before adding most suffixes except for those beginning with *i*.

4. Use *i* before *e*, except after *c*, or when sounded as *a* in *neighbor* and *weigh*, or in *weird* words such as *their*.

Memorizing the Spelling Demons

Some spelling demons just need to be memorized. A good example is *carrot*, *carat*, *karat*, and *caret*. Sound-symbol, roots and meanings, and English orthographic patterns are of no help here. By the way, the four are the vegetable, the gem stone weight, the unit of measure for the purity of gold, and the insert mark used in editing. When dealing with spelling demons, rote practice still works. Nancy Murphy (1997) reports that the look-say-write method, shown below, was developed by E. Horn in 1919.

1. Look at the word and say it to yourself.

2. Close your eyes and try to see the word as you spell it to yourself.

3. Check to see if you were right.

4. Cover the word and write it.

5. Check to see if you were right.

6. Repeat steps 4 and 5 two more times.

Do not eliminate this strategy just because it is old and not structured as a game. The important thing is to have students write the words from memory, not just copy. It may be one of the few activities that can strengthen visual memory. Because visual memory is so important, when students practice spelling words, they should write them rather than practice aloud (Matz, 1994).

> Because visual memory is so important, when students practice spelling words, they should write them rather than practice aloud.

WHAT ABOUT SPELLING TESTS? ■

One of the most balanced and manageable approaches to spelling tests is for the teacher to have a base list of words of varying difficulty for the week. The words should share either a common or a contrasting orthographic pattern, and the list may include some sight words. The teacher may select the words for the base list or use the spelling book if it is organized by pattern. The spelling book list may need to be altered to include some easier words that follow the pattern for the benefit of those students who are working at an earlier developmental level. When students have different lists, the spelling test is given in partners. There are some inherent problems with accuracy, but stapling a copy of the original list onto the completed spelling test provides for cross-checking by the teacher.

Adding words that the child has misspelled the previous week is very effective for transfer but logistically difficult to manage. It becomes possible when papers are returned once each week, just prior to the pretest. Those misspelled words go on the top of each student's personal list. The list is rounded out with the base words.

The most workable plan that I have come across is an ingenious blend that includes self-choice, a range of difficulty, a way to eliminate studying known words, and an overall related list. It is from Mary Jo Fresch and Aileen Wheaton (1997). It starts with a pretest similar to the one in Figure 10.5. Students fold the paper along the dotted line and are given the pretest from words in the first column. For every word they spell correctly, they can choose a word from the second column. If the pretest list has words with a range of difficulty, below-grade-level students can be incorporated easily into the week's activity at an appropriate level. Children who consistently score above 80% can choose their own words, but the words they choose must be based on the pattern of the week. Students copy their list three times. List one goes home, list two stays in school, and list three can be cut apart for word-sorting activities.

For the list in Figure 10.5, small groups of children in my class did open word sorts for different spellings of the /aw/ sound. They generated the rules, and it did not matter if all the students had the same words. The small groups then gathered together to do a large sort with the teacher as students added their insights and conclusions.

For about 15 minutes the next day, students participated in a word hunt, in which they searched their own reading materials for more examples of these patterns. On the third day, students used their word list in writing. Fresch and Wheaton (1997, p. 28) suggest, "These compositions [can] take on forms such as poetry, advertisements, riddles, limericks, and short stories. . . . The entire writing process is used as the texts are edited." On the fourth day, depending on the pattern, students could proofread, do dictionary work, work with compounds, or pretest by writing the words in columns headed with the appropriate pattern rule. Day five involved buddy testing.

In 1897, J. M. Rice wrote a journal article in *The Forum* entitled "The Futility of the Spelling Grind." If we use all that is known about teaching and learning spelling, perhaps in this century, Rice's thoughts will no longer hold true.

Figure 10.5 Sample list for a spelling test

Pretest	Base list	Choice list
	saw	drawn
	haunted	gnaw
	dawn	squaw
	launch	fraught
	law	laundry
	flaw	taunt
	caught	chalk
	talking	halt
	lawn	malted
	clawed	stalk
	walk	sought
	straw	ought
	draw	brought
	salt	fought
	off	naughty

Source: Adapted from Fresch, M. J, and Wheaton, A. "Sort, Search, and Discover." *The Reading Teacher,* 51, 1997.

11

Balanced Writing

Of all those arts in which the wise excel,
Nature's chief masterpiece is writing well.

—John Sheffield

Being able to write well is an admired skill, but it is a form of communication we use somewhat grudgingly when we cannot pick up the phone or meet face to face. Whether we are an adult or a child, writing is often a love-hate relationship that some of us take joy in, some find a tool for communication, and some just hate. It is a complex process involving planning, content selection, organization, revision, consideration of the audience and purpose, mastery of English skills, and sustained attention. Researchers (Scardamalia & Bereiter, 1986; Graham, Harris, & Larsen, 2001) have identified all these aspects as being difficult for school-aged children. These challenges are apparent in the most recent National Assessment of Educational Progress, which reported 14% of fourth graders, 15% of eighth graders, and 26% of twelfth graders below the basic level. Fourth- and eighth-grade scores had risen by one or two points between the 1998 and 2002 assessments, and girls outperformed boys at all three grade levels (National Center for Education Statistics, 2002).

Much research in writing was done in the 1980s and early 1990s, and the findings changed classroom practices and introduced the writing process and writers' workshop. Research has continued, with a special focus on teaching learning-disabled students and English language learners to write well.

ELEMENTS OF THE WRITING PROCESS ■

The writing process can be thought of as having five stages: prewriting, drafting, revising, editing, and publishing. It would be wonderful if the entire process actually progressed in a fixed, stable order, but no writer, child or adult, can keep the entire process from being messy. The process gets messier as the writer matures

179

and is able to mentally switch back and forth among the steps, anticipating how changes in one step will affect the others. However, for the sake of explanation, let us assume that it is an orderly process.

Prewriting

Prewriting is the planning stage and includes both deciding on a topic and planning the general development of the piece. Finding a topic can be a solitary activity or done as brainstorming with a group. Planning is more complex.

Brainstorming in student-directed writing, in which students write about a topic of their own choice, includes coming up with multiple topics that might interest a student. One idea will spark the imagination of the writer, or a topic might be tucked away for development at a later time. If the writing is teacher directed, in which a specific topic is assigned by the teacher, the brainstorming session will be narrower. It will focus on various ways to approach the topic or on the components that need to be included. During the brainstorming process, not only are ideas generated, but explicit language to express the ideas and supporting details emerges.

The point of brainstorming is not only to find a topic but also to consider the possibilities of different approaches and their relative merits. One outcome of brainstorming is that students learn not to simply take the first topic that pops into their heads but to choose a topic that will work out well, is well suited to the purpose, or is appealing to the student.

> Better writers take longer to plan their writing than average writers do.

Planning the development of a piece is an important phase of good writing. Better writers take longer to plan their writing than average writers do. Stallard (cited in Hillocks, 1986) found that good writers take 4.18 minutes to plan, but average writers take only 1.2 minutes to plan. All but the youngest writers can work from an outline of a few key words and phrases. The youngest writers, and sometimes older ones, plan by drawing or by talking.

Drafting, Revising, and Editing

For the youngest writers, there is only one draft. Done is done! The process of physically forming letters, spelling, and composing is a joyful but monumental task. They approach writing in a straightforward manner, producing text just for the pleasure in it, not for the product. There is no going back; they just go forward to the next thought and the next piece of primary writing paper. In second grade, students begin to make "sloppy copies" and then final drafts. For older students, revising means changing ideas, organization, and content, whereas editing refers to the mechanical aspects of spelling, punctuating, correcting grammar, and paragraphing.

Publishing

Publishing means polishing a draft and sharing it with a wider audience. The youngest writers love sitting in the Author's Chair, a chair specially reserved for reading the piece to the class. The listeners may give positive comments and suggestions and may ask the author questions. Young writers experience the pride of having composed a piece and then reading it to an appreciative audience. The audience's questions alert writers to missing details. Little ones can listen to two to three authors before becoming restless.

Another publishing technique is making bound classroom books of illustrated stories written by the young authors. Class anthologies can be compiled and shared with students in other classes, shared through a school publication, or sent home as a class project. Other teachers elect simply to post pieces on the bulletin board.

DEVELOPMENTAL STAGES OF WRITING ■

Students become increasingly sophisticated in their use of the elements of writing through growth in cognitive capabilities and good instruction. The developmental characteristics of writers are summarized briefly in the following sections.

Kindergarten and First and Second Grades

Emergent writing begins as scribble writing and then progresses to a combination of letters, numbers, or symbols. "My cat, Elliot, sleeps in the sun" might come out "FF3W+AA." With phonics and spelling instruction, compositions approximate Standard English to a greater and greater degree throughout the grades.

The youngest writers do not plan. Often the idea occurs through drawing, which expresses much of the content. Making a drawing first (rather than illustrating after) helps them remember their ideas when they take time out to decide what letter is required for the word they want to write. Second graders can decide on a topic through verbal rehearsals, or talking through the possibilities. Students at this age are rather concrete in their thinking and may need to actually write out whole sentences as they do not yet have the mental flexibility that allows more mature writers to internally manipulate, accept, and reject ideas and make changes before putting the first word on paper.

Writers often vocalize while they compose in order to hang on to their ideas or to sound out words. Students start writing by labeling pictures with single words and then with a declarative sentence. Next they write "all about" stories. These are distinguished by several similar, related sentences: "I like pizza. I like steak. I like brownies. They are good." Narrative stories that have a sequence and action develop later in first grade. Curiously, children begin writing narratives at about the same time they are able to draw figures in profile. Second graders write "bed to bed stories," all starting with "I got up in the morning" and giving the subsequent events in detail, all strung together with a seemingly endless supply of *and*s. Most children have not yet developed the ability to focus on one part of a story more than another.

Young children tend to write more pieces rather than longer pieces and seldom make any changes in previously written text. When the topic of a story goes astray, children often fix it by changing the title. Teachers can encourage elaboration by asking questions, and second-grade teachers often encourage stapling the added details to the piece rather than asking students to recopy. The additions are called spiders because the final piece, with all the stapled-on legs sticking out, resembles one. Editing should be saved until the end as the constant spelling concerns of young writers often interrupt their thoughts. Important pieces of writing can be brought to the publication stage via the teacher, who acts as editor-in-chief.

Third, Fourth, and Fifth Grades

Third graders have the ability to plan and begin to divide events or separate subtopics into paragraphs. Details are usually sparse, for although the student has the supporting details in mind, it just takes too long to include everything. Fourth and fifth graders are better able to focus on key points and can consider alternate plans in their minds without having to write down the alternatives. They can weigh one topic against another and anticipate a reader's response. Students in these grades learn to express shifts in time and intersperse dialogue.

Revision follows writing for third graders, but older children can handle simultaneous composition and revision. Asking students to reread their work to another student or to the teacher usually prompts new ideas and forces the children to reconsider their writing through the eyes of a reader. Children who have been read to or who read many books independently are more likely to write pieces that imitate a sophisticated style.

Older Students

Older students can plan well and write about complex topics. They can draft, revise, and edit simultaneously and shift back and forth among these tasks with ease. They write with much greater detail and learn how to connect ideas so that the reader can follow. This progress is partially due to the development of abstract thinking abilities and longer attention spans. Older students benefit from comparisons and rating scales and can make good use of peer editing.

■ BALANCED WRITING INSTRUCTION

Balanced writing instruction is somewhat different from balanced reading instruction. The big picture in writing (the first whole in whole-part-whole instruction) comes from wide reading, which serves as a model of genre, clarity, and cohesion. Reading helps children understand the purposes for writing. But where writing ideas come from and how the skills are developed and practiced can be conceptualized in terms of two different approaches. The most familiar philosophies can be categorized broadly as student-directed writing (the writers' workshop approach) and teacher-directed writing (structured writing).

The main advantages of student-directed writing are motivation and ownership, due to the students' choosing their own topics, and rich detail, because the content comes from students' personal experiences. Clarity is developed through reader responses to a piece. The optimum outcomes of student-directed writing are increased flexibility and fluency in writing.

The main advantages of teacher-directed writing are concentration on and refinement of one part of the writing process at a time, more-structured teacher guidance, development of criteria for good writing, and comparison and contrast of similar pieces of writing. The primary outcome of teacher-directed writing is craftsmanship.

Both approaches share the elements of the writing process and make use of peer discussion and revision groups, and both approaches are far superior to older practices of assigning without instruction and grading primarily for correct English conventions. You probably remember the venerable "What I Did During Summer Vacation," which was assigned without direction (so as not to inhibit creativity) and graded by some process shrouded in mystery (believed to have something to do with the throwing of darts). Teachers can use both the student-directed and the teacher-directed approach by providing direct instruction at times and encouraging student choice at others. The final whole in the whole-part-whole model has to do with writing for real purposes for which good written communication skills make a difference.

WRITERS' WORKSHOP ■

Writers' workshop was developed by Donald Graves (1983), Nancie Atwell (1987), and Lucy Calkins (1994), and continues with Shelly Harwayne (2001). Because children write about topics of their own choice, the hallmark of writers' workshop is personal ownership. Thus in a single classroom, children are writing about a multiplicity of topics, and each child may be at a different point in the writing process.

During workshop time, some children may be drafting independently while others may be at work with a partner, trying out new ideas, developing details, or determining organization. Other students may be looking for a peer to listen and respond to their paper. Students working in the drafting area, however, may not be disturbed by others or asked to peer edit. Peer partners may be found through a sign-up sheet or by waiting in a specified corner of the room, where two chairs and a workspace have been set aside just for peer editing. Other children may have finished the revision process and found peers who are helping them edit for spelling, sentence structure, punctuation, or paragraphing. Others may be preparing the final copy for publication. Students are free to move around but must stay quiet and on task.

Underlying Structure of Writers' Workshop

A strong organizational structure underlies writers' workshop. Early sessions begin with the whole class brainstorming to choose an idea to cultivate immediately or to store for later use. For accountability purposes, at the start of each session, the teacher asks for the status of the class, quickly asking students what their own agenda is for the session and recording the information on a chart. Although students generally move at their own pace, children occasionally need to be spurred along or are sometimes told what must be accomplished by the end of the session.

Some classes may start with a ten-minute minilesson on one aspect of the writing process if the teacher notices that several students are stuck at the same stage. The lessons may focus on leads, introducing different genres, or punctuation. Drafting centers with a large supply of papers, pens, markers, scissors, portfolios, glue, and staplers need to be prepared. During writing time, students draft independently or ask for assistance from peers. The teacher circulates, holding impromptu conferences, or has longer conferences with children who need feedback. On some days, the last seven to eight minutes are set aside for sharing. Some students will have final pieces to read aloud. Others may disclose a problem and ask for possible endings, motivations, or details to make the piece more descriptive. The procedures for writers' workshop need to be taught, and many of the initial minilessons are used for procedural issues.

To make peer conferences more productive, partners can be taught to make the following kinds of statements: (1) I like . . . , (2) I wonder . . . , (3) these are questions I have, and (4) (for the author) plans for action.

> Conferencing is one of the major ways teachers help lift the quality of students' work.

Writers' workshop allows for abundant social interaction. Children enjoy sharing ideas, working with a partner, and listening to and telling stories. This sharing is not only allowed but is encouraged and very necessary. To improve their writing, writers must practice and listen to readers' responses (Kruzich, 1995).

The Teacher's Role in Writers' Workshop

In writers' workshop, the teacher circulates asking open-ended questions to encourage children to evaluate their own work in order to make it more complete and understandable. On some days, just a minute or two is spent with each child. On other days, the teacher is available for longer conferences with writers. Because not all writers are at the same stage of the writing process, the teacher can confer individually with students instead of grading papers at night and writing copious notes to the students, who may or may not read them. Conferencing is one of the major ways teachers help lift the quality of students' work (Harwayne, 2001). Students can request conferences when the teacher asks for the status of each student. During a teacher conference, the teacher responds by asking open-ended questions, such as those in Figure 11.1. When the teacher takes a nondirective role, then the writer must make the decisions, which is the first step toward becoming a self-evaluating writer. Teacher nudging is occasionally allowed.

A predictable block of time for uninterrupted writing is one of the requirements for writers' workshop. Atwell (1987) recommends a minimum of three hours or three class periods each week. Children will always be on the lookout for some intriguing topic because they know writing time is coming up.

Children's personal writing and choice of topics are important components in writers' workshop. Students learn about clarity from audience response, develop fluency, and make their own meanings and decisions.

Figure 11.1 Open-ended questions for writers' workshop

---

1. Tell me about your story.

2. What part do you like best?

3. When you told me your favorite part, were there details that you didn't write?

4. What is the problem (or, what is the beginning) in your story?

5. How does it end?

6. How does the main character feel?

7. What questions might the other students have if they hear this?

8. Were you trying to write this the way your favorite author writes?

9. Have you chosen some words that help the reader see this?

10. Is it in order, the way it happened?

11. What can you borrow from the literature you have been reading?

12. Can you zero in on one part to let the reader really see what is happening?

Source: Adapted from N. Zaragoza and S. Vaughn, 1995.

STRUCTURED WRITING ■

While many teachers are pleased with the fluency and flexibility that develop through student-centered writing, they find that the explicit instruction and clear criteria used in structured writing instruction also help students become better writers. Hillocks (1986) found this to be true in a meta-analysis conducted for the United States Department of Education's Educational Resources Information Center, in which he analyzed 63 research studies encompassing 6,313 students in experimental groups and 5,492 students in control groups. Hillocks's work has remained the classic study of research-based instruction for 20 years. (An updated collection of writing research, the first in 20 years, titled *Research on Composition: Multiple Perspectives on Two Decades of Change,* edited by Peter Smorginski, has recently been published by Teachers College Press.)

The greatest gains in writing were made in what Hillocks called the environmental mode of writing instruction, which consisted of clear and specific objectives, a set of materials and problems selected to let students practice specific aspects of writing, and high levels of peer interaction. The average effect size for the environmental mode of writing was .75, compared with .26 for the writers' workshop style of instruction, which Hillocks termed natural process writing. Scales to judge writing and to develop criteria are often used in environmental writing.

Harris, Graham, and Mason (2003) also recommend a structured approach, especially for students experiencing problems with writing. "Mini-lessons might not offer the extensive, explicit, and supported instruction students need to master important strategies and abilities" (p. 4). Teaching writing strategies to students with learning disabilities can result in considerable benefits to writing quality and students' self-perceptions of their ability to write effectively (Baker, Gersten, & Graham, 2003).

Scales and Rubrics to Judge the Quality of Writing

Starting with the assessment can clarify learning objectives and activities. If process writing gives teachers the *how* of writing instruction, standards and rubrics inform teachers about *what* to teach. Rubrics translate the standards into understandable expectations for both teachers and students. The analytic scales (individual features) provide evaluation criteria for focus, support, organization, and English conventions, which are the most common criteria found in standards (although the wording may vary). Focus means sticking to one topic and not digressing throughout the entire piece. Support refers to the richness of elaboration, details, and examples. Organization describes an orderly development that transitions from one topic or event to another, and English conventions cover spelling, punctuation, and grammar. With nonfiction pieces, accuracy may be an additional criterion. There may also be standards for vocabulary, sentence structure, and voice in writing. It takes years to master and coordinate all these aspects of writing. Focus and organization are usually conquered before richness of detail and smooth transitions for connecting ideas.

Put all the scales together, and what you have is called a rubric. Checklists of writing features have long been used in the classroom, but a rubric is more specific because each performance level is specifically described. The usual genres are narrative, expository, persuasive, and descriptive, and the rubrics are similar for most features. Teachers develop their own rubrics for specific assignments or use student-friendly versions of rubrics from state assessments. Look at Rubistar, http://rubistar.4teachers.org, from Advanced Learning Technologies, and Teachnology, http://www.teach-nology.com, from Teachnology Inc., for ready-to-use rubrics. They can be altered to meet particular needs. The Landmark rubric generator at http://www.landmark-project.com provides a blank format.

Children sometimes use different criteria than adults do to judge the quality or effectiveness of writing. This mismatch of criteria occasionally produces pieces that are neat and spelled correctly but also long and devoid of coherent content. Rubrics provide common criteria so that students no longer have to guess how the writing will be evaluated or what the desired outcomes are for a particular format or genre of writing.

Scales and rubrics have many advantages. They can help children develop a set of standards for good writing, they can be used to clarify an assignment, they can be used as students self-revise or participate in revision groups, and they can be used for grading. Rubrics may be as complex as the one in Figure 11.2, which has a six-point scale for a persuasive essay, or they may be simplified to a three- or four-point scale for everyday classroom use. While it may take some effort to prepare a rubric, the result is well worth the trouble because of its multiple uses.

Prewriting and Planning in Structured Writing

Although rubrics may be used in all stages of writing, they are especially helpful for clarifying expectations. If children know the requirements, they will be better able to construct a plan and shape the purpose and organization of the final product. Clarifying expectations with a rubric can come before or after brainstorming.

Imagine **brainstorming** with students for whom reading and writing are integrated and who are going to read about a child who is left on his own in *Crispin: The Cross of Lead* (Avi, 2002). The teacher wants the class to empathize with the character's feelings of distress and not knowing where to turn. Children might activate their prior knowledge and develop empathy for the character by writing about a time when they were on their own and without help.

As the students brainstorm about their own experiences, the teacher acts as scribe, writing on chart paper or on the chalkboard so that ideas are not forgotten. Various students relate their own stories as the teacher helps the children bring to the forefront emotions and solutions to the problems they describe. As students relate being in a big, new school on the first day, being left to do a task while their parents were busy or away, figuring out how to get help, or being lost and determining how to find their way, images and stories begin to percolate, even in the minds of those students who usually protest that they have no stories to tell. All the aspects—character, plot, setting, sequence, emotion, and climax—begin to be set into motion. Brainstorming not only helps students come up with a topic; it encourages them to consider several stories before settling on a final choice. It also brings details and vocabulary to the surface for immediate use. Personal writing can be a part of structured writing. The difference between writer's workshop and this assignment is that all students are working on the same assignment for the same purpose.

Graphic organizers are the visual equivalents of outlines and are used for planning. They come in all shapes and organizational patterns. They are easy to devise and much less intimidating than the traditional outline. Depending on the type of writing desired, there is a graphic organizer to support it. Since persuasive and expository types of writing are organized on a topic-subtopic basis, as opposed to narratives and story writing, which are organized along sequential lines, the graphic organizers are different for each. Figure 11.3 is a graphic organizer for expository or persuasive pieces and helps students develop the introduction, body, and conclusion. Figure 11.4 is a primary expository organizer in which the teacher has modeled the opening and closing, and the students need only write the body (after studying an undersea unit). For a

Figure 11.2 Six-point rubric: "All Summer in a Day"

Criteria / Performance	1	2	3	4	5	6
FOCUS	• No focus • Wanders	• Focus unclear • Conflicting focus • Changes position • Retelling • Not cause and effect	• Focus clear but must be inferred • Introduction or conclusion may not match body	• Focus stated • Has introduction and conclusion • Introduction or conclusion may be unclear	• Focus stated • Has introduction and conclusion • Body matches	• Focus and reasons announced in introduction • Body matches in order • Conclusion matches
DETAIL	• Almost no detail	• Little detail • List of reasons with no detail	• Few details • Invalid argument • Inaccurate details • Cause of unhappiness unclear	• Major and some minor detail • At least one reason well explained • More general than specific	• Major and lots of minor detail • Two reasons well explained • Gives examples	• All reasons well explained with second order details
ORGANIZATION	• Rambling	• Lacks cohesion • Major digression	• Beginning clear, may drop off at end • More than one topic in a paragraph • Minor digression	• Has introduction, body, and conclusion • One topic/paragraph	• Argument carries throughout introduction, body, and end • Has main idea sentences	• Argument carries throughout • Clearly shows cause and effect • Paragraphed appropriately • Uses more than one transition
CONVENTIONS	• Cannot be understood because of grammar, structure, or inappropriate vocabulary	• Several sentences do not make sense • Inappropriate vocabulary • Many common spelling errors	• Many errors • Several sentence runons or fragments • Appropriate vocabulary	• Some errors • Appropriate vocabulary • Awkward sentences	• Minor errors • Appropriate vocabulary	• 1-2 errors at the most • Appropriate vocabulary

Source: Rubric for "All Summer in a Day" by Ray Bradbury.

narrative, Figure 11.5 helps develop the sequence of the story, and Figure 11.6 is a Venn diagram, used to plan comparison and contrast writing. Children love to make their own graphic organizers on Inspiration or Kidspiration (Inspiration Software, Inc.), the software that makes illustrated webs.

Once a plan is jotted down on a graphic organizer, there is a strong likelihood that the writer will follow the plan and not stray far afield in the middle of the piece. This works extremely well with children in third grade or older. Second graders often write the sequel to the plan instead of following it. It is just a matter of maturity until they have the cognitive skills to plan ahead.

Frameworks also help writers plan a story. The W-W-W, What=2 How=2 framework stands for the following questions:

Who is the main character?

When does the story take place?

Where does the story take place?

What do the main character and other characters do or want to do?

What happens then to the main character and other characters?

How does the story end?

How do the main character and the other characters feel? (Harris et al., 2003)

With those elements decided, the story has to be good. This planning framework is the beginning step of a three-step process: Pick my idea, Organize my notes, and Write and say more.

Planning discourages children from writing in the "what next?" style used by novices (Dahl & Farnan, 1998). In this mode, students write the first sentence and ask themselves, "What next?" The second sentence has a connection to the first, and the third has a connection to the second, but by the end of the process, the final sentence has absolutely no relation to the beginning. You probably know an adult who still carries on a conversation in this manner.

Opinions are mixed about **using children's literature as models** for prewriting. Undoubtedly some children love to imitate their favorite authors and borrow literary elements or ideas from them (Harwayne, 2001). For other children, a whole professionally written book seems like an impossible leap compared with their work. They may identify better with a classroom exemplar.

Teachers who have a stable curriculum often keep **exemplars**, or outstanding pieces from previous classes, to offer as models. Reading two or three exemplars will give students a feel for what a good paper looks like—perhaps the desired length or general organizational pattern that they are expected to incorporate into their own writing. Exemplars are powerful for helping students understand the different text structures used in narrative, persuasive, expository, and descriptive writing and other genres. Be sure to use two to four exemplars, or else all the papers will look exactly like the one sample that was shown.

Figure 11.3 Graphic organizer

GRAPHIC ORGANIZER

Introduction

A	

B	

C	

Conclusion

Note: This graphic organizer for persuasive or expository writing is used to help develop the introduction, body, and conclusion.

Figure 11.4 Primary expository organizer

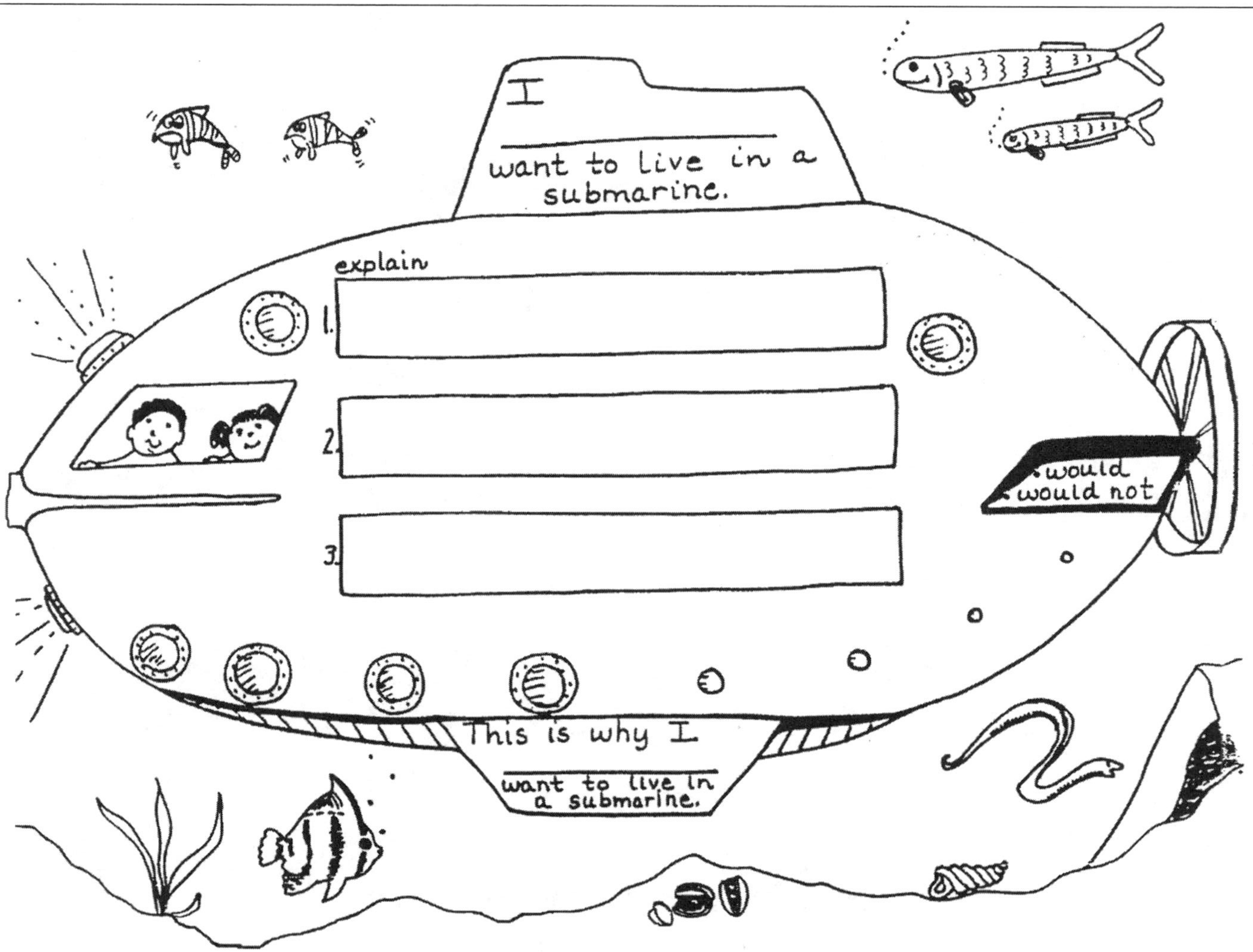
I
want to live in a submarine.
explain
1.
2.
3.
would
would not
This is why I
want to live in a submarine.

Note: In this primary expository organizer, the teacher has modeled the opening and closing. (Developed by Deborah Behm.)

Figure 11.5 Graphic organizer: Chain of events

GRAPHIC ORGANIZER: CHAIN OF EVENTS

Beginning
Topic
Setting

What happened?

What happened?

What happened?

Feelings

Feelings

Feelings

Wrap Up,
I learned, or
Overall

Reaction

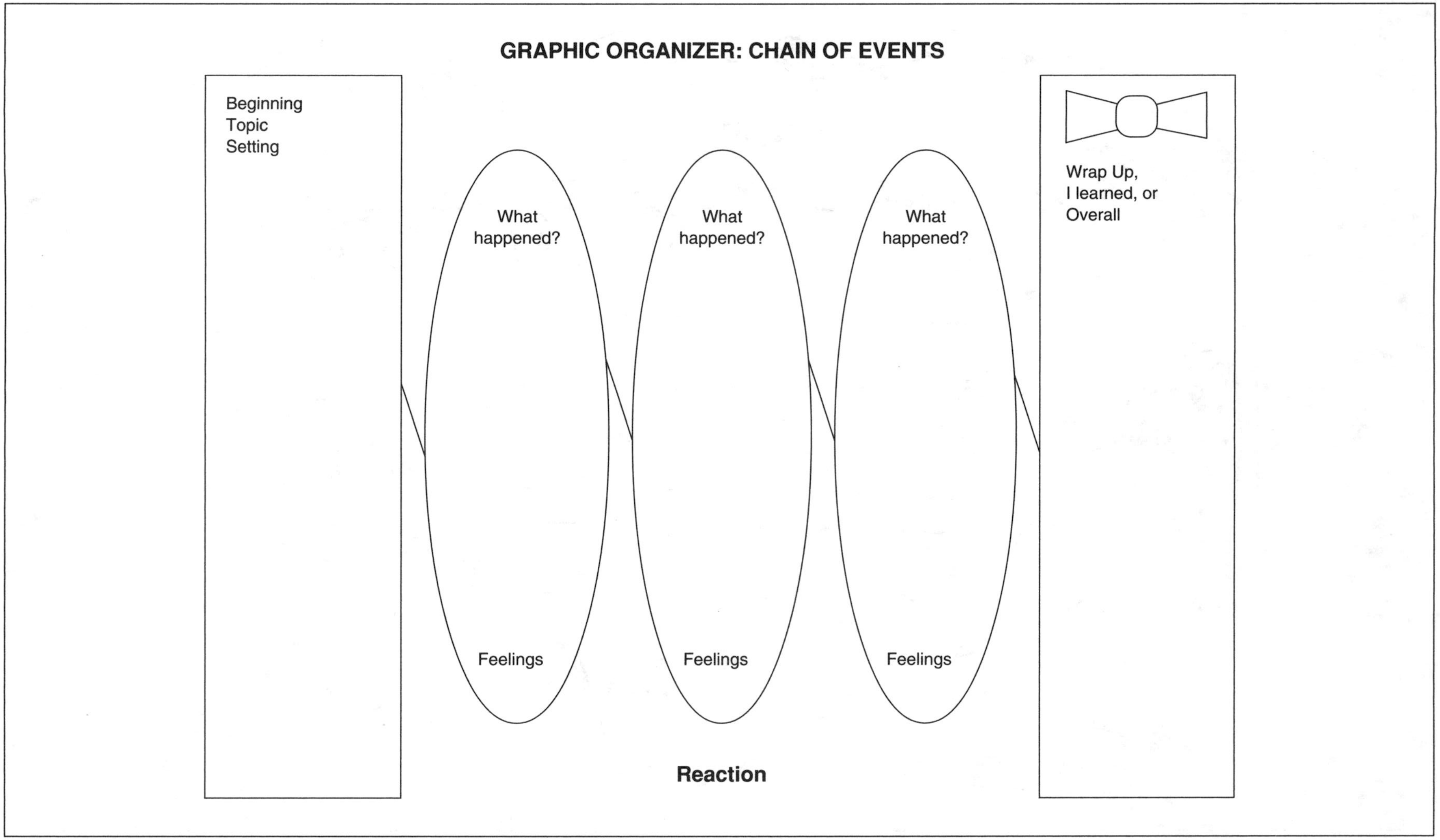

Note: This graphic organizer helps to develop the chain of events, or the sequence, of the story. (Developed by Sue Schulte.)

Figure 11.6 Venn diagram

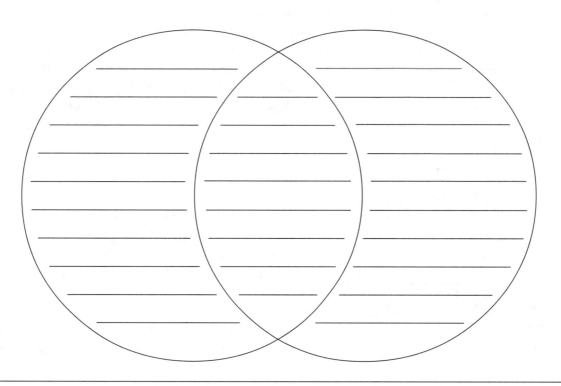

VENN DIAGRAM

Note: A Venn diagram is used to plan comparison and contrast writing.

Using Children's Literature as a
Prewriting Activity: A Sample Lesson

Using picture books as writing prompts can be fun for writers of any age. Many have beautiful illustrations, delightful language, and universal themes. *Wilfrid Gordon McDonald Partridge* (1985), a picture book by Mem Fox, describes a little boy who helps elderly Miss Nancy recover her memories. The following activity, developed by Patricia Braun, can also help students in any grade retrieve their memories for a writing assignment.

The teacher should read the book aloud and elicit from the class the qualities of memories: something warm, something from long ago, something that makes you cry, something that makes you laugh, and something as precious as gold. Artifacts similar to the ones that Wilfrid brought to Miss Nancy to restore her memories can make the experience more vivid. With the list of the characteristics of memories on the board, ask students to each write down a key word for a memory of their own that fits each category. Whip around the room and ask for a short answer from every student in each of the categories. The teacher should participate in each round but should answer last. Hearing the others may prompt some of the students to change their mind or to add a new memory. Students may pass when they do not wish to share something that is too personal.

Ask students to freewrite for five minutes on one or two of their choices and then to pair share. Something more will always surface in the discussion, and perhaps questions will be asked that will rouse a few more details. The final decision must then be made, and students can write. Undoubtedly, everyone will have a favorite story to tell, and the whole class will be engrossed for some time in writing their memoirs. The teacher's writing about a memory on the overhead while the students are drafting provides additional modeling. Later, the students will share, revise, edit, and perhaps publish the final piece, accompanied by an artifact or an illustration that represents the treasured memory. Expect a deluge of teddy bears, pictures, and family keepsakes.

Drafting

Drafting is actually the simple part for most children. When students have sufficient keyboarding skills, they can draft on the computer, providing they come prepared with a plan. Everyone appreciates the legibility afforded by word processing, and revision is simplified. Some students have absolutely no problem ignoring spelling and mechanics in their first draft, but for others, problems with mechanics block the flow of ideas.

> The real growth in writing comes between the first draft and the final product.

For children with disabilities in spelling or the physical act of writing, voice-activated software such as Dragon NaturallySpeaking (Dragontalk) can be used. Richards (2002) cautions that to use such software successfully, students must be able to state phrases and sentences fairly fluently without using filling words such as "uh." They must also speak clearly, organize material in advance, and have a basic understanding of word processing.

Revision

The real growth in writing comes between the first draft and the final product. Although lessons in specific writing skills (e.g., introductions, paragraphing, relevant details) may precede the writing process, the revision stage is when children are most interested in improvement. They now have a topic and a working draft, so they can concentrate on a writing skill and see where it fits. I have always had better results working with students within a whole composition than trying to teach some skill out of context. The kids just don't see the point. Think of this as balanced writing too.

Revision is the stage with which most writers and teachers struggle. Without instruction, students tend to revise at the word or sentence level, which has no impact on the quality of writing (Graham et al., 1995). At this stage, very significant gains occur when students apply standards or criteria to their own writing or to one another's (Hillocks, 1986). When revising with criteria, introduce one scale at a time so that students can learn its features and scoring. Too many aspects at one time just yield a diffused focus, and little is mastered. Then examine many samples and rate them. After students have learned the criteria of one scale, such as making sure all the details in a paragraph match the topic, others

Figure 11.7   Criteria scales

Scoring for Position and Support in a Persuasive Paper from 4th Grade Scoring Guide of the National Assessment of Educational Progress	Student-Generated Criteria for Details and Elaboration
Unsatisfactory: Takes a position but provides no support OR attempts to take a position (is on topic) but position is very unclear; may only paraphrase the prompt.	1. Nothing there, No details, Can't imagine the scene
Insufficient: Takes a position, but provides only minimal support (generalizations or a specific reason or example) OR attempts to take a position but the position is unclear.	2. Some details but some don't match topic, Partially wrong details
Uneven: Takes a position and offers limited or incomplete support; some reasons may not be clear or related to the issue.	3. Lots of details, Related to topic, Lots on some points, little on others
Sufficient: Takes a clear position with support that is clear and generally related to the issue.	4. Tons of details, Makes sense, Can really "see" it
Skillful: Takes a clear position and develops support with some specific details, reason, or examples.	
Excellent: Takes a clear position and develops support with well-chosen details, reasons, or examples across the response.	

Source: National Center for Education Statistics, 2005.

can be introduced, leading up to the use of an entire rubric. Criteria sheets can be elaborate and technical or simple and student designed, as shown in Figure 11.7, which includes one from the National Assessment of Educational Progress (NCES, 2005) and one developed by students.

Criteria rating can be introduced to the whole class with a short piece or section read orally or prepared on an overhead transparency. The rating scale must be visible on the board or a poster. After listening to or reading the piece, children hold up their fingers to give a number rating. Hands should be held in front of the chest rather than overhead so that everyone has to decide independently. The teacher calls on several students to justify their ratings and then does likewise so that everyone's criteria begin to develop along the same lines. It is a high-participation activity, and soon everyone is on the same page. The activity becomes even more worthwhile if students suggest revisions so that the sample will meet the highest standard. Several studies have shown that revising the work of others is as effective in improving the quality of writing as revising one's own work.

Working with criteria has both short- and long-term benefits. For the short-term, students are able to evaluate their own papers and make changes before handing in the paper for grading. After the grade has been given, postmortems hold little interest for students. The long-range gains are more important. What students learn with modeling, discussion, and criteria sheets today transfers to an independently written piece tomorrow as students internalize the criteria for good writing.

Teaching **revision techniques** starts with an interactive dialogue. The sample piece (preferably the same topic as the class is working on) should be typed and have all the grammatical and spelling errors removed so that editing corrections do not divert the students' attention. After ratings are made and discussed, revisions to improve the piece are suggested, such as taking out the third paragraph because it has nothing to do with the topic. Deletions are the most gut-wrenching revisions for students. They get to see what a messy process revision is and to hear multiple ideas for straightening out a problem. The teacher can think aloud about the relative merits of the suggestions and guide students toward the most effective ones. When learning about revision, the children must have their draft in front of them so that they can look for ideas that will work in their paper, too.

Students then repeat the process with their own paper and a partner or a small group, looking primarily for the same kinds of revisions that were modeled. Although this is called **peer** *editing,* peer *feedback* is more valuable for revision. When students work together, they make more revisions than they make when working alone (MacArthur, Schwartz, & Graham, 1991). Revision groups may or may not have a greater impact than teacher feedback does, depending on the specificity of the system for peer feedback (Hillocks, 1986; Wong, Butler, Ficzere, & Kuperis, 1996). Revision groups using specific criteria show more improvement than students who revise and edit independently, even with a set of scales.

Writers work long and hard with partners after observing modeling because they have a specific purpose and specific criteria to work with. Without criteria for evaluation, the judgment will be made in terms of whether the editor personally likes the author rather than whether the editor likes the piece. Students need to be taught both evaluation criteria and social skills for interacting with other students in the group. These social skills include learning not to complain when partners are assigned and listening without interruption to what the editor has to say. The author always has the option of making the suggested revision or not. Role-playing appropriate and inappropriate reactions can help students learn desired behaviors.

Do not be afraid to spend significant time revising a single aspect of writing. A whole class period spent working just on concluding paragraphs will yield a whole class that knows how to write a conclusion.

Revising With Comparisons

Some children may have criteria endlessly explained to them without apparent effect. What they need to see is an example, what a "good one" looks like. Exemplars and modeling of revision with a piece of writing on the overhead help students understand the criteria through comparing the various pieces of writing with their own work.

Have students read the work of several other children. Seeing how other writers developed the topic, crafted details, or supported reasons is especially useful to the writer who is lacking ideas or who is unfamiliar with a particular format. Comparison also demonstrates what can be expected when students are introduced to new or higher standards. What was acceptable in second grade is no longer the norm in third. On seeing the more complex work of classmates, most students are willing to work toward the higher expectations, and now they have an example to guide the way.

Editing

The best time to integrate language arts instruction and meet all the state standards is during editing. Between drafts is the best place to teach mechanics. When students have their own pieces in front of them and have just finished struggling with how to punctuate dialogue, they are ready to learn how to make their content more accessible to the reader. Students can apply what they have just been taught to their own work, which is always more meaningful than applying it to ten sentences from the English book.

Editing should be done after revising, although almost all writers start penciling in corrections as they go along. Editing partners can work with a checklist that can be moderately helpful, although partners are more effective if looking for just one or two types of editing problems, such as incomplete sentences or inappropriate punctuation.

Editing for Sentence Structure

Written sentence structure is much more formal and complex than sentence structure in speech. Formal study of grammar does not transfer to writing, but pattern clubs and sentence combining do make a difference.

Pattern clubs help students identify sentence patterns and produce similar sentences of their own. May (1998) cites the following sentences from a social studies book.

Unless Franklin got to the French on time, the money wouldn't be available.

Unless the money became available, the soldiers would receive no supplies.

Unless the supplies came soon, the soldiers would starve.

The teacher first models a similar sentence: "Unless my husband does the laundry tonight, the children will have no clean socks tomorrow." Students then suggest sentences with the same pattern until everyone is in the pattern club. Without getting entangled in formal patterns of grammatical explanation, students intuitively grasp the pattern.

In **sentence combining** activities, two separate sentences are combined into one sentence. Fluency increases, and the number of repeated ideas and simple constructions decreases (Joseph, Shafer, & Swindle, 2003). Students need multiple samples and multiple trials.

Jimmy was throwing paper airplanes. Jimmy was redirected by the teacher.

Jimmy, who was throwing paper airplanes, was redirected by the teacher.

Students combine several sets of sentences by following the pattern. This seems to work best when students work in partners so that they can talk out the patterns and check with each other to see if their sentences have retained the original meaning. "Jimmy, who was throwing the teacher, was redirected to paper airplanes" will not be counted as correct. As a follow-up, students return to their own pieces to find sentences to combine. The research on sentence combining is overwhelmingly positive. George Hillocks (1986) found that 60% of studies done on sentence combining reported significant gains in syntactic maturity. Other researchers, all cited in Hillocks, reported that sentence combining worked well with students of all levels, especially disadvantaged or remedial students, and that sentence combining instruction helped to build confidence because of its positive approach.

To convince children that a **variety of sentence structures** will improve the flow of their writing, have students do an exercise in which they list the first word of every sentence and then count the number of words in those sentences. Have them write the results on a page with two columns, one column for the first words and one with the word totals. If every sentence begins with *I* or *Then*, it is easy so see that some variety is needed in sentence structure. For those sentences with 52 words, there is a good chance that some run-on sentences might exist within the big one.

■ AUDIENCES AND GENRES

Students need to write for a valued reader because most writing is done to communicate ideas to others rather than for personal enjoyment. Most writing assignments are done for the teacher, but a different audience might provide an additional incentive. Mem Fox, author of *Wilfrid Gordon McDonald Partridge*, wrote about her students in teacher education who had to prepare an annual presentation, consisting of poems, passages from read-aloud picture books, and excerpts from children's novels, for their peers. It was "merely satisfactory," according to Fox, until she asked her students to present their projects to groups of school children. "Dreading the imminent and real audience galvanized them into quite a different sort of action: they ached with caring about the response and rehearsed for hours outside class times" (Fox, 1988, pp. 114–115).

Letters to real people, articles for newspapers, stories to be read to younger children in the school, movie reviews for the school newspaper, thank you notes, or even the promise that every paper will be stapled to the bulletin board may alter the level of engagement when students are writing. Regie Routman (2005) tells about a Washington state teacher who made up a reader of state writing tests (tired, bored, and yearning for something organized and exciting to read) so that her students had someone real to write to.

> Writing clarifies reading and thinking.

The teacher is still an important audience, and many students will put forth their best for the teacher. Since all students are not motivated by the same incentives, as in all aspects of teaching, it is good to offer students a variety of assignments and audiences.

■ WRITING IN RESPONSE TO READING

Personal writing in the form of stories, narratives, journals, and diaries is probably the most common genre of writing, especially in the lower grades. But what about those children who are private in nature and do not wish to share? Writing in response to reading—in response to literature and in response to text materials—allows all children to respond and can employ the entire range of formats. When reading and writing are taught together, research shows that "writing can have a positive affect on children's reading comprehension and on their critical thinking abilities" (Qian, cited in May, 1998, p. 307). Writing clarifies reading and thinking.

Genres and Formats

There are many possibilities for writing in response to reading, including narratives, persuasive essays, expository essays, newspaper articles, interviews, diaries, journals, poems, commercials, revised endings or sequels, advice columns, critiques, editorials, notes, reviews, plays, articles, and letters. Chapter 12 contains more ideas for writing assignments suitable for working with a content text. While some of these genres are great fun, the teacher needs to consider what aspect(s) of writing will be taught through the assignment. Short activities such as writing bumper stickers, greeting cards, and slogans may be motivational but are not rich enough in content or process to be useful for improving writing skills.

Roll of Thunder, Hear My Cry (Taylor, 1977) is the inspiration for an example of the variety of writing assignments that can be derived from a single source. This novel follows the life of the Logan family in Mississippi in the 1930s. All the assignments below not only provide opportunity for the development of writing skills but also require that the student revisit the text. If students listen and discuss the assignments in revision groups, then all the aspects of literacy are integrated.

1. Expository essay: Explain why Cassie's day in Strawberry was the worst day of her life.

2. Interview: Interview Mr. Logan about the night of the fire.

3. Narrative retelling: Retell how Cassie finally got even with Lillian Jean.

4. Newspaper articles: Jefferson Davis School Bus Disabled. Unknown Assailants Responsible for Death of John Henry Berry

5. Editorial: Accounts With the Company Store Leave Residents Without Choice and in Greater Debt

6. Advice column: There is this girl who has been mean to me and got me in trouble for something I didn't do. . . .

7. Expository essay: Explain why the Logans are a strong family.

8. Diary: Mrs. Logan contemplates whether her stance about the schoolbooks and her decision not to shop at the local store are worth losing her job for.

9. Persuasive essay: T. J. (should/shouldn't) be held responsible for his decisions. T. J.'s "friends" (have/have not) excessively influenced him.

10. Journal: Of what unfair circumstances does this book remind you?

11. Poem: The Night Men Are Riding

12. Commercial: Mr. Barnett's General Store

13. Persuasive essay: Racial prejudice is (as prevalent now/less prevalent now) than in Mississippi in the 1930s.

14. Play: Change the scene of shopping at the Barnett store into a script.

15. Letter: Mrs. Logan writes to Uncle Hammer telling him that the mortgage has come due but begging him not to come.

The diagnostic teacher decides which aspects of writing the students need to practice and chooses the appropriate writing assignment on the basis of those needs. Cassie's worst day will provide practice in sequence and elaboration. Writing a poem about the night men will surely be a fine platform for visualization, description, vivid vocabulary, and metaphor. Explaining why the Logans are a strong family will require that children examine their own beliefs about how families support each other. Once the objectives have been decided on, children always appreciate a choice of assignments. It is not very difficult to devise a similar assignment in the same genre so that options are available.

Retellings, Summaries, and Other Response Formats

A standard written response to reading is the retelling or summary. Just think of the involvement in rereading for sequence, the determination of major and minor events, visualization, relevant details, and required manipulation of the text to turn it into the student-writer's own words. Students make the text meaningful as they paraphrase, reinterpret, and set the events clearly into their memories.

A visual technique to help students learn to summarize is the tic-tac-toe picture summary. Older students as well as younger ones love to respond to a story through drawing. The tic-tac-toe nine-square has top, middle, and bottom rows for events from the beginning, middle, and end of the story. Scenes can be drawn with stick figures or with complex drawings that can be labeled or not. Once the events have been decided on and drawn in sequence, each picture idea is turned into a written sentence. The sentences can be written in paragraph form by a third grader, or they can be connected, elaborated on, and smoothed out by a high school freshman for a summary.

In **reading-response journals**, students write an entry, usually of their own choosing, responding to something they have read. Many students, especially culturally and linguistically diverse students, substantially improve their writing as a result of keeping these journals (Routman, 2005). Although the journals are ungraded, teachers model standard language and probe ideas in their responses. Many teachers respond to students on a rotating basis to keep the task of writing responses within manageable time limits.

Another written response to reading involves students' **interpreting characters or events**. Interpretation requires that students use their own experiences and the text to infer characters' motivations. After reading Rudyard Kipling's *The Jungle Book*, students may be asked to write a persuasive piece indicating whether they think Mowgli belonged with the men or with the animals. High school students might write why Odysseus was a tainted hero. The shared inquiry approach of Junior Great Books uses this method extensively for discussion groups. Many of the discussion questions can be turned into high-interest writing assignments. It can be much easier for students to debate moral dilemmas in literature than to reveal dilemmas in their own lives. Not only may considering consequences and multiple viewpoints make an interesting composition; it could have important effects in the lives of the writers.

Metacognitive responses are open-ended responses about the thoughts and reading processes of children as they read the story, passage, or chapter. Modeling and instruction are required for this response or it will turn into a summary of the chapter.

Comparison and contrast can be used to make connections between themes, plots, characters, settings, or any element of literature. Be sure to teach children how to set up these pieces, or they may write, "He was tall, but she was Norwegian." The Venn diagram, shown in Figure 11.6, is useful for planning this type of writing.

LOOKING BACK AT OBJECTIVES ■ AND BALANCED WRITING

A classroom teacher who decides to balance the writing program needs to know a wide variety of strategies and techniques. These include the abilities of the children in the class and the types of assignments and the classroom environment that will help the children blossom.

What should be the ultimate objective in teaching writing? The optimum outcome is that students be able to self-evaluate their own performance accurately because they have developed internal criteria for what a "good one" is. The goal must be for students to no longer be dependent on the grade of a teacher to know whether they have produced writing suited to the purpose and accessible to the reader. Students will have learned to communicate and write well independently.

12

Reading and Writing in the Content Areas

Not only is there an art in knowing a thing, but also a certain art in teaching it.

—Cicero

Nearly 20 years ago, I gave a conference presentation called "What to Do While Waiting for Reading to be Taught in the Content Areas." Today, I do not have to wait quite as much. The trend is changing to include more expository selections in both basals and trade books, and content teachers are thinking about ways to more effectively use their textbooks to help students learn content and handle expository text. Attitudes about reading and writing across the curriculum are different now.

Although adults read more expository text than narrative, expository reading had been neglected in all grades. Content teachers assumed that once children had been taught to read and write in language arts classes, they could automatically understand the content and management of textbooks as well as write organized content papers. However, being able to breeze through a John Grisham novel does not mean you can read an aeronautical engineering journal with ease and comprehension.

> Students need greater exposure to expository text, and reading strategies and study skills can be taught and learned in content-area classes.

The notion of balance, in this context, is to establish greater equity between the teaching of literature and the teaching of expository text. Students need greater exposure to expository text, and reading strategies and study skills can be taught and learned in content-area classes.

THE DIFFERENCES BETWEEN ■
A TEXTBOOK AND A NOVEL

Narrative text (stories) and expository text (textbooks) are considerably different. They differ in text structure—how the text is organized or structured. Expository texts have heavier vocabulary and concept loads, use more formal language, and have more visual aids such as graphs, charts, and diagrams than novels do. Even the purposes for reading are not the same. Whereas novels are likely to deal with the familiar, the content of textbooks is meant to be learned, so much of it will be new and unknown. Gaps in comprehension can be expected with lack of extensive previous knowledge. To make things more difficult, many textbooks are written above grade level.

Text Structures in Expository Texts

Readers who have only a narrative schema read in a chronological pattern or narrative text structure of "and then . . . , and then . . . , and then . . . , and then." Without understanding how other text structures function, students use their narrative schema and are reduced to trying to memorize long lists of information that is beyond the capacities of most people. Look at the following list for 30 seconds, and then try to write it from memory:

> Oranges, rye bread, pick up blouse at cleaners, ¾-inch screws, Dijon mustard, drop off pants at the cleaners, Spackle, sliced ham, recycling bags.

Most adults who are successful with this experiment categorize or group—grocery store, cleaners, and hardware store. They also count the number of items. Most children try to memorize without a structure.

The expository structures are listing, sequence, cause and effect, comparison and contrast, description, topic-subtopic, and problem-solution. Students need to learn to recognize these structures so that they can organize their thoughts and their notes in the same structures.

The following samples of text structure are in **list format**, a text structure in which the order is not important. Cue words are *another*, *several*, *also*, and *the following*.

Sequence is another text structure that is crucial for following the steps of weather formation or the chronology of English royalty. This expository structure is one of the few that fit well with the "and then" strategy. Cue words are *before*, *after*, *following*, *first*, *next*, *then*, *finally*, *during*, *by*, and *last*. Notice how important the order is in the following passage.

> Then a year later, on November 14, 1854, the Crimean War Allied fleet found itself anchored off the Russian port of Balaklava. . . . During the afternoon, violent rainstorms began to lash Balaklava, and by nightfall a full-scale hurricane was blowing. By morning the entire fleet had been sunk. (Burke, 1996, p. 136)

Cause and effect is another critical pattern in both science and social studies. Cue words are *so, because, if, then, as a result,* and *therefore.* The following excerpt does an especially good job at clarifying the relationships.

> The western part of the [Midwest] region is much drier than the central and eastern parts are. What causes this difference? The dry weather of the western Midwest is caused by the presence of mountain ranges to the west of the region. Because weather in the United States generally moves from west to east, much of the moisture in the air from the Pacific Ocean falls as rain on the western slopes of the Sierra Nevada and the Rocky Mountains. By the time the air gets to the eastern slopes it is very dry. (Scott Foresman's *Regions,* 2005, p. 229)

For **comparison and contrast,** cue words are *in comparison, on the other hand, in contrast, alike, same as, however,* and *but.* The teacher would have to point out the relationship in the following excerpt.

> To the Chinese, constellations told stories of everyday people, of great generals in battle, or of royal parades. These stars and their stories are used as a calendar to predict seasonal changes. The ancient Egyptians had many myths and gods represented in the stars. The brightest star in the sky, Sirius, represented the goddess Isis. When Sirius rose in the eastern sky just before sunrise, it was thought that the Nile River would soon flood. (Sipiera & Sipiera, 1997, pp. 29–30)

Although narrative contains a great deal of description, the description tends to be interwoven with the plot and enhances characterization or setting. **Expository description** is an end in itself. Cue words are *for example, characteristics are,* and *looks like.*

> Sun bears—also called dog bears . . . are the smallest bears in the world. Most are about the size of large dogs, weighing 60–100 pounds and standing about three feet tall. . . . On their chests, yellowish-orange crests resemble the rising sun for which they are named. (Muldoon, 1995, p. 36)

While researching this chapter, I found few experts listed **topic-detail** (topic-subtopic) as an expository pattern, perhaps considering them lists, but when I started examining students' texts, especially social studies texts, I found that an overwhelming amount of material was organized in this way.

> Trees are another important resource of the Southeast. Some farmers in the Southeast grow and harvest trees, just like other crops. . . . The trees are used to make boards for the lumber industry. They are also used for other wood products such as furniture. Some trees are made into pulp, a combination of ground-up wood chips, water and chemicals. Pulp is used in the production of paper. (Scott Foresman's *Regions*, 2005, p. 182)

If students use the topic and subtopic organizational pattern in their own writing, their reading comprehension may improve (Shanahan, 1997).

Problem and solution is a common pattern, but it is often confusing to students because in passages of this nature, the problem or solution may be implied rather than stated, or solutions are described before the problem is discussed. Cue words are *questions*, *answer*, *solved*, and *purpose*. To make things even trickier for students, the problem may be in one paragraph, and the solution several pages away.

> Leakey located a businessman who would pay the costs for Jane [Goodall]'s first six months in the field. However, British officials did not want Jane to live in the jungle alone. Jane solved this problem by inviting her mother along for the first months. (Jerome, 2004, p. 13)

Younger students can begin learning about expository structures through read-alouds and trade books so that they won't be as bewildered by these patterns when they begin reading textbooks. Biographies are an easy place to begin because of their narrative structure, as in *Martin's Big Words* (Rappaport, 2001). Other good choices are *Mars* (Adamson, 2004) and *Tyrannosaurus Rex* (Cohen, 2001), which both include topic headings, glossaries, and fabulous illustrations. *T Rex* is wonderfully gory!

To teach text structures, May (1998) recommends that teachers choose examples of a particular text structure, teach students the organizational pattern, and then apply that knowledge to passages with the same format in textbooks being used in their classes. In addition, writing pieces with the same structure gives students the insider's view on organization.

Special Features in Textbooks

Special features include charts, graphs, diagrams, pictures, headings, tables of contents, glossaries, indexes, end-of-chapter summaries, and preview and review questions. The most common reaction of students is to skip over them. Students need to be taught the usefulness of these features as well as how to use them.

Many students learn how to interpret charts, graphs, and diagrams by making their own. When I taught eighth grade, I saved the graph and chart unit until late May and June. The students found that making their own charts and graphs from provided and original information was much more challenging and intriguing than simply answering questions about prepared graphics. After constructing their own, they found it was a snap to read any others. While creating their own graphics, students discover the need for scale, titles, symbols, and labels. The same is true of maps, time lines, and other graphics.

Difficulty of Text

Many textbooks are not written at the appropriate grade level. Hill and Erwin (cited in Richardson & Morgan, 1997) found that more than half the textbooks they studied were written at least one level above their targeted grade.

Social studies textbooks intended for a single grade were found to have a range of six grade levels (Kinder, Bursuck, & Epstein, cited in Richardson & Morgan, 1997). Even if a text is written at grade level, not all the students in a typical class read at grade level.

It is hard to understand a text written above grade level, but it is even harder to improve reading skills when the book is too difficult. Ivey and Fisher (2005, p. 12) are explicit. "We know of no student who got better at reading by reading books that were too difficult for him, and we know of no student reading at a 4th grade level who learned to read at an 8th grade level by reading only 8th grade-level books."

A quick way to determine the level at which a text is written is to use the Fry Readability Graph (Fry, 1968). To find the grade level of a selection, determine the number of sentences and the number of syllables in a 100-word passage. The grade level is found at the intersection of the two lines in Figure 12.1. In addition, the readability level of 6,000 textbooks can be found online. Go to TASA Literacy, Touchstone Applied Science Associates, http://www.tasaliteracy.com. Click on Readability on the top line, and then on Readability of Textbooks Online. Type in the name of a book in the database, and the readability is given in Degrees of Reading Power (DRP) units, which can be converted to grade equivalencies with the conversion chart in Chapter 7.

> Even if texts have the "right" number of syllables and sentences per 100 words, many textbooks are still difficult to understand because they are not well written.

Even if texts have the "right" number of syllables and sentences per 100 words, many textbooks are still difficult to understand because they are not well written. The desire to fit in as much content as possible often makes the text disconnected and incoherent. Vocabulary words are not explained, and the relationships between ideas are not apparent.

I was working with fifth-grade teachers, helping them use a social studies text to develop prompts for writing. We looked for topics that had at least four supporting details and therefore could be used to write expository pieces. Because the book covered such a range of material—from prehistoric to current times on all seven continents—only about ten topics in the entire book had four supporting details, our criterion for sufficient information for writing a paper. The text consisted of 400 pages of sequential but unrelated facts. Good readers chunk and organize information so that recalling one idea calls up all the correlated details. Poor readers try to memorize information as a laundry list. This poorly written text made it impossible for good readers to use their efficient strategies unless they already possessed enough prior knowledge to connect the lists of unrelated facts.

A series of studies on incoherent texts done by Margaret McKeown, Isabel Beck, and their colleagues was summarized by Frank May (1998, pp. 418–420). The researchers found children's prior knowledge of historical periods to be too "vague and inaccurate" to supply the missing connections in the text. When McKeown et al. rewrote the text to have explicit definitions of new concepts and vocabulary and to explain relationships clearly, the children had better comprehension of the text. In the final study of the series, students were given

Figure 12.1 Fry Readability Graph

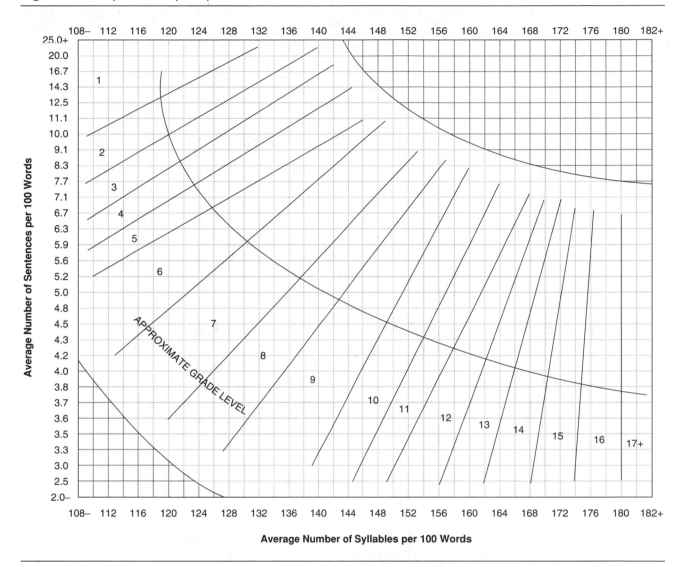

Average Number of Syllables per 100 Words

Source: Fry, Edward B., 1968, "A Readability Formula That Saves Time." *Journal of Reading*, 2(7), 513. Reprinted by permission.

a preparatory lecture to provide background and clarify relationships of the historical period. Those students who had the preparatory lecture and the revised texts did the best.

TRADE BOOKS AND TEXT SETS ■

To supplement poorly written texts, many teachers are using trade books, which are independently published content books for children. The number of trade books is increasing dramatically as the interest in expository texts grows, and the books are just gorgeous! They provide current, in-depth information on a huge variety of specific topics that textbooks cannot offer. Because they treat narrower topics, trade books are often more logically arranged and more coherent than textbooks are. Teachers can also accommodate the range of reading abilities in their classes better by using a text set, that is, a set of diverse books at varying levels on the same topic. Easy-reading trade books are terrific for providing background before students read the textbook, and the trade books are interesting enough that kids will read a lot. Ivey and Fisher (2005) recommend starting with intriguing aspects of a topic. They suggest using *Silent Witness* (Ferllini, 2002), which deals with fascinating details of solving crimes, to begin a genetics unit. The smaller size of trade books makes them less intimidating than textbooks.

Good resources for finding trade books are the National Science Teachers' Association: Outstanding Science Trade Books for Children resource, at http://www.nsta.org/ostbc; the National Council for Social Studies' Notable Children's Trade Books in the Field of Social Studies, at http://www.socialstudies.org/resources/notable; and the Children's Book Council Online, at http://www.cbcbooks.org/ (click "Reading Lists").

■ REMOVING OBSTACLES TO COMPREHENSION WITH PREREADING ACTIVITIES

When a selection of trade books is not available and rewriting the textbook is not a viable option, then the best solution is preparing students by providing them with a broader background before they read the textbook.

Wouldn't it be wonderful if background knowledge could be developed through direct experience! My first choice would be a unit on world cultures in which we started with a field trip to Mexico so students could see the shadows of Quetzalcoatl, the plumed serpent, slithering down the temple railings on the days of the equinoxes. They could experience a jungle without rivers, and they could walk on the steps of a temple that demonstrates how calendars and astronomy were related. These students would never forget the sights, the concepts, or specific vocabulary, and they would read historical accounts of Mexico with much greater comprehension. I am afraid that choice is not in this year's fieldtrip budget, however. Movies, videos, museums, picture books, discussions, and guest speakers will make a good second choice.

Prereading Plan

Many prereading activities begin with discussion so that readers can make connections between their own backgrounds and a new text. The Prereading Plan (PreP) (Langer, 1981) is a more formalized way of activating prior knowledge during a prereading discussion. The teacher says, "Tell anything that comes to mind when you hear the words ____." Students answer, and the teacher jots ideas on the board. To make students consciously aware of connections, the teacher probes, "What made you think of ___?" After all known information is listed, the teacher asks, "Based on our discussion and before you read, do you have any new ideas about ____?" Responses to the third question are often more refined as students add to their knowledge base (Unrau, 2004).

KWL

Another way to activate background is KWL. The *K* stands for what I *know,* the *W* for what I *want* to know, and the *L* for what I *learned.* Even young readers of nonfiction can use KWL to activate their prior knowledge and tickle their curiosity. Students set up a three-column chart and brainstorm in small groups all the things they know about the topic. Next they list the things they want to know. With older students, it often works better to do a KCL, using C for what I'm *certain* of, because the answer to "What do you want to know?" is occasionally "Nothing." I like to use KCL for all ages because the first column can be speculative, and anything not listed in the C column automatically functions as a topic for inquiry. KWL-Plus asks students to also predict what topics they might find in the text so they will be alert to the text structure.

KWL can be modeled with the whole class first, but deeper involvement happens in small-group work. Teachers can be very helpful, and a little manipulative, as they walk around from group to group asking the students to be as specific as possible with their lists. If the topic were sea turtles, the teacher might ask the groups to guess exactly how much the turtles weigh or whether the eggs are the size of ping-pong balls or baseballs or why mother turtles cry as they lay their eggs.

KWL, developed by Donna Ogle (1986), is an easy strategy for students to transfer to independent reading. Setting a purpose helps students ferret out information from difficult texts because they know what they are looking for. KWL works with all age levels. I have known exhausted teachers who are attending graduate classes in the evening after a hard day's work to exclaim, "Oh, you were right! I didn't think they were that big! I saw that on National Geographic!" when they found that turtles weigh up to 1,500 pounds, their eggs are the size of golf balls, and the turtle's tears keep her eyes free from loose sand.

Artifacts and Examples

Some firsthand experiences are available, and if the teacher can show students how common experiences relate to the text, it will suddenly have greater meaning. When studying atmosphere in a weather unit, ask children which bunk bed is warmer, the top or the bottom one. Have students hypothesize about where the water comes from on the outside of an icy drink on a hot day. Why does it look like steam is rising off a bald football player's head during a November game? Which direction does the water swirl down the toilet? Students who can connect text to real experiences have an easier time relating to new material than those who cannot.

Anticipation Guides

If the students are being introduced to a topic about which they have limited prior knowledge, an anticipation guide, shown in Figure 12.2, will give them a place to start because they can guess in this low-risk activity. Anticipation guide statements can be true, false, or ambiguous. The exercise can be extended by asking students to prove their answers during reading or by reanswering after reading.

Figure 12.2 Anticipation guide

Before Reading		Anticipation guide	After Reading	
Agree	Disagree		Agree	Disagree
_____	_____	1. Earth's population remained steady until about 500 years ago.	_____	_____
_____	_____	2. The increased productivity of crops due to the use of pesticides outweighs the medical problems caused by pesticides.	_____	_____
_____	_____	3. Carbon dioxide is one of the gasses that contributes to the greenhouse effect.	_____	_____
_____	_____	4. Composting yard waste will reduce trash put into landfills by 40%.	_____	_____

Note: An anticipation guide helps students ferret out information from difficult texts, especially if the students have limited prior knowledge.

Curiosity

Building enthusiasm or curiosity also provides a good start. The mysteries of ancient Egypt, such as the Giza pyramids without any interior decoration or written messages, the little birdlike *bas* with beards, the dismemberment and reassembling of Osiris, and the beautiful temple of Karnak, provide inspiration for students to enter a lost realm. After they become interested in the attention grabbers, the teacher can introduce irrigation, centralized government, and public works projects.

Structured Overviews

Previewing a text is similar to seeing a coming attraction that includes a movie's organization as well as its content. The previewing method called SQ3R (survey, question, read, recite, review) starts with a survey. An updated version to "steal" information prior to reading is named THIEVES (Manz, 2002), which stands for title, headings, introduction, every first sentence in a paragraph, visuals and vocabulary, end of chapter questions, and summary. It works especially well at the beginning of a new chapter. It has been used with fifth graders and college students, and one of my graduate students uses it with her social studies class of learning-disabled seventh graders. She reports that students are much more ready to tackle the reading after "thieving."

■ REMOVING THE OBSTACLES OF CONCEPT VOCABULARY

Most new content words are not in the speaking or meaning vocabulary of students. Unfamiliar vocabulary and technical jargon can be real obstacles to comprehension. New vocabulary can be divided into three categories: elaborate words for known ideas (such as *aspic* for *gelatin*), familiar words with new meanings (*plate* in *plate tectonics*), and new words for unfamiliar concepts (*magnetic alignment*). The third category provides the most challenge. Terms such as *magnetic alignment*, *Pangaea*, and *continental drift* represent whole concepts—and fairly abstract concepts at that.

> New concepts and terms will obstruct comprehension unless they become familiar to the student by the time the student meets the text.

These new concepts and terms will obstruct comprehension unless they become familiar to the student by the time the student meets the text. Techniques such as word splash and word sort will help students develop general familiarity and background.

Word Splash

In word splash, various words that are integral to the chapter are spread across a page or a transparency. Variety in the style of print seems to aid students' memory. The teacher elicits from the class what is already known about the terms, adding elaboration or clarifying definitions. Examples may be drawn from the class or provided by the teacher. Soon the teacher is asking students to develop sentences with the words.

The wider the discussion, the more likely that students will make a connection. Discussion of the vocabulary words in Figure 12.3 may elicit connections to the movie *The Tomb of the Mummy*, burn ointments, divinity fudge, an inscription on a friendship ring, characters in computer games, an account from a student

Figure 12.3 Word splash

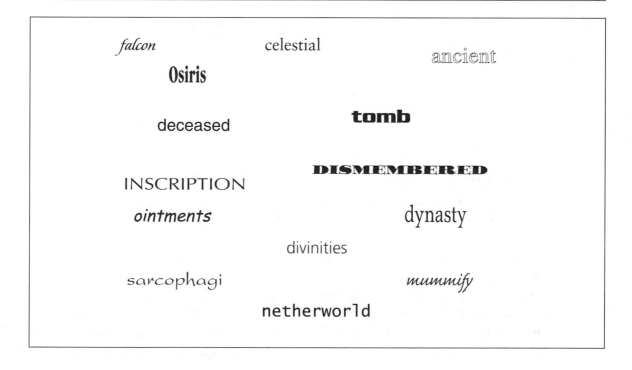

who is reading a book about the Middle Ages that includes falconry, and Celestial Seasonings Tea. This activity may not produce precision with vocabulary, but when the words are encountered in the text, they will not be complete strangers.

Word Sort

To do a word sort, randomly list important words from the chapter and have groups of students sort them into categories of their own choice or of the teacher's choice. Children may use their texts, their experiences, and any other reference sources to find out if an *acropolis* is a person, place, tool, or geographical feature. After the sorting is finished, groups must justify the placement and provide a rationale for their decisions. Other groups may challenge the placement if they can validate their claim. This activity is an excellent strategy for generating interest, encouraging discussion, developing concepts, and practicing one of the structures of expository writing: topic-subtopic. Figure 12.4 shows an example of a word sort for a chapter about ancient Greece.

Figure 12.4 Word sort for ancient Greece

ANCIENT GREECE

acropolis	citizen	monarchy	colony	Mt. Olympus
oligarchy	democracy	Athens	Athenians	Homer
agora	city-state	Sparta	javelin	Odyssey
armor	Athena	Parthenon	Socrates	bronze
Plato				

CATEGORIES

People	**Places**	**Government**	**Things**	**Related to Myth**
citizen	acropolis	oligarchy	armor	Athena
Athenians	agora	democracy	javelin	Mt. Olympus
Plato	city-state	monarchy	Odyssey	
Socrates	Athens		bronze	
Homer	Sparta			
	Parthenon			
	colony			

Webs and Semantic Maps for Vocabulary and Concepts

Webs and semantic maps are visual representations of relationships and can be used before, during, or after reading. They are relatively easy to use or to have students develop. Webs and semantic maps remove some of the barriers to comprehension of texts by activating prior knowledge, discussing new vocabulary and concepts, and refining some of the relationships among ideas before students reach that incoherent text.

Simple webs can be used for brainstorming in the prereading stage. The teacher places the key word, such as *volcano,* as in Figure 12.5, in the center of the web and asks students to contribute associated terms. In the earliest stages,

Figure 12.5 Semantic web for *volcano*

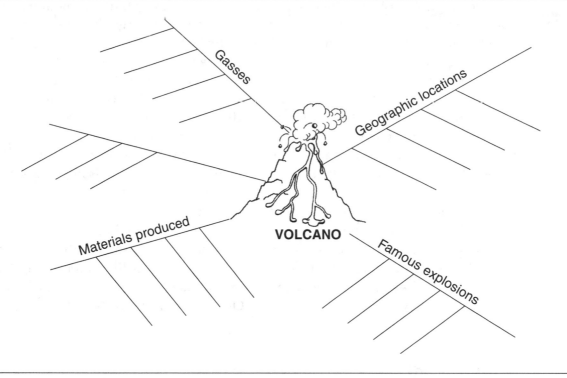

Note: A web of related words around a key word extracted from the story helps activate prior knowledge before reading a new book.

the teacher decides on the relationships of the suggested words. If the children start the web with the teacher, this activity can carry through to the reading stage as students fill in additional information. The clever teacher makes sure the categories in the web match the sections in the textbook.

Semantic maps, as developed by Camille Blachowicz and Peter Fisher (1996), are more thought provoking than simple webbing. In constructing a semantic map, the teacher first selects a key word and target words. The key word (the major concept) is written at the center of the map, and the target words (words related to the concept) are listed at the side. Students then generate examples related to the key word and target words, and relationships among the words are discussed and connected. The map can be constructed by the entire class, in small groups, or individually. Finally, the students add to the map as they read or work on the topic. Students have more responsibility for determining the relationships and subtopics with semantic mapping than they do with webbing. The more thought required about the structure, the greater the recall and understanding.

GUIDING COMPREHENSION ■
DURING THE READING PROCESS

To help students during reading, the teacher can use guided reading (yes, it can be used for nonfiction text) or some form of study guide that acts as a vicarious teacher, pointing out vocabulary, ideas, or relationships that are important. Not only young readers need guidance. As students progress through middle school, high school, and then into college, the complexity of the content materials increases. At every grade level, students need to learn organizational patterns and methods of incorporating new ideas so that education entails more than just one long list after another of boring items to be memorized until the test.

One of the pieces of advice I recently read on how to help students conquer textbooks was this: Ask them to focus on the big ideas or key concepts, not just to memorize the small details. It is sound advice, but the problem is that students have absolutely no clue which pieces are the key concepts. I found myself in the same situation when I recently attended a marvelous lecture about the history of the Silk Road. Much of the talk centered on Turkmenistan, Uzbekistan, Azerbaijan, and great civilizations that sprang from those regions, and I was awash in unfamiliar geography, unpronounceable names, and unknown events. Marco Polo was the only name I could remember by the end of the evening. I had no idea which pieces of information were more central than others in the history of the Silk Road.

Students often feel the same way. They have a hard time identifying key themes until they have gathered enough comprehensible information to be able to sort the relevant from the irrelevant. One way to help students is through a study guide.

Study Guides

Study guides are prepared by teachers to accompany textbook reading and help students determine the main ideas, relevant details, and application to other situations, although application is usually a "beyond the text" section. Study guides can be used as students are reading or afterwards (for more capable students who find the guide interrupts the flow of ideas). One team of teachers organized a yearlong world history class around the theme that ideas are transferred through trade, travel, and warfare. In their study guides, the teachers highlighted the parts of the text that told about how ideas spread through time and distance. They asked the students to work mostly with those sections.

Study guides come in many formats. Some look like partially filled-in outlines, some look like semantic maps, some are folded to fit over a page and match up exactly with the text, and some are in chart or graphic organizer form.

Graphic Organizers as Study Guides

Graphic organizers are often used to make relationships more evident and to capitalize on the brain's aptitude for remembering patterns (Sousa, 2005). The effectiveness of graphic organizers may also simply have to do with working with the materials a second time as the organizer is filled in or constructed.

Graphic organizers can be started as prereading activities and finished during independent reading. A good graphic organizer requires that both relationships and topics be labeled. Figure 12.6 shows a graphic organizer for a textbook segment about the Middle Ages. Teachers who are emphasizing cause and effect create graphic organizers that look like flowcharts so students can see how a particular effect may be the cause of another occurrence. If the text has a

Figure 12.6 The Middle Ages

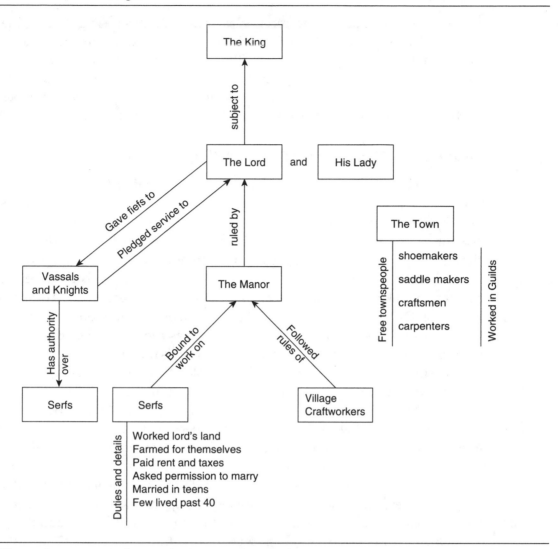

Note: This graphic organizer is for a textbook section about the Middle Ages.

coherent organizational pattern, the study guide can emphasize the pattern. If connections are lacking, the study guide can provide them.

With instruction, students can develop their own graphic organizers. Joseph Boyle and Mary Weishaar (1997) conducted a study comparing learning-disabled high school students who used teacher-generated graphic organizers, students who created their own organizers, and a control group. All used the same text materials. Those students who created their own graphic organizers outperformed the other groups on both literal and inferential comprehension. Those using teacher-generated organizers did better than the control group. Boyle and Weishaar concluded, "Using cognitive organizers during reading can help [students] to become more actively involved in the reading process, particularly if students construct their own organizers" (1997, p. 234).

T Notes

This form of note taking received its name because a big T is written on the page. The topic name is written above the T, main ideas are written to the left of the T, and supporting details are written to the right. The main advantage is that the paper can be folded down the middle, along the stem of the T, and the notes can be used for self-testing. No other form of note taking is as amenable to independent study as T notes are, and they can be used at many grade levels, including college.

Discussions During or After Reading

Classroom discussion in the middle of or following the reading of a textbook section is such a time-honored procedure because it is rich with possibilities. Students can hear the answers to questions they were too timid to ask and can consider possibilities that never previously crossed their minds. Because a significant part of learning is social, much interaction is needed.

The same researchers who rewrote textbooks, as described earlier in this chapter, to make them more coherent also developed Question the Author (better known as **QtA**) for discussing text (Beck, McKeown, Hamilton, & Kucan, 1997). QtA asks students to do much the same thing as the researchers did when they rewrote the texts: consider what is there and what is missing and make "revisions" in order to make the text more comprehensible. What makes these queries different from ordinary questions is that they seldom contain specific content. Instead they take forms such as What is the author trying to say here? Does the author explain this clearly? Does this make sense when compared with what the author told us before? Does the author tell us why? Answering queries like these requires active processing by the students, rather than just searching for answers. The teacher develops the queries anticipating what problems the inexperienced reader might have, especially in terms of missing background knowledge or incoherent text. This technique has proven results and is worth reading more about.

During discussion, do not forget to ask students to **visualize.** Let them do it verbally and draw and sketch too. What did Kublai Khan's palace look like when Marco Polo arrived? Is the wind blowing hard as you walk along the Great Wall of China, and what do you see? How anxious was Christopher Columbus's crew after not sighting land for so long? These scenes, these emotions are what make learning memorable. Visualizing is likely to increase learning for students in and above Grade 3 (Tierney & Cunningham, 2002).

■ RESPONDING TO TEXTS AFTER READING

When I think about responding to reading, I always remember Roger Farr's statement, "Children can read without thinking, but they cannot write without thinking." After reading is the time to work on some strategies and consolidate ideas through written responses (Farr, 1990).

Summarizing and Paraphrasing

Summarizing and paraphrasing are difficult but worthwhile skills to learn. They must be taught, and struggling readers need instruction the most. It is not that they need skills that are different from the skills other students need; they need instruction that is more explicit and intensive (Torgesen, 2004).

To explicitly teach summarization to beginners, use a **paragraph frame**, shown in Figure 12.7. Having the format gives young readers the freedom to look for the content. Students can first pair-share information that they learned while reading and then complete the paragraph frame. A variation is **skeletal writing** (Unrau, 2004). The teacher provides the skeleton (the main ideas), and the students flesh it out with the details, as in Figure 12.8. They add a sentence for every star in the skeleton.

Figure 12.7 Expository paragraph frame

I learned many interesting things about how plants grow.

First, I learned that _____.

Next, I learned that _____.

Third, I learned that _____.

Finally, I learned that _____.

It was interesting to learn how plants grow.

A knowledge of the genetics of populations has practical applications in medicine, education, and government. This knowledge is important because _____.

It also _____

_____ . . . In addition _____

_____ . . . A third use is _____

_____ . . . This knowledge helps to solve many kinds of problems.

Figure 12.8 Skeletal writing

Inventions of the Industrial Revolution

Eli Whitney invented the cotton gin in 1793. **Cyrus McCormick made it easier to harvest grain in 1831. **Thomas Alva Edison invented the light bulb. **All these inventions made life easier.

Duke and Pearson (2002) report on a rule-governed method for summarizing that draws on the work of several researchers. In the first draft of a summary, (1) delete unnecessary material. (2) Delete redundant material. (3) Compose a word to replace a list of items. (4) Compose a word to replace individual parts of an action. (5) Select a topic sentence. (6) Invent a topic sentence if one is not available. Any teacher who has worked on summarization knows that this sounds difficult, and it is.

An entirely different approach is GIST (Cunningham, 1982), in which students create summaries of 15 words or less for increasingly large amounts of text. Both GIST and rule-governed methods were found effective for learning summarization and for improving comprehension (Duke & Pearson, 2002).

Paraphrasing for notes or for a summary is always difficult. **In Your Own Words** helps students paraphrase. With new material, students read silently for one minute. Their pencils must not be in their hands. Then they cover the text and for two minutes write notes about what they can remember. On a signal, they read again for one minute, either going back to clarify what they wrote or continuing reading from where they left off. Again they write. Having to write without looking certainly cuts down on the copying, and students find out immediately, as they try to write notes, whether they understood the text. After a few rounds of reading and note taking, students write summaries in complete sentences using only their notes. Last, students compare their summary with each other's and with the original text. This technique is especially helpful to students before they write research reports.

Open-Ended Responses

Students can also be asked to make more open-ended responses to reading. **Learning logs** can feature five minutes of free writing, summaries, personal reactions, implications, or observations during a science lab. Writing about how a mathematical operation functions is very effective for clarifying thinking. A log to summarize, elucidate thinking, or extend learning can be a one-time response or a daily occurrence.

Entrance or exit slips are completed before the lesson begins or in the last few minutes of the class. An entrance slip helps focus students' attention and can ask for a connected piece of prior information, a prediction, a recollection from the preceding night's reading assignment, or an "I wonder" question. Exit slips can ask for a fact recalled from the text or class discussion, an everyday example or application of the lesson, a point unclear to the student, or a personal reaction. When students know a daily exit slip is required, they make sure to fix in their memories at least one segment of the lesson so they will have something to write.

Predicting Test Questions

Another way to respond to the text is to predict test questions. Students think that it is fun to write questions instead of answers. Asking for and modeling certain types of questions, such as cause and effect, discussion questions, or application questions, can direct the students to a broader range of questioning.

Formal Written Responses

Formal writing can take the form of expository essays, all-about books, alphabet books, or reports. These are usually assigned at the end of a chapter to consolidate aspects of the unit. In the middle grades, a class collaborative report not only reviews the information but models the process of putting a report together: deciding on the topics, choosing relevant information, deciding on an organizational pattern, writing introductions and conclusions, citing sources, revising, editing, and producing copies of the finished product.

Creative Drama, Newspaper Articles, Diaries, and Letters

These formats turn plain facts into real and vivid events. Human aspirations and frailties become causes of historical events. The effects of sweeping changes are translated into the repercussion on a single life. Dramatic vignettes can provide a stage for ethical concerns in science. A letter may be sent from Benjamin Franklin in France or from a scientist surveying the Yucca Mountain area in Nevada to decide whether it is a safe place for nuclear waste storage. A diary may be kept by a child on the Mayflower. A drama may portray decision making in the control room of NASA. A newspaper article may recount the devastating effects of the 1906 earthquake in San Francisco. Not only are important facts sequenced and summarized, but empathy is developed.

Writing in Math

Just in case this chapter is getting too long and your eyes are glazing over, here is a puzzle to arouse the mind.

Suppose a three-inch cube is painted blue. Assume the cube is cut into 27 one-inch cubes. How many of the smaller cubes will have blue paint on one face only? On two faces only? On three faces only? On no face? Show your work and explain in words how you arrived at your answer. (Illinois State Board of Education, 1995, Grade 10 sample assessment item)

You could probably solve the problem, but did you attempt to write it out in words? The National Council of Teachers of Mathematics has called for mathematics instruction to be based on the process of problem solving, which means math textbooks now have more written text than in the past. Learning how to communicate verbally in math is a new skill for students and for many teachers. By the way, the answer is that 6 cubes have paint on 1 face only, 12 cubes have paint on 2 faces only, 8 cubes have paint on 3 faces only, and 1 cube has no paint.

> Learning how to communicate verbally in math is a new skill for students and for many teachers.

STANDARD TECHNIQUES THAT ■
DO NOT WORK WELL

A standard technique that students use, or are asked to use, for setting a purpose for reading is to turn titles and headings into questions that they can answer while reading the text. This works fairly well with modeling from the teacher, but it is not very interesting. And often, using titles and headings to make an outline does not work well because many texts contain irrelevant or superfluous information that does not match the heading. Just think of all those sidebars and extra text boxes in modern textbooks! Students are left wondering what to do with these off-topic bits of information, or they create headings that are too general to categorize information.

Asking students to find the main idea of paragraphs does not work well either. The problem with texts is that main ideas occur in only one of every eight paragraphs (Donian, cited in May, 1998), and the problem for readers is that the ability to construct main-idea statements develops later than summarization skills (Brown & Day, cited in Richardson & Morgan, 1997).

The goal is for students to eventually use all these strategies independently. Toward this end, students should be taught a variety of techniques for untangling the complexities of textbooks so that they have multiple methods from which to choose.

13

Assessment

And still they gazed, and still the wonder grew,
That one small head should carry all it knew.

—Oliver Goldsmith

Testing happens occasionally, but assessment is continual. Tests are summative, that is, they occur at the end of a unit of study and are used to determine achievement. Assessment is formative, which means it is used throughout the process of learning to gauge students' current understanding and to make instructional decisions about what is needed to help children achieve.

Literacy teachers need to understand several types of assessment. They need to know how to determine a child's reading level, make accurate diagnoses, use informal classroom assessment, and make use of information from standardized tests.

DETERMINING READING LEVEL WITH ■ AN INFORMAL READING INVENTORY

At the beginning of the year, children are commonly assessed to determine their reading levels. Teachers assess for initial placement into reading groups and continue to assess periodically to check on progress and to reassess reading group placement.

To determine a child's reading level, teachers use an informal reading inventory (IRI). Basic assessment for reading level is a rather mathematical affair. Experienced teachers can make it diagnostic as well, but let's start with a simple reading level assessment. There are several published informal reading inventories, such as the Bader Reading and Language Inventory (Bader, 2005), the Basic Reading Inventory (Johns, 2005), and the QRI Qualitative Reading Inventory (Leslie & Caldwell, 2006). The advantage to using one of the published IRIs is that they come prepared with leveled passages, usually preprimer to Grade 12, and have alternate forms for retesting. The word lists and comprehension questions are prepared, and the publisher has already counted the number of words in the passage. Often there is a quick scoring guide at the bottom of the page that says "Word recognition: 2 or fewer words missed is independent level, 3–5 instructional, 6 or more frustration," and there is quick guide for the needed number of comprehension responses, too. Teachers no longer need to calculate to obtain a percentage-correct score. The Basic Reading Inventory has a Spanish version and comes with a CD that shows a sample assessment. The QRI includes both narrative and expository pieces at each level. Although directions and cut-off points may vary slightly among the inventories, they follow the same general guidelines.

The teacher starts with the leveled word lists to get an approximate idea of the child's reading level. The general rule is that if 90% of the words at a particular level are correct, the child can try the next higher list. If 90% are not correct on the first word list, drop down one list and continue dropping down until the student reaches 95% correct to find the independent level. Since the word lists are usually 10 or 20 words long, the general guidelines are as follows:

95–100% correct = independent word recognition level

90% correct = instructional word recognition level

85% correct or lower = frustration word recognition level (McCormick, 1999)

For example, if Tommy had 100% of the words right at the third-grade level, 90% right at the fourth-grade level, and 70% right at the fifth-grade level, his instructional word recognition level is fourth grade.

Since the word lists are short and can be administered quickly, they provide a fast way to get an idea about where to start with the comprehension passages. To determine which comprehension passage to start with, drop down one level from the instructional level for the word list since many students have better word recognition than comprehension. For Tommy, the teacher would start with the third-grade comprehension passage. Usually the student retells the story, and then the teacher prompts with questions about any parts that were missed. The general comprehension guidelines are as follows:

90–100% correct = independent level

70–89% correct = instructional level

69% correct or lower = frustration level (McCormick, 1999)

Several passages may need to be read to get the frustration, instructional, and independent levels. If the word-recognition instructional level and the comprehension instructional level are not the same, choose the lower score for determining instructional level materials.

If teachers do not have an IRI, they can make their own. The leveled passages must be carefully selected to be representative of their level. The teacher could check one of the readability Web sites to find the reading level of the book selected or use the leveled downloadable books from Reading A-Z at http://www .readinga-z.com. Comprehension questions should include both explicit and implicit questions. However, it is much easier and not very expensive to buy an IRI.

Dynamic Indicator of Basic Early Literacy Skills

The Dynamic Indicator of Basic Early Literacy Skills (DIBELS; University of Oregon Center on Teaching and Learning) can be used in much the same way as an IRI. Often all primary students in a school are screened at the beginning of the year and tested periodically to determine groupings and identify children at risk. A huge advantage is that each DIBELS subtest takes exactly one minute. The testing materials are free at http://dibels.uoregon.edu, and schools can subscribe for a reasonable fee to a Web-based database that generates numerous reports from the school's accumulated scores. On the basis of extensive research, DIBELS identifies cutoff points in the scores to identify children at risk, at some risk, and at low risk. The tests include initial sounds fluency, letter naming fluency, phoneme segmentation fluency, nonsense word fluency, oral reading fluency, retell fluency, and word use fluency.

Reading Level Self-Assessment

For quick self-assessment, the rule of thumb, or in this case a rule of hand, is to have students read a full page of text, putting down one finger for every word they do not know. If all five fingers go down, the book is not at the independent reading level and may not be a suitable choice. Since the number of words per page differs greatly from book to book, this is not a highly technical method, but it is a technique that youngsters can quickly learn to use by themselves.

DIAGNOSTIC ASSESSMENT ■

Experienced teachers can use an IRI to obtain diagnostic information by recording and analyzing a student's errors. Several of the published versions have checklists for fluency, repetitions and substitutions, and organized retelling. Passages can also be timed to obtain a fluency rate. Beginning teachers or teachers who want to focus on one aspect of reading at a time can use various additional assessments.

Assessing Word Recognition

Decoding is best assessed with nonsense words because children will not be able to pronounce them as sight words. Figure 13.1, the BAF test for phonics (May, 1998; May & Rizzardi, 2002), will quickly yield diagnostic information about all the graphophonic relationships. The teacher can check off 59 different consonant sounds and combinations in less than three minutes. This brief test is systematic and efficient, and it could be given several times a year to determine growth.

Parts A and B are more suitable for first grade than parts C and D, but this test could be used at any grade level when the teacher needs to know whether students have learned all the letter-sound relationships. The teacher needs one copy for marking, and the child needs an enlarged copy to read.

Sight words can be best assessed with word lists or flash cards. The Dolch list was developed in 1935. A more up-to-date list is the Fry 1,000 list, which can be found in *The Reading Teacher's Book of Lists* (Fry, Kress, & Fountoukidis, 2000) or in *1000 Instant Words by Dr. Fry* (Fry, 2000). The first 600 words can be found

Figure 13.1 The BAF test for phonics

Read these directions to the child: "These words are nonsense words. They are not real words. I'd like you to think about what sound the letters stand for; then read each word out loud without my help. Don't try to go fast; read the list slowly. If you have trouble with a word, I'll just circle it and you can go on to the next one. The first word is /baf/. Now you say it. All right, now go on to the rest of the words in row 1."

Part A: Consonant Letters

1.	baf	caf	daf	faf	gaf	haf	jaf	
2.	kaf	laf	maf	naf	paf	raf	saf	
3.	taf	vaf	waf	yaf	zaf	baf	bax	

Part B: Consonant Digraphs

4.	chaf	phaf	shaf	thaf	whaf	fack	fang	fank

Part C: Consonant Clusters

5.	blaf	braf	claf	craf	draf	dwaf	flaf	fraf
6.	glaf	graf	fand	plaf	praf	quaf	scaf	scraf
7.	skaf	slaf	smaf	snaf	spaf	splaf	spraf	squaf
8.	staf	straf	swaf	thaf	traf	twaf		

Part D: Vowel Letters, Vowel Digraphs, and Vowel Clusters

9.	baf	bafe	barp	baif	bawf		
10.	bef	befe	berf	beaf			
11.	bof	bofe	borf	boaf	bouf	boif	boof
12.	bif	bife	birf				
13.	buf	bufe	burf				

Source: May, Frank B.; Rizzardi, Louis, *Reading as Communication,* 6th edition. © 2002, Phonics Test. Adapted by permission of Pearson Education, Inc., Upper Saddle River, NJ.

at http://www.sd129.org/hall/fry_words.html, and the first 100 are included in Chapter 10 of this book. Sight words are an odd mix. They are the high-frequency words, and some are decodable, while others, such as *of* and *one*, are among the most irregular in the language. Students should be able to say the words rapidly if they truly recognize them by sight.

Running Records

Running records are like making your own IRI. They are used to assess students' reading performance as they orally read from one of a set of benchmark books (books at progressively difficult levels and set aside for assessment). A student reads aloud from the unfamiliar book as the teacher makes a record of the student's reading. Usually a passage of 100–150 words is sufficient. Some teachers record on a blank piece of paper, using check marks for correct words and other symbols for errors, but I prefer a copy of the text to write on. Substitutions, insertions, omissions, repetitions, self-corrections, and teacher-provided words are noted. It might look like Figure 13.2. Repetitions are not counted as errors. A self-correction rate of 33% indicates a basic level of monitoring for meaning.

Figure 13.2   Running record sample

Pattie Ann B.   12/5/05

"Lazy cat, lazy cat what will you do? What will you do this morning?"

                 and   *This   will   all SC*
"I'll sit in the sun, ∧ then maybe I'll run. That's what I'll do this morning."

                                        non
"Lazy cat, lazy cat what will you do? What will you do this noon?"

                 water   *P*
"I'll come to be fed <u>at my dish</u> white ~~and~~ red. That's what I'll do this noon."

"Lazy cat, lazy cat what will you do? What will you do this night?"

     h-his ball   *fall*   *my*
"My ball has a bell. See where it fell. I like to play ∧ ball at night.

Word	*Word*	
Substituted word	Inserted ∧ word	Omitted ~~word~~
	word SC	*P*
Repeated <u>word</u>	Self-corrections	Provided words

90 words, 11 errors − 1 self-correction = 10. Repetition not counted as an error.

80/90 words correct, or 88% correct

1/11 words self-corrected = 9% self-correction rate

Pattie Ann's word recognition was 88%, just a little less than instructional level. The teacher then asks the student to retell and prompts with comprehension questions. Running records are more diagnostic than an IRI because the teacher notes the kinds of errors that are made. The errors can be diagnosed further with a miscue analysis.

Miscue Analysis

Miscue analysis, developed by Kenneth Goodman (1967), analyzes errors to gain insight into the cues and strategies used to construct meaning from a text. Miscues are errors or, more kindly, deviations from the text. They are analyzed for semantic similarity (the miscue means the same as the text word), syntactic similarity (the miscue could grammatically fit in the sentence in place of the text word), and phonetic similarity (the miscue partially looks or sounds the same as the text word). Phonetic similarities are analyzed further. On a miscue chart, first mark whether a phonetic similarity exists. Then analyze whether the similarity is in the beginning, middle, or end of the word. Students usually are able to identify beginning letter-sound relationships first, then ending sounds, and finally medial or middle sounds. The teacher can judge whether the reader is reading for sense, is using sentence structure, and is using letter-sound relationships.

Goodman and Goodman (1998) recommend that passages for analysis be several paragraphs or several pages in length. The material needs to be "long and challenging enough to produce sufficient numbers of miscues for patterns to appear. In addition, readers receive no help and are not interrupted" (p. 103). They recommend that the teacher wait a full 30 seconds before supplying a word, but that seems uncomfortably long. An analysis might look like this:

Text: Stan saw a dog. It was on the side of the street. The dog gave a happy bark.

LaDonna: Stan was a dog. It was on . . . Stan saw a dog. It was on the side of the store. The dog got a happy bark.

Miscue	Text	Semantic similarity	Syntactic similarity	Phonetic similarity				Nonword	Self-correct
				Yes	Beg	Mid	End		
was	saw		x	x		x			x
store	street		x	x	x				
got	gave		x	x	x				

Note: Beg = beginning; Mid = middle.

LaDonna is reading for meaning even though she substituted some of the words. She read the passage word by word without fluency, so she could probably use some practice with sight words and pay more attention to ending sounds. Children often repeat as they pause to figure out the next word; they repeat the prior word(s) so that the phrase sticks together. This is not really an error.

Text: Stan saw a cat. It was sitting under a blue car.

Tom: Stan saw a cat. It was beneath a blue car.

Miscue	Text	Semantic similarity	Syntactic similarity	Phonetic similarity				Nonword	Self-correct
				Yes	Beg	Mid	End		
beneath	under	x	x						

Note: Beg = beginning; Mid = middle.

Proficient readers often make semantically acceptable miscues. Since the brain can process information faster than the reader can read aloud, good readers know what is coming and sometimes substitute synonyms or phrases that sound more comfortable to their ears. These types of miscues are hardly errors at all and need not be corrected.

Text: He saw the little bugs. They were everywhere. There was a cat with a long tail. It chased the bugs.

Charles: He saw the little bugs. There where eight. Three was a cat with a long tall. It chas-ed the bugs.

Miscue	Text	Semantic similarity	Syntactic similarity	Phonetic similarity				Nonword	Self-correct
				Yes	Beg	Mid	End		
there	they			x	x				
where	were			x	x		x		
eight	everywhere			x	x				
three	there			x	x				
tall	tail			x	x		x		
chas-ed	chased			x	x	x	x	x	

Note: Beg = beginning; Mid = middle.

Charles's miscues are typical of struggling readers. They tend to rely solely on phonetic cues and fail to monitor for sense. Nonwords are the most serious errors; the student does not expect the text to be sensible. "The errors that interfere with meaning and the errors that are syntactically unacceptable are the most serious because the student doesn't realize that reading should make sense" (Tompkins, 1997, p. 447).

If the passage is long enough, or the miscues are recorded over several days, a pattern will emerge. If no miscues are made, try a harder passage so the reader has to use strategies for determining words. Let's look back at Pattie Ann.

Miscue	Text	Semantic similarity	Syntactic similarity	Phonetic similarity				Nonword	Self-correct
				Yes	Beg	Mid	End		
this	that's			x	x		x		
will	what			x	x				
all	I'll			x			x		x
non	noon			x	x		x	x	

Note: Beg = beginning; Mid = middle.

Miscue	Text	Semantic similarity	Syntactic similarity	Phonetic similarity				Nonword	Self-correct
				Yes	Beg	Mid	End		
water	white			x	x				
his	has			x	x		x		
ball	bell		x	x	x		x		
fall	fell	x		x	x		x		
Number		1/8	1/8	8/8	7/8	0/8	6/8	1/8	1/8
Percent		12%	12%	100%	87%	0%	75%	12%	12%

Note: Beg = beginning; Mid = middle.

It is a lot easier to see strengths and weaknesses with a miscue analysis. Pattie Ann is a bit unclear about her short vowels. She is probably monitoring for sense a little more than the numbers indicate because she was aware of the rhyming pattern in the last line and changed *fell* to *fall* to make it rhyme with her miscue on *bell*. Continuing the miscue analysis on another day will make the pattern clear.

Insertions and omissions do not fit well on a miscue chart, and if they are frequent, they need to be analyzed separately. Readers who consistently insert words may be overrelying on background knowledge rather than attending to the print (Almasi, 2003). Phonetic miscue analysis does not work quite as well with two-syllable words. Often children will pick out some letters from the original word and include them in a substituted multisyllable word, but the patterns take slightly more analysis. Running records and miscue analysis are not quite the same, but they are compatible. They help the teacher diagnose which strategies a child is using, and they provide a direction for instruction.

Assessing Comprehension

Assessing comprehension is not as easy. It is usually done through questioning. Answers to individual questions will tell a teacher whether a student remembered the answer to a particular question or not, but they do not always reveal the degree to which the child understood the entire passage. If answers are analyzed by question type—right there, think and search, author and you, and on your own—the teacher can get a better idea whether the child comprehends at the literal, inferential, or critical level.

Much too late in my career, I learned to ask "What made you think that?" I remember Tyler, who said the scene could not possibly be by the ocean, despite clues of lapping waves, gulls, and sand. He said that the passage stated it was "by the sea," which to him meant an inland lake, and thus it could not possibly be by the ocean. He understood reasonably well, but without questioning him, I thought his answer was completely wrong. Comprehension can be assessed by oral or written retelling or by answering questions; I much prefer retelling.

Retelling and Summarizing

For a retelling, simply ask children to retell the story in their own words, remembering as much as they can. Young students may retell an entire picture book, but older ones are more likely to retell a chapter or a significant event in the plot. Gambrell, Pfeiffer, and Wilson (cited in May, 1998) found that children who had practice in retelling improved in both comprehension and recall. "They also gain in the ability to organize and retain text information" (p. 388). As young readers retell the story orally, the teacher checks off significant events from a prepared summary of the story. Primary teachers have flannel board figures, cutouts, or manipulatives available for the child to use to aid in the storytelling.

Teachers can question the student about any events that were missed during the retelling. Pearson and Duke (2002) suggest questions similar to these:

What kind of character was X? What makes you think so?

Is it important that the story took place there? in that time period?

What did X want to do? Why was X having trouble?

What happened after X did Y?

How did X solve the problem?

How did the story turn out?

Beyond third grade, students usually write the retelling as a summary, which is more condensed than a retelling. Although a teacher can learn a great deal about students' comprehension in oral discussion and individual retellings, a question is usually answered by no more than a few students. When answers are written, everyone responds, and all students can be assessed. A positive aspect of summaries is that every student will be able to respond at some level of specificity. Students receive credit for all the things they do know. Summaries can reveal a great deal about the breadth and depth of students' comprehension.

The following questions aid in assessment of summaries:

1. Is trivial information deleted from the summary? Are redundancies deleted from the summary? Grade-school children should be able to make these deletions (Brown & Day, cited in Baker & Brown, 2002).

2. Is everything included, or are lists of items or actions summarized with category words?

3. Is it just a list of facts (and then . . . , and then . . . , and then . . .), or are the facts connected in ways that show how they are related?

4. Does the child understand a character's motivation, or do events just happen without apparent reason?

5. Is the summary accurate? Are relevant details included?

6. Did the student miss or misinterpret something that caused an understanding that is different from the author's?

7. Does the summary have a main-idea sentence that was constructed by the student? This is the most difficult part of a summary and may be beyond the capabilities of fifth graders. Tenth graders typically use a main-idea sentence on only a third of those occasions when it would be appropriate (Baker & Brown, 2002).

Greater depth of comprehension is usually demonstrated by retelling than by responding to a set of quiz questions, and students learn that they have to read the whole section to be able to tell how it fits together. A different sense of accountability exists than when merely skimming to find the answers to questions. Some children like to be succinct, some have difficulty with the physical process of handwriting, and some think a few lines about the main events are sufficient. The teacher should model a response of the expected depth so students understand how much they need to tell in a summary to demonstrate comprehension. Comparing several papers with different levels of elaboration or developing a class rubric will also work. Unclear expectations of depth are often more of a problem than lack of student knowledge and comprehension. "Instruction of summarization improves memory for what is read, both in terms of free recall and answering questions" (Trabasso & Bouchard, 2002, p. 182).

> Unclear expectations of depth are often more of a problem than lack of student knowledge and comprehension.

Probing for Comprehension

When students' understanding does not match the author's intentions, sometimes a mismatched schema is the culprit. A class was reading Langston Hughes's "Thank You M'am," about a woman living in a boarding house who was mugged by a young boy. Instead of turning him in to the police, she took him home, fed him, and gave him money for his fondest desire, which was a pair of suede shoes. Several students thought it was no big deal for a rich woman to give a boy some money. On closer questioning, they revealed their reasoning. She lived in a three-story house with many bedrooms and had dinner in the dining room every night with several other people. Their schemas did not include *boarding house,* other *boarders,* and *hot plate,* so they paid attention only to the clues they could interpret. When the confusion was straightened out—so that their schemas matched the author's—the students understood the compassion and personal sacrifice of the woman. The teacher also learned that this particular story needed some preteaching. Quizzes with specific questions would not have revealed the students' mismatched schemas.

■ INFORMAL CLASSROOM ASSESSMENT

Informal assessments are done in the context of daily instruction, using materials in the curriculum. Frequent assessments provide the information for data-driven decision making. It is only when teachers gather and interpret data that they have a sound basis for deciding which children need additional instruction and practice or whether students are ready to tackle a new objective.

Observation, Checklists, and Anecdotal Records

Information can be gathered informally and unobtrusively as teachers watch their students participating in daily activities. Individual observations yield diagnostic information, and state standards and benchmarks help teachers interpret observations.

Checklists lend themselves to those questions that can be answered yes or no. For example, during classroom activities, a teacher might observe whether a student knows letter-sound relationships or can identify a word-family word by analogy or whether a student stops at punctuation. Editing concerns in writing make for good checklist items, too. Evaluating comprehension is too complex for a checklist format.

Anecdotal records are appropriate for recording student behaviors that cannot be checked off in a yes-or-no fashion. Teachers use anecdotal notes to record examples of strategies and cueing systems that students are using, to record book selections, or to note cooperative group behaviors. Teachers may jot down revealing comments during story discussion or comments that divulge students' attitudes toward literacy. Some teachers carry sticky-note pads or index cards on a clipboard so that nothing has to be recopied, and the note can be dated and placed in the teacher's file or a child's folder. A good time to take notes is when the students are working harder than you are and when you are doing more listening than talking.

In order to find observation time, a teacher might divide the class into groups of three children, then specifically observe one set of students during the morning on Monday, another on Monday afternoon, and the remaining sets on the remaining days. This method will yield more than 35 individual observations per child in a year's time.

Assignments as Assessment

Assignments that are completed individually are assessments. Additional testing is duplicative and takes unnecessary time. Students might be assessed through written responses or drawn responses or through performance assessments.

Writing as an Assessment of Reading

There are more interesting ways to assess reading comprehension than having students answer written questions. The caveat is that writing as a reading assessment must demonstrate comprehension of the material; it cannot merely be related to the text. Writing assignments on the same topic, creative responses, and stories of the same genre make good extension activities, but they are not good assessments. The teacher needs to communicate expectations clearly when assigning an assessment project, especially if previous writing experiences have been creative responses to the material rather than assessment-based responses.

Writing assignments that make good assessments include a diary or letter from a character (either of which is a variation of retelling), a postcard from a character (a five-minute evaluation of plot and sequence and perhaps character), a newspaper article (evaluates plot, sequence, setting, and characters), an advice column (assesses whether the student understands the conflict and can generate evaluative solutions), and an interview with a character (reveals understanding of motivation and characterization).

Another writing assignment is an epilogue to the story. Only a few stories leave enough loose ends to allow for different but realistic epilogues. A student's epilogue cannot change any facts from the story and must logically follow the events and characterization in the story. A book that begged for an epilogue is *Julie of the Wolves*, by Jean Craighead George. Ms. George finally wrote the epilogue herself, *Julie*, published nearly 25 years after *Julie of the Wolves*. Figure 13.3 provides an example of a rubric for assessing children's epilogues.

A persuasive essay is an excellent way to judge critical reading because the student evaluates options and makes a decision. Certain stories and most novels are suitable for persuasive writing; there must be enough viable options in the story to allow students to choose a position.

These assessment assignments are graded with rubrics. One or two of the analytical features must assess content from the story; an assessment cannot be graded only in terms of the quality of writing. If teachers choose to take these pieces though all the steps of the writing process (i.e., use them as integrated language arts assignments), they may want to evaluate reading comprehension from the first draft, before peers suggest revisions to the content.

When students know they will have to respond to what they read, they are more likely to monitor their comprehension. Just think about your reading habits when you know you are going to be held accountable for information and when it does not make any difference. A few comprehension questions give the teacher an indication that the students are on track, but a more complex assignment will give greater depth of assessment.

Drawing as an Assessment of Reading

Drawing is an appropriate response for every grade level. Most students find drawing a welcome and creative break from written responses. Students can draw the sequence of events of a book or chapter by making the nine-square grid (like a tic-tac-toe game) discussed elsewhere in this book and drawing events from the beginning, middle, and end of the story.

More complex endeavors include constructing a flipbook. Use three pages of blank paper. Fold each piece with a horizontal fold but at a different point on the page, so that when the three pages are tucked together at the fold, each edge sticks out farther than the previous edge. You should be able to see the bottom edge of each of the six pages. See the top half of Figure 13.4. An eight-page fold book is a similar idea, but the pages are very tiny, making the eight-page fold book more suitable for the upper grades. Fold one piece of paper along the lines indicated in the bottom half of Figure 13.4. Cut where indicated. These little books are perfect for making selections about key events and retelling a story in sequence.

Performance Assessment

A performance assessment is the most logical way to evaluate oral performances and projects. Performance assessments require students to produce a product or to demonstrate a process. There may be more than one right answer

Figure 13.3 Rubric for *Julie of the Wolves* epilogue

RUBRIC FOR *JULIE OF THE WOLVES* EPILOGUE

	1	2	3	4
Plausibility	Has nothing to do with *Julie*	Implausible Unclear how and why	Plausible Most parts clear Picks up where story ends	Plausible extension of the story Clear how and why Picks up where story ends and relates epilogue to past
Supporting Details	1–2 details	3–5 details	6–10 details Includes feelings of characters	More than 10 details Includes feelings of characters
Focus	Can't stay on topic No introduction or conclusion	Some straying off topic Introduction or conclusion missing or don't match body	Mostly stays on topic Introduction and conclusion match body	Stays on topic Introduction and conclusion match body
Organization	No paragraphing Everything lumped together	Illogical paragraphing	Correct paragraphing	Correct paragraphing One topic per paragraph Details match topic sentences
Conventions	Difficult to understand	More than eight errors in grammar	3–8 errors in spelling and punctuation	Fewer than three errors in spelling and punctuation No incomplete or run-on sentences
Drafts	Only rough draft submitted	Only final draft submitted	Final draft and rough draft submitted	Final draft, rough draft, and revisions submitted

(Developed by Debra Davidson.)

Figure 13.4 Drawing-response formats for retelling

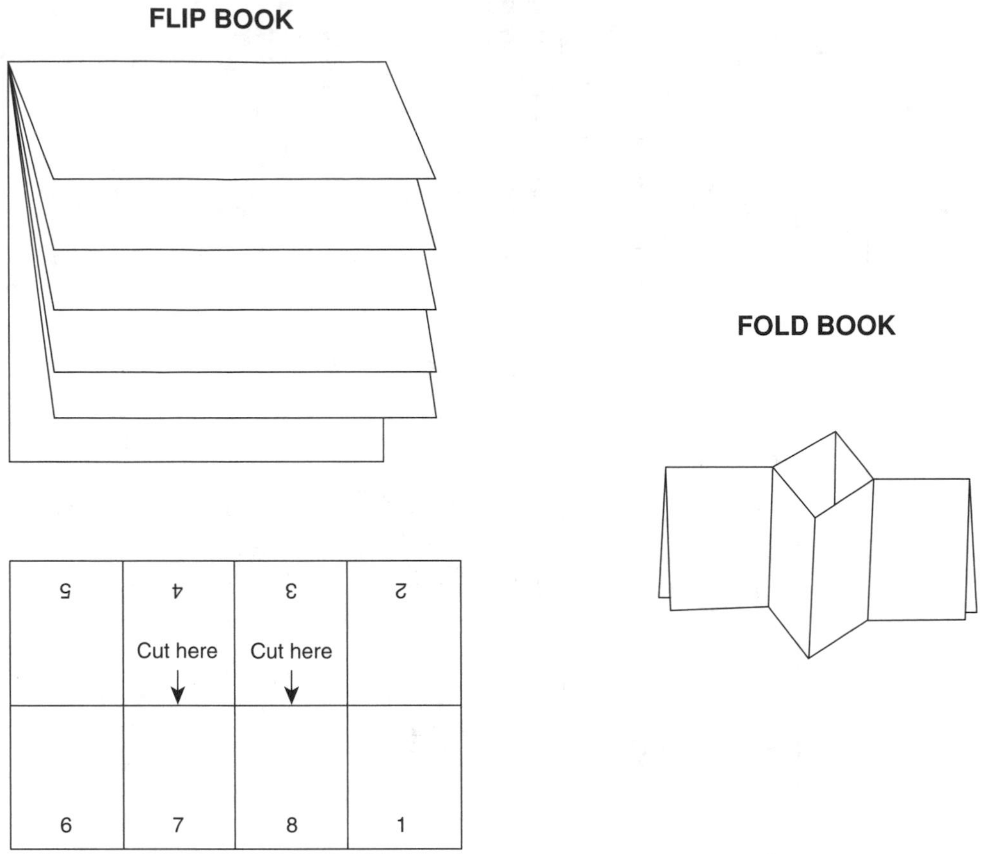
FLIP BOOK
FOLD BOOK
5
4
3
2
Cut here
Cut here
6
7
8
1

or more than one way to complete the process. The key to effective performances is setting the standards and criteria in advance. These types of assessments are also graded with a rubric. Performance tasks are often classroom assignments that are integral to the curriculum, so they fit more fluidly into classroom activities than forced-choice testing does. They require more than simple recall, and they help students apply what they have learned.

My favorite performance assessment was an assignment called Court of the Gods. Pairs of students were asked to research a story in Greek mythology in which a punishment occurred (usually some poor mortal was entrapped by a capricious god). Students acted as opposing advocates for the mythical characters and had to be ready to tell the story orally to an adult judge, although only one actually did so during the trial. Students had to submit a written brief that told the facts of the case (which each pair wrote cooperatively) and argued for or against the original penalty (a statement each student wrote individually). The briefs ended with an appeal that the punishment in the myth be overturned and damages awarded or that the original punishment was justified. A decision was made by the judge based on the arguments presented. Students had to find and read the myths, interpret them carefully, work cooperatively, evaluate the actions of the characters, find reasons to support or condemn those actions, reflect on ethical issues, apply the information in written briefs, use word processing, and present their recommendation in a mock trial. It sure beat fill in the blank!

Rubrics

Rubrics are the most efficient and objective ways to grade written compositions and performance assessments. They are used for assignments that cannot be graded in terms of percentage correct. See the writing rubric in Figure 11.2. In addition to grading, rubrics can be used by students for revision and editing in writing, when preparing for a speech, or as a checklist before a final project is presented. Teachers also use rubrics to clarify expectations when explaining a new assignment.

A rubric is a grading grid that can be written in a general manner, such as a rubric for expository essays, or for a specific purpose, such as a rubric for a newspaper article based on *Number the Stars* (Lowry, 1990). Customarily, the levels of development an assignment uses are written across the top of the page, and the analytical features or subcategories are listed down the side. The lowest developmental level usually represents the performance of the least knowledgeable student, and the highest level represents an outstanding performance. The levels or stages of development should number either four or six so that the student or teacher must decide if the assignment basically meets the standards or is not there yet.

The analytical elements are the subfeatures of the assignment. In a writing rubric, the elements may be focus, support and elaboration, organization, accuracy, and English conventions. For a speech, they may be volume and pace, lack of distracting movements, organization, clarity of speech, eye contact, and content. The characteristics of each trait are specifically described across the developmental levels.

A mere list of the objective and several numbers to designate the quality of the student's work does not constitute a rubric; it is a grading scale. While grading scales are helpful to illuminate the objectives, the characteristics are not defined, nor is the degree of quality assigned to each number specified.

In a rubric, within each box of the grid, the characteristics are described as accurately and succinctly as possible so that two people, grading independently, would render the same score. This is called interrater reliability. Using percentages rather than comparative descriptors such as *seldom* ensures that everyone has the same criteria in mind. The language in a rubric should be written so that the

> Both student and teacher can use the rubric as a diagnostic tool.

terms can be understood by students and parents as well as by teachers. Look again at Figure 13.3, the rubric for the epilogue to *Julie of the Wolves*, which demonstrates specificity in all the categories.

Rubrics can also be used to help students learn to appraise their own work and set new goals. Ask students to grade themselves on the rubric after the performance is finished or when the written assignment is completed. The teacher can grade on the same sheet and the two evaluations can be compared. It is the perfect time to confer and find out if the student did not understand or just did not put enough time and effort into the project to meet a higher standard. Because the scores are analytic (separate scores for different categories) rather than holistic ("Your grade is a B"), both student and teacher can use the rubric as a diagnostic tool. The more often students are asked to self-evaluate, the more they will internalize the criteria and understand the application. Rubrics can also help students develop goals. Because of the developmental nature of a rubric, a student can easily see what is needed for the next level of achievement.

Analytical grades can be added up, weighted, or reviewed diagnostically. If standard ABC grades are to be given, it works better to assign grades, 24 = B, rather than to calculate percentages (24/30 = 80% = C). Rubrics just do not convert to percentages very well. Although it takes time to develop a rubric, it is time well spent because teachers must clarify in their own minds the desired qualities of the product.

Tests

From a very early age, children think that tests are exceedingly important. They develop ideas about what is significant in school by the kinds of tests they are given. If teachers ask only for informational tidbits, then students will believe that collecting tidbits is the ultimate goal of an education.

Students benefit from assessment when they receive feedback on their work and then use that knowledge to develop criteria for future work. However, students seldom view assignments or assessments as diagnostic and helpful unless their teachers show them how to assess their progress on a developmental scale and set future goals. If teachers could develop tests to show progress, then students might view schooling differently. The kinds of tests teachers give and the information that is gathered for the test influence the attitudes and actions of both teachers and students.

End-of-the-book tests are acceptable as long as the teacher knows that what is being tested is a combination of reading comprehension and listening comprehension. If both guided reading and discussion took place as the reading progressed, there is no way to tell how the child learned the information for the final test. For an assessment of reading comprehension only, assess immediately after silent reading. For a broader assessment of comprehension, one that includes the ability to change one's mind after hearing conflicting evidence, then test after discussion.

Self-Evaluation

Students learn to self-assess when they choose and critique a limited number of pieces for inclusion in a portfolio or end-of-the-quarter conference. They must complete a reflection or analysis sheet explaining why they made their choices. Students who do not know how to evaluate the quality of their own work finish their assignments and turn them in without a second thought. They depend on the teacher's grade to determine the quality. Thus they are handicapped when faced with future assignments and are always dependent on the teacher's directions. Self-assessment helps students build internal criteria about what makes a "good one."

Reflection sheets often use stem starters such as the following:

This is an example of my best work because . . .

I chose this piece because . . .

In order to do this well, I had to know . . .

Two things I liked about my selection are . . .

What was hard for me to do on this piece was . . .

My special strengths are . . .

One thing I would like to work on in the next quarter is . . .

Until children become familiar with metacognition or self-evaluation, they may be tempted to choose the pieces with the highest grades. Much discussion is needed about how to select a piece that shows growth, took effort, showed insight, or represents a high standard of work. It is helpful for students to hear the reasoning behind someone else's choices and the wording that can be used for their own reflection sheets.

STANDARDIZED ASSESSMENT ■

Many teachers are beleaguered by the increase in standardized testing. The abundance and importance of these tests have increased in the last decade, but teachers are learning how to live with them and make use of the results.

Norm-Referenced and Criterion-Referenced Tests

Let's start by looking at what these tests are supposed to do and how they are constructed. Standardized tests were meant to be quick, inexpensive, indicative, and comparative. They are quick and inexpensive because they are administered to groups, in contrast to tests individually administered by specialized personnel such as a reading specialist or a school psychologist. They are indicative because they are a snapshot of achievement; they are not diagnostic. They are meant to compare achievement with the achievement of other students at the local, state, or national levels. Any college admissions officer will admit that grades are almost meaningless, and the only way to compare is when all students across the state or country take the same test. Sometimes growth indicators (comparisons of a child's early work to later work) are needed, but sometimes comparative indicators are needed for evaluating the effectiveness of instruction and curriculum and for decision making. Standardized testing is akin to asking a knowledgeable, unbiased outsider to take a quick peek into the classroom and give an indication of how well the kids are doing.

Norm-referenced tests use a normal curve of distribution (Gall, Borg, & Gall, 1996). The norms (expected normal distribution) are developed through initial testing of large sample groups. The mean score of the group is designated to be at grade level, so 50% score below grade level and 50% above grade level. When you read a headline such as "About 40% of 10-year-olds can't read at grade level" ("Why use volunteers," 1997, 12A), you should not be shocked. If every child were reading "at grade level," then the norms would be readjusted to reflect the higher achievement and rebalanced as described above. Figure 13.5 shows how percentile scores and standard deviations match the

Figure 13.5 National curve equivalency

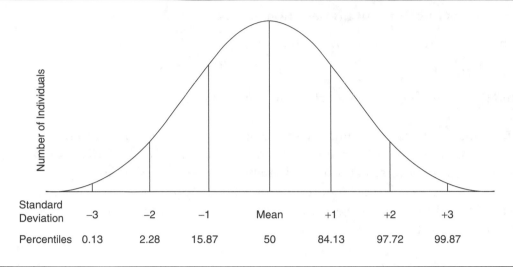

Source: Gall, M. D., Borg, W. R., and Gall, J., *Educational Research: An Introduction* (6th ed.). © 1996. Published by Allyn and Bacon, Boston, MA. Copyright © 1996 Pearson Education. Reprinted by permission of the publisher.

curve. If a child scored at the 45th percentile, 55% of the sample scored higher than that child did, and 44% scored lower.

Criterion-referenced tests are constructed according to specific standards or criteria for a grade level. They are not comparative or competitive. A cut point is set, and students who score above that point meet the standards, and those below the cut point do not. Theoretically, *all* students could meet the criteria. Most state tests are constructed in this manner, with the criteria determined by the state standards. Many educational leaders believe that attainable, uniform standards should be used because both teachers and students know the target for which they are aiming. Goal setting is easier, and teachers can develop instructional activities with clear objectives in mind.

It takes a little training to learn how to interpret standardized test reports, but they provide highly useful data for examining classrooms, grade levels, and schools. Evaluation of a curriculum or program needs to start with the data.

High-Stakes Testing

In the past decade, standardized tests, especially statewide tests, have become high-stakes tests. These assessments are central to the standards-based reform movement that stresses the use of measurable outcomes to monitor students' progress. Tests are high-stakes if they are used for making decisions about promotion or graduation, about closing schools or putting them on probation, about tracking, about high school placement, or about whether special services will be offered or withheld. Not to mention that superintendents can be fired, principals and supervisors can turn neurotic, and teachers are in a tizzy.

John Guthrie (2002) describes five stages of teachers' reactions to these tests: (1) Teachers feel shame, embarrassment, guilt, anger, and disappointment and feel they could have done better to prepare their classes. (2) Teachers then wonder if these tests actually measure "real reading." (3) Teachers are concerned about the emotional impact and stress levels of their students. (4) Teachers resent the loss of instructional time due to testing. (5) Teachers adapt to tests, often narrowing the curriculum and making activities more test-like.

These attitudes, if not the sequence, were confirmed in a national survey carried out by the National Board on Educational Testing and Public Policy and reported by Abrams, Pedulla, and Madaus (2003). They also compared teacher attitudes in high-stakes states, such as Florida, California, Texas, and North Carolina, to teacher attitudes in low-stakes states, such as Hawaii, Maine, and Wyoming, where no consequences are attached to test scores.

Teachers whose students take high-stakes tests do change classroom instruction. Some 43% of teachers in high-stakes states and 17% in low-stakes states reported greatly increased time spent on instruction in tested areas. Sometimes this is viewed positively and sometimes negatively. Jones and colleagues (1999) found a narrowing of curriculum to reading, writing, and math, subjects tested in North Carolina, and Stecher and Barron (1999) found increased instructional emphasis on fourth-grade problem solving, reasoning, pictorial representation, and writing in math in Kentucky. They also found increased instructional emphasis in seventh-grade writing instruction. Both increases were in grade levels in which those subjects were tested. Vogler (2002) investigated changes in instruction by tenth-grade teachers in Massachusetts in reaction to statewide performance-based tests in English, science, and math. More than 50% of the teachers reported an increase or large increase in the use of open-response questions (81.6%), creative/critical thinking questions (68%), problem-solving activities (63.7%), the use of rubrics or scoring guides (61.3%), writing assignments (59.8%), and inquiry/investigation (56.3%). These six practices represent the same types of questions or activities tested and evaluated by the Massachusetts tests. Change of instruction is viewed negatively when teachers concentrate on lower-level reading skills, usually literal questions. The type of questions asked on high-stakes tests does make a difference in classroom preparation for the tests. Proponents of assessment-driven reform have argued for assessments that require the use of higher-level thinking. "If you test it, they will teach it" (Popham, cited in Vogler, 2002).

Teachers do feel stressed. In the Abrams study, 57% of teachers in high-stakes states strongly agreed that they felt pressure from their district superintendents, and 41% felt pressure from their principals, to raise scores on state tests, compared with 41% and 17%, respectively, in low-stakes states.

Instructional practices involving test-preparation materials have changed too. In high-stakes states, 70% of teachers prepared students for state tests throughout the year and 63% used test preparation materials developed commercially or by the state, as compared with 43% and 19%, respectively, in low-stakes states (Abrams et al., 2003). "In some cases preparing, administering, and recovering [from] tests may cost 100 hours of instructional time" (Guthrie, 2002, p. 373). Some experts are wondering whether highly focused test preparation is artificially raising state scores. Maryland's and Virginia's state scores have gone up almost every year in every grade level and subject, but the National Assessment of Educational Progress scores show no gains or only slight gains in those states (de Vise, 2005).

Test Preparation That Makes a Difference

Does all this test prep make a difference? Guthrie (2002) reports some very interesting research based on how different types of tests correlate. First, he reports on the components that influence test performance and then recommends how much and what types of activities are useful for test preparation.

Reading ability accounts for 40% of the difference between students, and knowledge about the content of the reading passages accounts for 20%. Motivation accounts for 15%, format of the test and test-taking strategies for 10%, and unknown sources of error in the process of measurement for 15%. On the basis of this research, recommendations can be made for test preparation that makes a difference.

Since the largest chunk has to do with reading ability, the largest amount of time, 40%, should be spent teaching expository and narrative reading and writing, not practicing taking tests on it. Another 20% of the time should be spent teaching real reading strategies that can be used in the tests. Guthrie lists reading strategies commonly needed for tests. They include using background knowledge and searching to locate information. In my state, the expository sections have some picky questions that require that students return to the text

> Reading ability accounts for 40% of the difference between students [on test performance], and knowledge about the content of the reading passages accounts for 20%.

to confirm the answer. I had to convince my children that rereading parts of the passage to find the answer was not cheating, which they considered it to be. Understanding how the text is structured is helpful for locating information.

Other needed strategies are summarizing, self-monitoring, concept mapping to synthesize text, and self-questioning and self-explaining—explaining ideas to oneself and asking why and how ideas are connected (Guthrie, 2002). Although some experts recommend spending three months prior to testing working on these strategies, I do not know why a teacher would not use the entire year because all these strategies are basic components of comprehension. Effective test preparation depends on a sustained, long-term plan of instruction and opportunities to practice.

Guthrie further recommends that 20% of test preparation time be spent in engaged, independent reading to solidify strategies, build fluency (because the tests are timed), and learn content. The strongest predictor of achievement on standardized tests for children in Grades 3–6 was the amount and variety of reading they did. It outweighed intelligence, economic background, and gender (Guthrie, Wigfield, Metsala, & Cox, 1999).

Format practice, teaching students strategies for responding in multiple choice formats or other formats used on the test, should take about 10% of the time. Here are some test-taking strategies (Millman and Bishop, cited in Guthrie, 2002) and a few additions for multiple choice tests.

1. Use time efficiently by beginning to work rapidly.

2. Temporarily omit items that seem too difficult and go back when the questions are completed. If guessing is not penalized, guess rather than leave an answer blank.

3. Pay attention to directions and check all answers after completing the test.

4. Rule out unlikely alternatives and answers that are only partly correct.

5. Read the questions first, before reading the passage, to determine a purpose for reading.

6. Avoid extreme words such as *never*.

7. Examine the longest answer carefully as the longest is often the correct answer.

For writing tests and other tests requiring open-ended responses, teachers need to learn the criteria and teach them. Most provide good formats and criteria for clarity and organization for writing.

Motivation for reading and test taking should be 10% of test preparation time. Guthrie reports, "Motivational support can include alleviating students' anxieties, providing meaningful reasons for test success, enabling students to feel self-efficacy toward reading, and most important, fostering extensive amounts of reading throughout the year" (2002, p. 337).

Pressley, Wharton-McDonald, and Hampston (2002) found that the exemplary teachers they observed were busily providing instruction and practice in reading with little decontextualized test prep occurring in their classrooms.

I do not know a single teacher who is not a little grumpy about statewide testing, but the best teachers learn what skills are required for the test, align curriculum with the standards, and incorporate instruction into meaningful balanced teaching of reading and writing all year long.

ASSESSING ASSESSMENT   ■

Assessment is a complex issue that intimidates many teachers. It is complex because it serves so many masters—individual diagnosis, class progress, informed teaching decisions, grades and progress reports for parents, criteria to be internalized, application of standards, and goal setting. In addition to multiple purposes, it is intertwined with emotional issues concerning competition and self-esteem, compounded by an overlay of statistics and technical terms. Yet, it does not have to be intimidating if teachers know the criteria and standards and are methodical and cumulative in instruction. A broad repertoire of assessment techniques can be learned and used successfully in every classroom.

References

Abrams, L., Pedulla, J., & Madaus, G. (2003). Views from the classroom: Teachers' opinions of statewide testing programs. *Theory into Practice, 42*(1), 18–29.

Adams, M. J. (1991). *Beginning to read: Thinking and learning about print* (4th ed.). Cambridge, MA: MIT Press.

Adams, M. J., Foorman, B. R., Lundberg, I., & Beeler, T. (1998). *Phonemic awareness in young children.* Baltimore: Paul H. Brookes.

Advanced Learning Technologies in Education Consortia. Retrieved October 23, 2005, from http://rubistar.4teachers.org

Allen, J. (1999). *Word, words, words: Teaching vocabulary in grades 4–12.* Portland, ME: Stenhouse.

Allington, R. L. (2001). *What really matters for struggling readers.* New York: Addison-Wesley, Longman.

Allington, R. L. (2002a). Research on reading/learning disability interventions. In A. E. Farstrup & S. J. Samuels (Eds.), *What research has to say about reading instruction* (3rd ed., pp. 261–290). Newark, DE: International Reading Association.

Allington, R. L. (2002b). What I've learned about effective reading instruction from a decade of studying exemplary elementary classroom teachers. *Phi Delta Kappan, 83*(10), 740–747.

Almasi, J. F. (2003). *Teaching strategic processes in reading.* New York: Guilford Press.

American Guidance Service Publishing. *Test of phonological processing* and *test of phonological awareness in Spanish.* Circle Pines, MN. (http://www.agsnet.com)

Anderson, R. C., Hiebert, E. H., Scott, J. A., & Wilkinson, I. A. G. (1985). *Becoming a nation of readers: The report of the commission on reading.* Urbana, IL: Center for the Study of Reading.

Anderson, R. C., & Pearson, P. D. (1984). A schema-theoretic view of basic processes in reading comprehension. In P. D. Pearson, R. Barr, M. L. Kamil, & P. Mosenthal (Eds.), *Handbook of reading research* (pp. 255–291). New York: Longman.

Anderson, R. C., Wilson, P. T., & Fielding, L. G. (1988). Growth in reading and how children spend their time outside of school. *Reading Research Quarterly, 23,* 285–303.

Atwell, N. (1987). *In the middle: Writing, reading, and learning with adolescents.* Portsmouth, NH: Heinemann.

Au, K. (2002). Multicultural factors and the effective instruction of students of diverse backgrounds. In A. E. Farstrup & S. J. Samuels (Eds.), *What research has to say about reading instruction* (3rd ed., pp. 392–413). Newark, DE: International Reading Association.

Bader, L. (2005). *Bader reading and language inventory* (5th ed.). Upper Saddle River, NJ: Pearson Merrill Prentice Hall.

Baker, L., & Brown, A. L. (2002). Metacognitive skills and reading. In P. D. Pearson (Ed.), *Handbook of reading research* (pp. 353–394). Mahwah, NJ: Erlbaum.

Baker, S., Gersten, R., & Graham, S. (2003). Teaching expressive writing to students with learning disabilities: Research-based applications and examples. *Journal of Learning Disabilities, 36*(2), 109–123.

Ball, E. W., & Blachman, B. A. (1991). Does phoneme awareness training in kindergarten make a difference in early word recognition and developmental spelling? *Reading Research Quarterly, 26*(1), 49–66.

Baumann, J. F., Hoffman, J. V., Moon, J., & Duffy-Hester, A. M. (1998). Where are teachers' voices in the phonics/whole language debate? Results from a survey of U.S. elementary classroom teachers. *The Reading Teacher, 51*(8), 636–650.

Baumann, J., Hooten, H., & White, P. (1996). Teaching skills and strategies with literature. In J. Baltas & S. Shafer (Eds.), *Scholastic guide to balanced reading 3–6* (pp. 60–70). New York: Scholastic.

Beatty, J. (2001). *The human brain: Essentials of behavioral neuroscience.* Thousand Oaks, CA: Sage.

Beck, I. L., McKeown, M. G., Hamilton, R. L., & Kucan, L. (1997). *Questioning the author: An approach for enhancing student engagement with text.* Newark, DE: International Reading Association.

Beers, K. (2003). When kids can't read: What teachers can do—A guide for teachers 6-12. Portsmouth, NH: Heinemann.

Berliner, D. C. (1981). Academic learning time and reading achievement. In J. T. Guthrie (Ed.), *Comprehension and teaching: Research reviews* (pp. 203–226). Newark, DE: International Reading Association.

Biancarosa, G. (2005). After third grade. *Educational Leadership, 63*(2), 16–22.

Blachowicz, C., & Fisher, P. (1996). *Teaching vocabulary in all classrooms.* Englewood Cliffs, NJ: Merrill-Prentice Hall.

Blachowicz, C., & Fisher, P. J. (2006). *Teaching vocabulary in all classrooms* (3rd ed.). Upper Saddle River, NJ: Pearson Education.

Bond, G. L., & Dykstra, R. (1967). The cooperative research program in first-grade reading instruction. *Reading Research Quarterly, (2)*, 5–141.

Boyle, J., & Weishaar, M. (1997). The effects of expert-generated versus student-generated cognitive organizers on the reading comprehension of students with learning disabilities. *Learning Disabilities Research and Practice, 12*(4), 228–235.

Brown, A. (1997). *Changes for effective schools.* Unpublished manuscript.

Brown, K., Sinatra, G., & Wagstaff, J. (1996). Exploring the potential of analogy instruction to support students' spelling development. *The Elementary School Journal, 97*(1), 81–99.

Burke, J. (1996). *The pinball effect: How renaissance water gardens made the carburetor possible and other journeys through knowledge.* Boston: Little, Brown and Company.

Burns, B. (1998). Changing the classroom climate with literature circles. *Journal of Adolescent and Adult Literacy, 42*(2), 124–129.

Burns, B. (2005-2006, December-January). I don't have to count syllables on my fingers anymore: Easier ways to find readability and level books. *Illinois Reading Council Journal, 34*(1), 34–40.

Button, K., Johnson, M. J., & Furgerson, P. (1996). Interactive writing in a primary classroom. *The Reading Teacher, 49*(6), 446–454.

Byrne, B., & Fielding-Barnsley, R. (1993). Evaluation of a program to teach phonemic awareness to young children: A 1-year follow-up. *Journal of Educational Psychology, 85*(1), 104–111.

Caldwell, J. S., & Ford, M. (2002). *Where have all the bluebirds gone? How to soar with flexible grouping.* Portsmouth, NH: Heinemann.

Calkins, L. M. (1994). *The art of teaching writing.* Portsmouth, NH: Heinemann.

Chall, J. S. (1967). *Learning to read: The great debate.* New York: McGraw-Hill.

Chard, D. J., Vaughn, S., & Tyler, B. (2002). A synthesis of research on effective interventions for building reading fluency with elementary students with learning disabilities. *Journal of Learning Disabilities, 35*(5), 386–406.

Clark, C. H. (1995). Teaching students about reading: A fluency example. *Reading Horizons, 35*(3), 251–265.

Coiro, J. (2005). Making sense of online text. *Educational Leadership, 63*(2), 30–35.

Cole, A. D. (1998). Beginner-oriented texts in literature-based classrooms: The segue for a few struggling readers. *The Reading Teacher, 51*(6), 488–501.

Cunningham, A. (1990). Explicit versus implicit instruction in phonemic awareness. *Journal of Experimental Child Psychology, 50*, 429–444.

Cunningham, J. W. (1982). Generating interactions between schemata and text. In J. A. Niles & L. A. Harris (Eds.), *New inquiries in reading research and instruction* (pp. 42–47). Rochester, NY: National Reading Conference.

Cunningham, P. M., & Allington, R. L. (1999). *Classrooms that work: They can all read and write* (2nd ed.). New York: Longwood.

Cunningham, P. M., & Cunningham, J. W. (2002). What we know about how to teach phonics. In A. E. Farstrup and S. J. Samuels (Eds.), *What research has to say about reading instruction* (3rd ed., pp. 87–109). Newark, DE: International Reading Association.

Cunningham, P. M., Hall, D. P., & Defee, M. (1998). Nonability-grouped, multilevel instruction: Eight years later. *The Reading Teacher, 51*(8), 652–664.

Dahl, K., & Farnan, N. (1998). *Children's writing: Perspectives from research.* Newark, DE: International Reading Association & National Reading Conference.

Davey, B. (1983). Think aloud: Modeling the cognitive processes of reading comprehension. *Journal of Reading, 27*(1), 44–47.

de Vise, D. (2005, October 24). State gains not echoed in federal testing. *Washington Post.* Retrieved October 24, 2005, from http://www.washingtonpost.com/wp-dyn/content/article/2005/12/23/AR2005102301330

Donahue, P. L., Daane, M. C., & Jin, Y. (2005). *The nation's report card: Reading 2003.* Washington, DC: U.S. Government Printing Office.

Don Johnston, Inc. *Write: OutLoud.* Retrieved October 29, 2005, from http://www .donjohnston.com

Dragon NaturallySpeaking. Retrieved October 12, 2005, from http://www .dragontalk.com

Duke, N., & Pearson, P. D. (2002). Effective practices for developing reading comprehension. In A. E. Farstrup & S. J. Samuels (Eds.), *What research has to say about reading instruction* (3rd ed., pp. 205–242). Newark, DE: International Reading Association.

Duke, N., & Stewart, B. (1997). Standards in action in a first-grade classroom: The purpose dimension. *The Reading Teacher, 51*(3), 228–237.

Ehri, L. C., & Nunes, S. R. (2002). The role of phonemic awareness in learning to read. In A. E. Farstrup & S. J. Samuels (Eds.), *What research has to say about reading instruction* (3rd ed., pp. 110–139). Newark, DE: International Reading Association.

Elbaum, B., Schumm, J., & Vaughn, S. (1997). Urban middle-elementary students' perceptions of grouping formats for reading instruction. *The Elementary School Journal, 97*(5), 475–499.

Elley, W. B. (1996). The benefits of reading stories aloud. In D. Berliner and U. Casanova (Eds.), *Putting research to work in your school* (pp. 77–82). Arlington Heights, IL: IRI/SkyLight Training and Publishing.

Farr, R. (1990). Inservice presentation in River Forest, IL.

Fink, R. P. (1998). Successful dyslexics: A constructivist study of passionate interest reading. In C. Weaver (Ed.), *Reconsidering a balanced approach to reading* (pp. 387– 408). Urbana, IL: National Council of Teachers of English.

Flyleaf Publishing. *Books to remember.* Lyme, NH. Retrieved October 29, 2005, from http://www.flyleafpublishing.com

Foorman, B. R., Francis, D. J., Fletcher, J. M., Schatschneider, C., & Mehta, P. (1998). The role of instruction in learning to read: Preventing reading failure in at-risk children. *Journal of Educational Psychology, 90* (1), 37–55.

Fountas, I., & Pinnell, G. S. (1996). *Guided reading: Good first teaching for all children.* Portsmouth, NH: Heinemann.

Fountas, I., & Pinnell, G. S. (2006). *The Fountas and Pinnell Leveled Book List, K-8.* Portsmouth, NH: Heinemann.

Fox, M. (1988). Notes from the battlefield: Towards a theory of why people write. *Language Arts, 65*(2), 112–125.

Frayer, D. A., Frederick, W. C., & Klausmeier, H. G. (1969). *A schema for testing the level of concept mastery* (Working Paper No. 16). Madison: University of Wisconsin, Wisconsin Center for Education Research.

Fresch, M. J., & Wheaton, A. (1997). Sort, search, and discover: Spelling in the child-centered classroom. *The Reading Teacher, 51*(1), 20–31.

Frey, B. B., Lee, S. W., Tollefson, N., Pass, L., & Massengill, D. (2005). Balanced literacy in an urban school district. *The Journal of Education Research, 98*(5), 272–280.

Fry, E. B. (1968). A readability formula that saves time. *Journal of Reading, 11*(7), 513.

Fry, E. B. (2000). *1000 Instant Words by Dr. Fry.* Westminster, CA: Teacher Created Materials Publishing.

Fry, E. B. (2002). Readability versus leveling. *The Reading Teacher, 56*(3), 286–291.

Fry, E. B., Kress, J. E., & Fountoukidis, D. L. (2000). *The reading teacher's book of lists* (4th ed.). San Francisco: Jossey-Bass.

Gall, M. D., Borg, W. R., & Gall, J. (1996). *Educational research: An introduction* (6th ed.). Boston: Allyn & Bacon.

Gambrell, L. (1996). Creating classroom cultures that foster reading motivation. *The Reading Teacher, 50*(1), 14–25.

Gambrell, L., & Almasi, J. (1996). *Lively discussions! Fostering engaged reading.* Newark, DE: International Reading Association.

Gaskins, I. W., Ehri, L. C., Cress, C., O'Hara, C., & Donnelly, K. (1997a). Analyzing words and making discoveries about the alphabetic system: Activities for beginning readers. *Language Arts, 74*, 172–184.

Gaskins, I. W., Ehri, L. C., Cress, C., O'Hara, C., & Donnelly, K. (1997b). Procedures for word learning: Making discoveries about words. *The Reading Teacher, 50*(4), 312–327.

Gaskins, R. W., Gaskins, I. W., Anderson, R. C., & Schommer, M. (1995). The reciprocal relationship between research and development: An example involving a decoding strand for poor readers. *Journal of Reading Behavior: A Journal of Literacy, 27*, 337–377.

Gentry, J. R. (1982). An analysis of developmental spelling in GNYS at WRK. *The Reading Teacher, 36*, 192–200.

Gentry, J. R. (2000). A retrospective on invented spelling and a look forward. *The Reading Teacher, 54*(3), 318–332.

Gentry, J. R., & Gillet, J. W. (1993). *Teaching kids to spell.* Portsmouth, NH: Heinemann.

Goldenberg, C. (2005). An interview with Claude Goldenberg. *Reading Today,* August/September, 8.

Goodman, K. (1967). Reading: A psycholinguistic guessing game. *Journal of Reading Specialist, 6*, 126–135.

Goodman, Y., & Goodman, K. S. (1998). To err is human: Learning about language processes by analyzing miscues. In C. Weaver (Ed.), *Reconsidering a balanced approach to reading* (pp. 101–126). Urbana, IL: National Council of Teachers of English.

Goswami, U. (2001). Early phonological development and the acquisition of literacy. In S. B. Neuman & D. K. Dickinson (Eds.), *Handbook of early literacy research* (pp. 111–125). Mahwah, NJ: Erlbaum.

Graham, S., Harris, K. R., & Larsen, L. (2001). Prevention and intervention of writing difficulties with students with learning disabilities. *Learning Disabilities Research and Practice, 16*, 74–84.

Graham, S., MacArthur, C. A., & Schwartz, S. (1995). Effects of goal setting and procedural facilitation on the revising behavior and writing performance of students with writing and learning problems. *Journal of Educational Psychology, 87*, 230–240.

Graves, D. H. (1983). *Writing: Teachers and children at work.* Portsmouth, NH: Heinemann.

Graves, M. E., Graves, B. B., & Braaten, S. (1996). Scaffolded reading experiences for inclusive classes. *Educational Leadership, 53*(5), 14–16.

Graves, M., & Watts-Taffe, S. (2002). The place of word consciousness in a research-based vocabulary program. In A. Farstrup & S. J. Samuels (Eds.), *What research has to say about reading instruction* (3rd ed., pp. 140–165). Newark, DE: International Reading Association.

Gunning, T. (2003). *Creating literacy instruction for all children* (4th ed.). Boston: Allyn & Bacon.

Gunning, T. (2005). *Creating literacy instruction for all students* (5th ed.). Boston: Allyn & Bacon.

Guthrie, J. T. (2002). Preparing students for high-stakes test taking in reading. In A. Farstrup & S. J. Samuels (Eds.), *What research has to say about reading instruction* (3rd ed., pp. 370–391). Newark, DE: International Reading Association.

Guthrie, J. T., Wigfield, A., Metsala, J. L., & Cox, K. E. (1999). Motivational and cognitive predictors of text comprehension and reading amount. *Scientific Studies of Reading, 3,* 231–256.

Hanna, P. R., Hodges, R. E., & Hanna, J. S. (1971). *Spelling: Structure and strategies.* Boston: Houghton Mifflin.

Harding, C. (1998). *Intervention strategies.* Unpublished manuscript.

Harris, K. R., Graham, S., & Mason, L. H. (2003). Self-regulated strategy development in the classroom: Part of a balanced approach to writing instruction for students with disabilities. *Focus on Exceptional Children, 35*(7), 1–16.

Hart, B., & Risley, T. R. (1995). *Meaningful differences in the everyday experiences of young American children.* Baltimore: Paul H. Brookes.

Hart, B., & Risley, T. R. (2003). The early catastrophe: The 30 million word gap by age 3. *American Educator, 27,* 4–9.

Harwayne, S. (2001). *Writing through childhood: Rethinking process and product.* Portsmouth, NH: Heinemann.

Heggerty, M. (2004). *Phonemic awareness: The skills they need to help them succeed!* River Forest, IL: Literacy Resources.

Henry, M. (1997). The decoding/spelling continuum: Integrated decoding and spelling instruction from preschool to early secondary school. *Dyslexia, 3,* 178–189.

Hicks, L. (1997). How do academic motivation and peer relationships mix in an adolescent's world? *Middle School Journal, 28*(4), 18–22.

Hillocks, G. (1986). *Research on written composition: New directions for teaching.* Urbana, IL: ERIC Clearinghouse on Reading and Communications Skills and the National Conference on Research in English.

Hughes, M., & Searle, D. (1997). *The violent e and other tricky sounds: Learning to spell from kindergarten through grade 6.* York, ME: Stenhouse.

Hunt, L. (1997). The effect of self-selection, interest, and motivation upon independent, instructional, and frustrational levels. *The Reading Teacher, 50*(4), 278–282.

Illinois State Board of Education. (1995). *Performance assessment in mathematics: Approaches of open-ended problems.* Springfield, IL: Department of School Improvement Services.

Inspiration Software Inc. *See what's new in Inspiration.* Retrieved October 29, 2005, from http://www.inspiration.com

Interest-Driven Learning, Inc. *Dr. Peet's TalkWriter!* Retrieved October 29, 2005, from http://www.drpeet.com

International Reading Association. (1997). *Position statement on phonics.* Retrieved October 1, 2005, from http://www.reading.org/resources/issues/positions_phonics.html

Intervention Central. *OKAPI Reading Probe Generator.* Retrieved July 11, 2005, from http://www.interventioncentral.org

Irvin, J. (1990). *Vocabulary knowledge: Guidelines for instruction.* Washington, DC: National Education Association.

Ivey, G. (2002). Building comprehension when they're still learning to read the words. In C. C. Block & M. Pressley (Eds.), *Comprehension instruction: Research-based best practices* (pp. 234–246). New York: Guilford.

Ivey, G., & Fisher, D. (2005). Learning from what doesn't work. *Educational Leadership, 63*(2), 9–14.

Johns, J. (2005). *Basic reading inventory* (9th ed.). Dubuque, IA: Kendall Hunt.

Johnston, F. R. (1998). The reader, the text, and the task: Learning words in first grade. *The Reading Teacher, 51*(8), 666–675.

Jones, M. G., Jones, B. D., Hardin, B., Chapman, L., Yarbrough, T., & Davis, M. (1999). The impact of high-stakes testing on teachers and students in North Carolina. *Phi Delta Kappan, 81*(3), 199–203.

Joseph, N., Shafer, G., & Swindle, S. (2003). What activity do you recommend for teaching grammar? *English Journal, 92*(3), 28–30.

Juel, C. (1988). Learning to read and write: A longitudinal study of 54 children from first through fourth grades. *Journal of Educational Psychology, 80*(4), 437–447.

Kamil, M. (2004). Vocabulary and comprehension instruction. In P. McCardle & V. Chhabra (Eds.), *The voice of evidence in reading research* (pp. 213–234). Baltimore: Paul H. Brookes.

Kismaric, C., & Heiferman, M. (1996). *Growing up with Dick and Jane.* New York: Collins.

Kruzich, K. (1995). *Classroom writing strategy analysis.* Paper presented to the Skylight/St. Xavier Field-Based Masters Program, Orland Park, IL.

Kucan, L., & Beck, I. (1997). Thinking aloud and reading comprehension research: Inquiry, instruction, and social interaction. *Review of Educational Research, 67,* 271–299.

Kuhn, M. (2004). Helping students become accurate, expressive readers: Fluency instruction for small groups. *The Reading Teacher, 58*(4), 338–344.

Laflamme, J. G. (1997). The effect of the multiple exposure vocabulary method and the target reading/writing strategy on test scores. *Journal of Adolescent and Adult Literacy, 40*(5), 372–381.

The Landmark Project. Retrieved October 23, 2005, from http://www.landmark-project.com

Langer, J. (1981). From theory to practice: A prereading plan. *Journal of Reading, 25,* 152–156.

Lapp, D., & Flood, J. (1997). Where's the phonics? Making the case (again) for integrated code instruction. *The Reading Teacher, 50*(8), 696–700.

Leap Frog Enterprises. *LeapPad books.* Retrieved October 25, 2005, from http://www .leapfrog.com/

Leslie, L., & Caldwell, J. (2006). *QRI-4 Qualitative reading inventory.* Boston: Pearson, Allyn & Bacon.

Levy, B., & Lysynchuk, L. (1997). Beginning word recognition: Benefits of training by segmentation and whole word methods. *Scientific Studies of Reading, 1*(4), 359–387.

Library of Congress. *American memory.* Retrieved February 1, 2006, from http:// memory.loc.gov/ammem

Lindamood-Bell Learning Processes. (2005). *LiPS, The Lindamood Phonemic Sequencing Program.* Retrieved on October 24, 2005, from http://lblp.com

Lovett, M. W., Lacerenza, L., Borden, S. L., Frijters, J. C., Steinbach, K., & Depalma, M. (2000). Components of effective remediation for developmental reading disabilities: Combining phonological and strategy-based instruction to improve outcomes. *Journal of Educational Psychology, 92,* 263–283.

Lundberg, I., Frost, J., & Petersen, O. P. (1988). Effects of an extensive program for stimulating phonological awareness in preschool children. *Reading Research Quarterly, 23*(3), 263–284.

MacArthur, C. A., Schwartz, S. S., & Graham, S. (1991). Effects of reciprocal peer revision strategy in special education classrooms. *Learning Disabilities Research & Practice, 6,* 201–210.

MacMall. Retrieved September 1, 2005, from http://www.macmall.com

Manz, S. L. (2002). A strategy for previewing textbooks: Teaching readers to become THIEVES. *The Reading Teacher, 55*(5), 434–435.

Martinez, M., Roser, N., & Strecker, S. (1999). "I never thought I could be a star": A readers' theatre ticket to fluency. *The Reading Teacher, 52,* 326–334.

Matz, K. (1994). 10 things they never taught us about teaching spelling. *The Education Digest, 59*(7), 70–72.

May, F. (1998). *Reading as communication: To help children write and read* (5th ed.). Upper Saddle River, NJ: Merrill-Prentice Hall.

May, F. B., & Rizzardi, L. (2002). *Reading as communication* (6th ed.). Upper Saddle River, NJ: Pearson Education.

McCormick, R. L., & Paratore, J. R. (1999). *"What do you do there anyway," teachers ask: A reading teacher's intervention using grade-level text with struggling third grade readers.* Paper presented at the National Reading Conference, Orlando, FL.

McCormick, S. (1999). *Instructing students who have literacy problems.* Upper Saddle River, NJ: Pearson, Merrill, Prentice Hall.

McCormick, S., & Becker, E. Z. (1996). Word recognition and word identification: A review of research on effective instructional practices with learning disabled students. *Reading Research and Instruction, 35*(1), 5–17.

McGuffey, W H. (1866). *McGuffey's new fifth eclectic reader: Selected and original exercises for schools.* Cincinnati, OH: Wilson, Hinkle & Co.

Metametrics, Inc. *The Lexile Framework.* Retrieved June 25, 2005, from http://www.lexile.com

Moats, L. C. (1995). *Spelling: Development, disability and instruction.* Baltimore: York Press.

Moats, L. C. (2005). Teaching decoding. In Z. Fang (Ed.), *Literacy teaching and learning: Current issues and trends* (pp. 81–90). Upper Saddle River, NJ: Pearson.

Morris, D. (2005). Preventing reading failure in the primary grades. In Z. Fang (Ed.), *Literacy teaching and learning: Current issues and trends* (pp. 184–196). Upper Saddle River, NJ: Pearson.

Morris, D., Blanton, L., Blanton, W. E., & Perney, J. (1995). Spelling instruction and achievement in six classrooms. *Elementary School Journal, 92,* 145–162.

Morrow, L. M., & Tracey, D. H. (1997). Strategies used for phonics instruction in early childhood classrooms. *The Reading Teacher, 50*(8), 644–651.

Moustafa, M. (1998). Reconceptualizing phonics instruction. In C. Weaver (Ed.), *Reconsidering a balanced approach to reading* (pp. 135–157). Urbana, IL: National Council of Teachers of English.

Murphy, N. (1997). A multisensory vs. conventional approach to teaching spelling. ERIC Document Reproduction Service No. (ED 405 564).

Nagy, W. (1988). *Teaching vocabulary to improve reading comprehension.* Urbana, IL: National Council of Teachers of English.

Nation, K., & Hulme, C. (1997). Phonemic segmentation, not onset-rime segmentation, predicts early reading and spelling skills. *Reading Research Quarterly, 32,* 154–167.

National Center for Education Statistics. (1995). Listening to children read aloud: Oral fluency. *NAEP Facts, 22,* 3–4. Retrieved January 25, 2006, from http://nces.ed.gov/pubs95/web/95762.asp

National Center for Education Statistics. (2001). *Fourth grade reading highlights 2000: The nation's report card.* Washington, DC: U.S. Department of Education.

National Center for Education Statistics. (2002). *The nation's report card: Writing highlights 2002.* Retrieved October 14, 2005, from http://nces.ed.gov/nationsreportcard/pdf/main2002/2003531.pdf

National Center for Education Statistics. (2004). *NAEP 2004 trends in academic progress: Three decades of student performance in reading and mathematics: Findings in brief.* Retrieved January 28, 2005, from http://nces.ed.gov/nationsreportcard/pdf/main2005/2005464_3pdf

National Geographic. (2005). *Spring 2005 school publishing PreK-12 nonfiction literacy catalog.* Des Moines, IA: National Geographic.

National Reading Panel. (2000). *Report of the national reading panel: Teaching children to read.* Washington, DC: U.S. Department of Health and Human Services.

NCES (National Center for Education Statistics). *NAEP questions grade 4 scoring guide.* Retrieved October 28, 2005, from http://nces.ed.gov/nationsreportcard/itmrls/itemdisplay.asp

Ogle, D. (1986). K-W-L: A teaching model that develops active reading of expository text. *The Reading Teacher, 39,* 564–571.

Opitz, M. F., & Ford, M. P. (2001). *Reaching readers: Flexible & innovative strategies for guided reading.* Portsmouth, NH: Heinemann.

Opitz, M. F., & Rasinski, T. (1998). *Good-bye round robin: Twenty-five effective oral reading strategies.* Portsmouth, NH: Heinemann.

Otto, W., Wolf, A., & Eldridge, R. (2002). Managing instruction. In P. D. Pearson (Ed.), *Handbook of reading research* (pp. 799–828). Mahwah, NJ: Erlbaum.

Palincsar, A. S., & Brown, A. L. (1986). Interactive teaching to promote independent learning from text. *The Reading Teacher, 39*(8), 771–777.

Pearson Learning Group. *Developmental reading assessment.* Retrieved October 17, 2005, from http://www.pearsonlearning.com/dra

Pearson, P. D., & Duke, N. (2002). Comprehension instruction in the primary grades. In C. C. Block & M. Pressley (Eds.), *Comprehension instruction: Research-based best practices* (pp. 247–258). New York: Guilford.

Podl, J. B. (1995). Introducing teens to the pleasures of reading. *Educational Leadership, 53*(1), 56–57.

Post, Y. (2003). Reflections teaching the secondary language functions of writing, spelling, and reading. *Annals of Dyslexia, 53,* 128–148.

Prescott-Griffin, M. L., & Witherell, N. L. (2004). *Fluency in focus: Comprehension strategies for all young readers.* Portsmouth, NH: Heinemann.

Pressley, M. (1996). Concluding reflections. In E. McIntyre & M. Pressley (Eds.), *Balanced instruction: Strategies and skills in whole language* (pp. 277–286). Norwood, MA: Christopher-Gordon.

Pressley, M. (2002). *Reading instruction that works: The case for balanced teaching* (2nd ed.). New York: Guilford Press.

Pressley, M. (2006). *Reading instruction that works: The case for balanced teaching* (3rd ed.). New York: Guilford Press.

Pressley, M., Almasi, J., Schuder, T., Bergman, J., Hite, S., El-Dinary, P. B., et al. (1994). Transactional instruction of comprehension strategies: The Montgomery County, Maryland, SAIL Program. *Reading and Writing Quarterly: Overcoming Learning Difficulties, 10,* 5–19.

Pressley, M., Rankin, J., & Yokoi, L. (1996). A survey of instructional practices of primary teachers nominated as effective in promoting literacy. *Elementary School Journal, 96,* 363–384.

Pressley, M., Roehrig, A., Bogner, K., Raphael, L. M., & Dolezal, S. (2002). Balanced literacy instruction. *Focus on Exceptional Children, 34*(5), 1–14.

Pressley, M., & Wharton-McDonald, R. (2002). The need for increased comprehension instruction. In M. Pressley (Ed.), *Reading instruction that works: The case for balanced teaching* (2nd ed., pp. 236–288). New York: Guilford Press.

Pressley, M., Wharton-McDonald, R., Allington, R., Block, C. C., Morrow, L., Tracey, D., et al. (2001). A study of effective first-grade literacy instruction. *Scientific Studies of Reading, 5,* 35–58.

Pressley, M., Wharton-McDonald, R., & Hampston, J. M. (2002). Expert primary-level teaching of literacy in balanced teaching. In M. Pressley (Ed.), *Reading instruction that works* (2nd ed., pp. 181–235). New York: Guilford.

PRO-ED Inc. *Test of Phonological Awareness.* Austin, TX. Retrieved February 11, 2006, from www.proedinc.com

Raphael, T. E. (1986). Teaching questions answer relationships revisited. *The Reading Teacher, 39*(6), 516–522.

Rasinski, T. (1995). Fast start: A parent involvement reading program for primary grade students. In W. Linek & E. Sturtevant (Eds.), *Generations of literacy: The 17th yearbook of the College Reading Association* (pp. 301–312). Harrisonburg, VA: College Reading Association.

Rasinski, T. (2000). Speed does matter in reading. *The Reading Teacher, 54,* 146–151.

Rastle, K., & Coltheart, M. (2000). Lexical and non-lexical print to-sound translation of disyllabic words and nonwords. *Journal of Memory and Language, 42,* 342–364.

Read Naturally: The Fluency Company. http://www.readnaturally.com

Reading a-z.com the online reading program. Retrieved October 24, 2005, from http://www.readinga-z.com

Reading Recovery Council of North America. *Book leveling.* Retrieved July 6, 2005, from http://www.readingrecovery.org/sections/reading/book.asp

Renaissance Learning, Inc. *Accelerated reader.* Retrieved November 1, 2005, from http://www.renlearn.com/store

Reutzel, D. R., & Cooter, R. B. (2003). *Strategies for reading assessment and instruction* (2nd ed.). Upper Saddle River, NJ: Merrill Prentice Hall.

Richards, R. (2002). Strategies for the reluctant writer. *LD Online.* Retrieved October 8, 2005, from http://www.ldonline.org

Richardson, J., & Morgan, R. (1997). *Reading to learn in the content areas.* Belmont, CA: Wadsworth.

Richgels, D. (2004). Paying attention to language. *Reading Research Quarterly, 39*(4), 470–477.

Robinson, H. (1960). The unity of the reading act. In H. Robinson (Ed.), *Sequential development of reading abilities* (pp. 237–244). Chicago: University of Chicago Press.

Roe, B. D., Smith, S. H., & Burns, P. (2005). *Teaching reading in today's elementary schools* (9th ed.). Boston: Houghton Mifflin.

Rosenshine, B., & Stevens, R. (2002). Classroom instruction in reading. In P. D. Pearson, R. Barr, M. L. Kamil, & P. Mosenthal (Eds.), *Handbook of reading research* (pp. 745– 798). New York: Longman.

Routman, R. (2005). *Writing essentials: Raising expectations and results while simplifying teaching.* Portsmouth, NH: Heinemann.

Rupley, W. H., Logan, J. W., & Nichols, W. D. (1999). Vocabulary instruction in a balanced reading program. *The Reading Teacher, 52,* 336–346.

Samuels, S. J. (1997). The methods of repeated reading. *The Reading Teacher, 50*(5), 376–381. Originally published in January 1979.

Samuels, S. J. (2002). Reading fluency: Its development and assessment. In A. Farstrup & S. J. Samuels (Eds.), *What research has to say about reading instruction* (3rd ed., pp. 166–183). Newark, DE: International Reading Association.

Scardamalia, M., & Bereiter, C. (1986). Written composition. In M. Wittrock (Ed.), *Handbook of research on teaching* (3rd ed., pp. 778–803). New York: MacMillan.

Schlagal, B. (2001). Traditional, developmental, and structured language approaches to spelling: Review and recommendations. *Annals of Dyslexia, 51,* 147–176.

Schlagal, B. (2002). Classroom spelling instruction: History, research, and practice. *Reading Research and Instruction, 42,* 44–57.

Schneider, W., Roth, E., & Ennemoser, M. (2000). Training phonological skills and letter knowledge in children at risk for dyslexia: A comparison of three kindergarten intervention programs. *Journal of Educational Psychology, 92,* 284–295.

Scholastic, Inc. *Scholastic reading counts.* Retrieved November 1, 2005, from http://teacher.scholastic.com/products/readingcounts/index.htm

Schwartz, R. M. (1997). Self-monitoring in beginning reading. *The Reading Teacher, 51*(1), 40–48.

Scott, J., & Nagy, W. (1997). Understanding the definitions of unfamiliar verbs. *Reading Research Quarterly, 32,* 184–200.

Shanahan, T. (1997). Reading-writing relationships, thematic units, inquiry learning . . . In pursuit of effective integrated literacy instruction. *The Reading Teacher, 51*(1), 12–19.

Shanahan, T. (1998). Twelve studies that have influenced K-12 reading instruction. *Illinois Reading Council Journal, 26*(1), 50–58.

Shanahan, T., & Shanahan, S. (1997). Character perspective charting: Helping children to develop a more complete conception of story. *The Reading Teacher, 50*(8), 668–677.

Silven, M., & Vauras, M. (1992). Improving reading through thinking aloud. *Learning and Instruction, 2,* 69–88.

Smith, C. B. (2003). *Phonological awareness: ERIC topical bibliography and commentary.* Bloomington, IN: ERIC Clearinghouse on Reading.

Snow, C. E. (2005). From literacy to learning. *Harvard Education Letter,* July/August 2005. Retrieved August 30, 2005, from http://www.edletter.org/current/snow.shtml

Snow, C. E., Burns, M. S., & Griffin, P. (1998). *Preventing reading difficulties in young children.* Washington, DC: National Academy Press.

Snowball, D., & Bolton, F. (1999). *Spelling K-8: Planning and teaching.* Portland, ME: Stenhouse.

Sousa, D. (2005). *How the brain learns to read.* Thousand Oaks, CA: Corwin Press.

Stahl, S. A. (1992). Saying the "p" word: Nine guidelines for exemplary phonics instruction. *The Reading Teacher, 45*(8), 618–625.

Stahl, S. A. (1997). Words, words, words. *Illinois Reading Council Journal, 25*(1), 58–62.

Stahl, S. A. (2003). No more "madface": Motivation and fluency. In D. M. Barrone & L. M. Morrow (Eds.), *Research-based practices in early literacy.* New York: Guilford Press.

Stahl, S. A. (2004). What do we know about fluency? In P. McCardle & V. Chhabra (Eds.), *The voice of evidence in reading research* (pp. 187–211). Baltimore: Paul H. Brookes.

Stahl, S. A., Heubach, K., & Cramond, B. (1997). *Fluency-oriented reading instruction.* Athens, GA, and Washington, DC: National Reading Research Center and U.S. Department of Education, Office of Educational Research and Improvement, Educational Resources Information Center.

Stahl, S. A., Osborn, J., & Lehr, F. (1990). *"Beginning to read: Thinking and learning about print" by Marilyn Jager Adams. A summary.* Urbana-Champaign, IL: Center for the Study of Reading; Cambridge, MA: Bolt, Beranek and Newman.

Stanovich, K. E. (1986). Matthew effects in reading: Some consequences of individual differences in the acquisition of literacy. *Reading Research Quarterly, 21*(4), 360–407.

Stauffer, R. (1969). *Teaching reading as a thinking process.* New York: Harper & Row.

Stecher, B. M., & Barron, S. I. (1999). *Quadrennial milepost accountability testing in Kentucky* (CSE Technical Report 505). Los Angeles: National Center for the Study of Evaluation; Center for Research on Evaluation, Standards, and Student Testing.

Strickland, D. (1998). What's basic in beginning reading? Finding common ground. *Educational Leadership, 55*(6), 6–10.

Strickland, D. (2002). The importance of effective early intervention. In A. Farstrup & S. J. Samuels (Eds.), *What research has to say about reading instruction* (3rd ed., pp. 69–86). Newark, DE: International Reading Association.

Strommen, L. T., & Mates, B. F. (1997). What readers do: Young children's ideas about the nature of reading. *The Reading Teacher, 51*(2), 98–107.

Sunburst. *Max's attic.* http://www.starfall.com

Swanson, H. L. (1999). Reading research for students with LD: A meta-analysis of intervention outcomes. *Journal of Learning Disabilities, 32*, 504–532.

TASA Literacy, Touchstone Applied Science Associates. Retrieved September 10, 2005, from http://www.tasaliteracy.com

Taylor, B. M., Pearson, P. D., Clark, K., & Walpole, S. (2000). Effective schools and accomplished teachers: Lessons from primary grade reading instruction in low-income schools. *Elementary School Journal, 101*, 121–165.

Teachnology Inc. Retrieved October 23, 2005, from http://www.teach-nology.com

Tierney, R. J., & Cunningham, J. W. (2002). Research on teaching reading comprehension. In P. D. Pearson (Ed.), *Handbook of reading research* (pp. 609–655). Mahwah, NJ: Erlbaum.

Tindal, G., Hasbrouck, J. E., & Jones, C. (2005). *Oral reading fluency: 90 years of measurement.* Technical Report #33. Eugene, OR: Behavioral Research & Teaching. Retrieved August 1, 2005, from http://brt.uoregon.edu/techreports/ORF_90Yrs_Intro_TechRpt33.pdf

Tompkins, G. E. (1997). *Literacy for the 21st century: A balanced approach.* Upper Saddle River, NJ: Merrill-Prentice Hall.

Topping, K., & Ehly, S. (1998). *Peer assisted learning.* Mahwah, NJ: Erlbaum.

Torgesen, J. K. (1998, January). *Phonological awareness*. Presentation in Oak Park, IL.

Torgesen, J. K. (2004). Lessons learned from research on interventions for students who have difficulty learning to read. In P. McCardle & V. Chhabra (Eds.), *The voice of evidence in reading research* (pp. 355–382). Baltimore: Paul H. Brookes.

Trabasso, T., & Bouchard, E. (2002). Teaching readers how to comprehend text strategically. In C. C. Block & M. Pressley (Eds.), *Comprehension instruction: Research-based best practices* (pp. 176–200). New York: Guilford.

Tracey, D. J., & Morrow, L. M. (2002). Preparing young learners for successful reading comprehension. In C. C. Block & M. Pressley (Eds.), *Comprehension instruction: Research-based best practices* (pp. 219–233). New York: Guilford.

University of Oregon Center on Teaching and Learning. *Dynamic Indicator of Basic Early Literacy Skills, DIBELS*, Retrieved November 1, 2005, from http://dibels.uoregon.edu

Unrau, N. (2004). *Content area reading and writing: Fostering literacies in middle and high school cultures*. Upper Saddle River, NJ: Pearson Merrill Prentice Hall.

Vellutino, F., Scanlon, D. M., Sipay, E. R., Small, S. G., Chen, R., Pratt, A., et al. (1996). Cognitive profiles of difficult-to-remediate and readily remediated poor readers: Early intervention as a vehicle for distinguishing between cognitive and experiential deficits as basic causes of specific reading disability. *Journal of Educational Psychology, 88*(4), 601–638.

Vogler, K. E. (2002). The impact of high-stakes, state-mandate performance assessment on teachers' instructional practices. *Education, 123* (1), 39–55.

Vygotsky, L. (1978). *Mind in society*. Cambridge, MA: Harvard University Press.

Wagstaff, J. M. (1997). Building practical knowledge of letter-sound correspondences: A beginner's word wall and beyond. *The Reading Teacher, 51*(4), 298–304.

Webbing Into Literacy: A Head Start program. Retrieved October 1, 2005, from http://curry.edschool.virginia.edu/go/wil/home.html

Wharton-McDonald, R., Pressley, M., & Hampston, J. M. (1998). Outstanding literacy instruction in first grade: Teacher practices and student achievement. *Elementary School Journal, 99*, 101–128.

White, T. (2005). Effects of systematic and strategic analogy-based phonics on grade 2 students' word reading and reading comprehension. *Reading Research Quarterly, 40*(2), 234–255.

Why use volunteers when pros are available? (1997, November 10). *USA Today*, p. 12A.

Wigfield, A., & Guthrie, J. (1997). Relations of children's motivation for reading to the amount and breadth of their reading. *Journal of Educational Psychology, 89*(3), 420– 432.

Wilde, S. (1992). *You kan red this!* Portsmouth, NH: Heinemann.

Winicki, B. A. (2004). Guiding students' literature discussions. *Illinois Reading Council Journal, 32*(1), 30–37.

Wong, B. Y. L., Butler, D. L., Ficzere, S. A., & Kuperis, S. (1996). Teaching low achievers and students with learning disabilities to plan, write, and revise opinion essays. *Journal of Learning Disabilities, 29*(2), 197–212.

Worthy, J., & Hoffman, J. (Eds.). (1997). Critical questions. *The Reading Teacher*, 51(4), 338–340.

Wylie, R. E., & Durrell, D. D. (1970). Teaching vowels through phonograms. *Elementary English, 47*, 787–791.

Yopp, H. K. (1992). Developing phonemic awareness in young children. *The Reading Teacher, 45*(9), 696–703.

Yopp, H. K. (1995a). Read-aloud books for developing phonemic awareness. An annotated bibliography. *The Reading Teacher, 48*(6), 538–542.

Yopp, H. K. (1995b). A test for assessing phonemic awareness in young children. *The Reading Teacher, 49*(1), 20–29.

Zaragoza, N., & Vaughn, S. (1995). Children teach us to teach writing. *The Reading Teacher, 49*(1), 42–47.

Zutell, J. (1996). The directed spelling thinking activity (DSTA): Providing an effective balance in word study instruction. *The Reading Teacher, 50*(2), 98–108.

Zutell, J. (1998). A *student-active learning approach to spelling instruction* (pamphlet). Columbus, OH: Zaner Bloser.

■ CHILDREN'S LITERATURE CITED

Adamson, T. (2004). *Mars.* Mankato, MN: Capstone Press.

Avi. (2002). *Crispin: The cross of lead.* New York: Hyperion.

Bradbury, R. (1984). All summer in a day. *Junior Great Books.* Series 6, Vol. 2. Chicago: Great Books Foundation.

Bradbury, R. (1984). The veldt. *Junior Great Books.* Series 6, Vol. 2. Chicago: Great Books Foundation.

Brown, M. W. (1947). *Good night moon.* New York: Harper.

Burnett, F. H. (1987). *The secret garden.* New York: Holt & Co.

Cohen, D. (2001). *Tyrannosaurus Rex.* Mankato, MN: Capstone Press.

Creech, S. (1994). *Walk two moons.* New York: HarperCollins.

Edwards, W. (2002). *Alphabeasts.* Tonawanda, NY: Kids Can Press.

Ferllini, R. (2002). *Silent witness.* Richmond Hill, Ontario: Firefly Books.

Fox, M. (1985). *Wilfrid Gordon McDonald Partridge.* New York: Kane Miller.

George, J. C. (1972). *Julie of the wolves.* New York: Harper & Row.

George, J. C. (1994). *Julie.* New York: HarperCollins.

Gwynn, F. (1988). *The king who rained.* New York: Simon & Schuster.

Hughes, L. (1975). Thank you m'am. *Junior Great Books.* Series 5, Vol. 1. Chicago: Great Books Foundation.

Jerome, K. B. (2004). *Jane Goodall: Protecting primates.* Washington, DC: National Geographic.

Kipling, R. (1955). The jungle book. In M. Martignoni (Ed.), *The illustrated treasury of children's literature* (pp. 257–264). New York: Grosset and Dunlap.

Lessing, D. (1984). Through the tunnel. In *Junior Great Books*. Series 6, Vol. 1. Chicago: Great Books Foundation.

Lowry, L. (1990). *Number the stars.* New York: Houghton Mifflin.

Martin, B. (1967). *Brown bear, brown bear, what do you see?* New York: Holt.

Maupassant, G. de. (1978). The necklace. In R. V. Cassil (Ed.), *The Norton anthology of short fiction* (pp. 928–935). New York: W. W. Norton & Co.

Muldoon, K. (1995). The smallest bears in the world. In E. Crooker (Ed.), *Cambodia* (pp. 36–37). Peterborough, NH: Cobblestone.

O'Dell, S. (1980). *Sarah Bishop.* New York: Scholastic.

O'Dell, S. (1983). *Island of the blue dolphins.* New York: Dell.

Paulsen, G. (1987). *Hatchet.* New York: Puffin.

Pinkwater, D. (1977). *The big orange splot.* New York: Scholastic.

Polacco, P. (2003). *G is for goat.* New York: Philomel Books.

Potter, B. (1903). *The tale of Peter Rabbit.* New York: Scholastic.

Rappaport, D. (2001). *Martin's big words.* New York: Hyperion.

Regions. (2005). Glenview, IL: Pearson Scott Foresman.

Richter, C. (1980). *The light in the forest.* Toronto: Bantam.

Roth, C. (2002). *The little school bus.* New York: North-South Books.

Sachar, L. (1998). *Holes.* New York: Dell Yearling.

Saroyan, W. (1984). The parsley garden. *Junior Great Books.* Series 6, Vol. 1. Chicago: Great Books Foundation.

Sendak, M. (1964). *Where the wild things are.* New York: Harper & Row.

Shaw, N. (1986). *Sheep in a jeep.* Boston: Houghton Mifflin.

Showers, P. (1961). *The listening walk.* New York: HarperCollins.

Sipiera, D. M., & Sipiera, P. (1997). *Constellations.* New York: Children's Press.

Soto, G. (1997). *Novio boy: A play.* San Diego, CA: Harcourt Brace.

Speare, E. G. (1983). *The sign of the beaver.* New York: Yearling.

Taylor, M. (1977). *Roll of thunder, hear my cry.* New York: Dial.

Taylor, T. (1969). *The cay.* New York: Avon Camelot.

Weeks, S. (2004). *If I were a lion.* New York: Atheneum.

Wilson, S. (1995). *Good zap, little grog.* Bergenfield, NJ: Candlewick.

Yolen, J. (1991). *Greyling.* New York: Philomel Books.

Index

**CORWIN
PRESS**

The Corwin Press logo—a raven striding across an open book—represents the union of courage and learning. Corwin Press is committed to improving education for all learners by publishing books and other professional development resources for those serving the field of PreK–12 education. By providing practical, hands-on materials, Corwin Press continues to carry out the promise of its motto: **"Helping Educators Do Their Work Better."**